D1479196

The Missing Spanish Creoles

The Missing Spanish Creoles

Recovering the Birth of Plantation Contact Languages

JOHN H. MCWHORTER

University of California Press

BERKELEY   LOS ANGELES   LONDON

University of California Press
Berkeley and Los Angeles, California

University of California Press, Ltd.
London, England

© 2000 by the Regents of the University of California

Library of Congress Cataloging-in-Publication Data

McWhorter, John H.
    The missing Spanish creoles: recovering the birth of plantation
contact languages / John H. McWhorter.
        p.   cm.
    Includes bibliographical references and index.
    ISBN 0-520-21999-6 (alk. paper)
    1. Creole dialects—Caribbean Area History. 2. Pidgin
languages—History. 3. Blacks—Africa, West Languages.
I. Title.
PM7834.C37M38   2000
467'.9729—dc21   99-41957
                                                           CIP

Manufactured in the United States of America

09 08 07 06 05 04 03 02 01 00

10 9 8 7 6 5 4 3 2 1

To my mother,
SCHELYSTURE ANNE GORDON McWHORTER
This is for both of us.

Contents

Acknowledgments

I have benefited immensely from conversations and correspondence with Philip Baker, Anthony Grant, Ian Hancock, Magnus Huber, George Lang, William Samarin, John Singler, and Sally Thomason. Special thanks go to William Jennings, who sent me the bizarrely neglected Martinique text of 1671, and Tim Thomas, at the Oriental and India Office Collections.

John Rickford and Elizabeth Traugott not only ushered me into the world of scholarship, but were directly responsible for restraining me at a critical juncture from deserting linguistics for pastures unknown. Thank you to these two consummate scholars.

I am sincerely grateful to the Committee on Research at the University of California, Berkeley for funding my research in London and Paris.

Chris Corne read Chapters 5 through 7 with a thoroughness far beyond the call of duty, always with his trademark constructive skepticism. His receptiveness and encouragement have been a rare delight. Armin Schwegler examined the entire manuscript with exemplary care; his authority and sharp eye were especially crucial to Chapter 2.

I am most indebted, however, to Mikael Parkvall. His close reading of my arguments, combined with the miracle of electronic mail, led to a voluminous and challenging correspondence, without which this would surely be a different and lesser book.

All remaining errors, of course, are strictly *mea culpa*.

1 Introduction

This book is written out of a conviction that creole studies, at this writing, is a field on the brink of a serious mistake.

One would never know this from current creolist literature, in which the reigning tone is that the past thirty years have witnessed great progress in our understanding of creole languages. Indeed, creole studies is currently passing from its pre-paradigm stage—that is, the free-for-all of competing hypotheses typical of scientific inquiries in their infancy—into the maturity of a basic paradigm agreed upon by all (to borrow the terminology of Kuhn 1962).

The paradigm is one so deeply rooted in creolist thought that few would even consider it to be a position, as opposed to a verity (a prime sign that a paradigm has set in). That paradigm is what we will call the *limited access model.*

This model stipulates that the plantation creoles of the New World and the Indian Ocean developed as a result of African slaves having had limited access to the lexifier spoken on plantations, due to the disproportion of blacks to whites in such settings. This conception depicts plantation creole genesis as an attempt by slaves to forge a viable lingua franca on the basis of unusually constrained input from a socially dominant lexifier. Thus plantation social structure is seen as having filtered lexifier input to most slaves.

In a field which prides itself upon its contentiousness, it will surprise many to hear that there is any fundamentally accepted tenet in creole studies. To be sure, no creolist subscribes explicitly to anything called the "limited access model." Most important, limited access is not the sum total of anyone's model—creole studies comprises a healthy variety of fascinating genesis theories. However, all work on plantation creole genesis uses some version of the limited access conception as a springboard.

For example, Bickerton's Language Bioprogram Hypothesis (1981, 1984a) identifies "dilution" of lexifier input, as slaves' access to the dominant language recedes, as the source of creole genesis. Meanwhile, substrate-oriented models, while diametrically opposed to Bickerton's in many ways, nevertheless concur in associating creole genesis with distance from the lexifier, assuming that substrate influence would have been strongest among slaves with the least contact with Europeans (e.g., Alleyne 1971: 180). In their broad-ranging typology of language contact phenomena, Thomason and Kaufman (1988) sharply separate creoles from pidgins, identifying creoles as responses to fragmentary transmission of a lexifier on plantations. Chaudenson (1979, 1992) treats creoles as mere evolutions of their lexifiers, but nevertheless associates what distance there is between lexifier and creole to the advent of disproportion between slave and master (i.e., "Zone C'" in Chaudenson 1992: 120−1). Though Chaudenson emphasizes that the transformation of a lexifier into a creole would have been through a series of gradual steps, the fundamental concept is the same: plantation creoles resulted from an unusually low level of direct contact with the lexifier.

The transformation of the limited access conception from a hypothesis into a paradigm is evident in how frequently current theorists refer to it as a given. Bickerton (1991: 22) writes as assumed fact that "in the dilution process that immediately precedes, and indeed accompanies, creolization, many superstrate morphemes and most substrate morphemes are lost completely." Subscribing to a different, yet still limited access–based, model, Mufwene (1994b: 70) writes in passing that "in the case of New World and Indian Ocean settlements . . . the new generation of field slaves had less and less exposure to the European language varieties, which were replaced as models by the approximations spoken by the earlier Creole or, simply 'seasoned' slaves." Chaudenson (1992: 176) considers the socio-historical and sociolinguistic foundations of his model nothing less than "confirmed and reinforced" by the linguistic data he has presented.

However, the very nature of creole studies is such that the limited access model, like all creole genesis models, is after all just a guess. The weight of three decades of articles, books, conferences, and new generations of creolists makes it sobering to recall that no one living has ever seen a plantation creole form, no one ever will, and meanwhile no one alive while a creole was forming ever wrote anything about it.

The uninitiated could come away from creolist literature under the impression that writers on creole genesis are basing their pronouncements upon remarks by planters on odd dialects developing among their slaves, and upon ample citations of creoles developing during the first decades of plantation colonies' existence. However, this is not the case. Documentation of any kind on Caribbean or Indian Ocean plantations during the crucial foundation stages is extremely sparse: by the time travelers' accounts and planters' records appear, the creole has already become well established. Similarly, the first relatively reliable linguistic records capture creoles long established as full languages, and thus cannot be said to reveal a great deal about creole "birth" (e.g., the Herlein Fragment for Sranan [Voorhoeve and Lichtveld 1975: 280–2], DuCoeurjoly 1802 for Haitian Creole).

Thus, essentially, any creole genesis account must be evaluated according to how good a guess it is. Since sociohistorical documentation is not only insufficient, but is also not the only source of data available to us, it follows that a viable creole genesis model will be based only partly upon sociohistorical extrapolation. Equally important will be that the model is situated within the general tenets of language contact and change, and that it be able to explain as much synchronic data as possible.

An analogy is the growing field of paleosociobiology. The depictions of dinosaurs engaged in dynamic mating patterns, child-rearing practices, and migrations, recently enshrined in *Jurassic Park,* are ultimately based on incomplete skeletons, mere shadows of the living creatures. No one was alive to observe living dinosaurs, and short of the genetic wizardry accomplished by the scientists in *Jurassic Park,* no one will ever observe them. Thus paleosociobiological reconstructions are evaluated strictly according not only to how well they are supported by the fossil evidence, but also to how well they are situated within universal laws of nature and how plausible they are in view of the behavior of living animals.

In creole studies, however, it is difficult to avoid the conclusion that the limited access model has yet to undergo this brand of scrutiny. In the first few chapters of this book, I will show that the limited access model leaves a great many questions unanswered. A few examples will suffice to show the nature of the problem:

(1) In a great many Spanish colonies, plantation slaves simply learned Spanish under the very conditions which are considered to have constituted "limited access" to the lexifier for slaves under other powers.

(2) Recent work in creole studies has called increasing attention to evidence that all of the Atlantic English-based creoles share a single common ancestor. Yet genesis work continues to be written locating the birth of a given creole in its individual colony. This leaves

a disjunction between basic principles of comparative reconstruction, which motivate reconstructing the common ancestor, and creole studies as a whole.

(3)   Other current work has shown that plantation creoles existed in many colonies long before blacks even outnumbered whites, raising further questions about the limited access model.

In themselves, these recent discoveries are signs that creole studies remains a viable discipline. However, the impact of these findings upon the core assumptions in the field has yet to be fully evaluated.

Upon attempting just such an evaluation, it has become my opinion that the limited access model of creole genesis, while an eminently plausible response to the range of data available to creolists in the 1950s and 1960s, is unable to account for the range of data which has since become available, and must be discarded. This book is an attempt to pull creole studies from the brink of coalescing around a questionable paradigm. I propose a new account of creole genesis which not only accounts for the questions the limited access hypothesis founders upon, but also answers other long-standing questions. This new model will be called the Afrogenesis Hypothesis.

Before proceeding, a word will be necessary about my use of the terms *pidgin* and *creole* in this book. My conception of the application of these two terms is fairly conventional, perhaps even recidivist. I believe that plantation creoles began as pidgins, be this on the plantations themselves (as most creolists believe) or on the West African coast (which I believe, and will argue for in this book). They became creoles when they were expanded into fully referential languages via use as Mediums for Interethnic Communication, in the terminology of Baker (1990), be this by children or adults.

I do not subscribe to the view of Chaudenson (1979, 1992) and Mufwene (1996) that plantation creoles are merely moderately transformed varieties of their lexifiers, with their distance from the lexifier due to widespread second-language acquisition (with Mufwene adding high typological variation among mother tongues as another factor). Under their analysis, there is no pidgin stage in the development of a plantation creole. I disagree, however, for reasons outlined in Section 5.5.3. and McWhorter (1996c, 1997a).

Thus throughout the text, I refer to the emergence of plantation creoles as having occurred via the *pidginization* of the lexifier. This is not meant to imply that the new language has remained a pidgin; it is assumed that the pidgin stage of any plantation creole was relatively brief and now lost to history.

Thus I assume that creole genesis begins with *pidginization*. I make little reference, then, to *creolization*, as I take this to refer to the expansion of a pidgin into a creole, a vital process but of minor import to this particular hypothesis. This differs from Chaudenson and Mufwene, who refer to the development of a plantation creole as *creolization*, with no intervening pidgin stage, and treat *pidginization* as a separate process leading to nonnative, structurally minimal trade vehicles like Chinese Pidgin English and Russenorsk.

2 Where Are the Spanish Creoles?

2.1 INTRODUCTION

Forty years of articles, books, dissertations, and presentations have enshrined limited access to a lexifier language as a driving force behind the emergence of plantation creoles. As noted in the previous chapter, while there is great variety among the genesis theories proposed in the field, all of them share the limited access conception as a pivotal component. It is important to recall, however, that the limited access mechanism has never been observed, and documentation sheds only the dimmest of light on the facts. Unlike, say, an interpretation of the causes of World War I, the limited access hypothesis springs not from an examination of empirical documentation, since this would be impossible, but simply from a natural interpretation of the fact that creoles are so often spoken in former plantation colonies, leading to the supposition that something about plantations created the creoles. It is a thoroughly plausible induction that demographic disproportion was the key.

However, what is plausible is not always true. Truth can be identified only via systematic testing, and the limited access conception has yet to be tested *per se*. To truly test it, creolists would have to search out as many plantation contexts as possible where demographic disproportion developed along the lines typical of European plantation colonies, and to ascertain that creoles have emerged in all or most such contexts.

When we actually test the limited access model in this fashion, we find that while superficially plausible when reconstructed for former English, French, Portuguese, or Dutch colonies, the model founders when applied to Spanish colonies. This is a first indication that a large-scale revision of creole genesis theory is necessary.

6

2.2 COLOMBIA, ECUADOR, PERU, VENEZUELA, AND MEXICO
2.2.1 THE CHOCÓ, COLOMBIA

Creole genesis work on Spanish colonies has generally assumed that under the Spaniards, massive African labor crews were a phenomenon of nineteenth-century Cuba and Puerto Rico. The supposition appears to be that until then, while other powers had developed full-scale plantation economies by the late 1600s, the Spanish were using Africans mostly as domestic help and on small farms.

However, the restriction of this work to the Spanish Caribbean islands is odd, given that it is general knowledge that Spanish colonization of the New World extended much further than these islands. In fact, the Cuban and Puerto Rican explosions of the 1800s were merely the last act in a long tradition of large-scale exploitation of African slave labor by the Spanish. From the early seventeenth century on, the Spanish had gathered massive African plantation and mining crews in their mainland colonies, while their island colonies were still subsisting on small-scale farming. The mainland societies were very much of a kind with the plantation colonies which would emerge later in the century under England, France, and Holland.

Importantly, creoles simply are not spoken in these mainland Spanish settings, contrary to what all leading models of creole genesis would predict. For example, starting in the late seventeenth century, the Spanish began importing massive numbers of West Africans who spoke a wide variety of languages into the Pacific lowlands of northwestern Colombia to work their mines. This context shortly became one which, according to the limited access model, was a canonical breeding ground for a contact language of extreme structural reduction.

In the Chocó region, for example, there were no fewer than 5,828 black slaves by 1778, while there were only about 175 whites—a mere 3 percent of the total population (West 1957: 100, 108). Slaves had little sustained contact with whites. The slaves were organized into large teams, or *cuadrillas*, each formally supervised by a white overseer but actually directed by a black *capitanejo* (131–2). *Cuadrillas* typically consisted of two hundred blacks or more, with ones as large as 567 reported (115–6). One of the most numerically precise hypotheses regarding creole genesis (Bickerton 1981: 4) specifies one in five as the minimum ratio of speakers to learners necessary to produce a creole sharply divergent from its lexifier language. It is significant, then, that in the Chocó, even in the very smallest *cuadrillas*, the proportion of whites would have been, on a day-to-day basis, roughly 3.3 percent, and in most *cuadrillas* the proportion would have been virtually negligible. Furthermore, slaves were forbidden to communicate with what freed blacks there were (139–40), eliminating the latter as possible sources of Spanish input.

Some creolists might guess that the absence of a creole in the Chocó might be due to there having been a long initial period during which whites and blacks worked in equal numbers, the blacks being thereby able to acquire relatively full Spanish and then pass this on to the larger influxes of blacks later on. For example, Chaudenson (1979, 1992) and Baker and Corne (1982) have observed that a long period of this type prevented the emergence of a French creole on Réunion as opposed to Mauritius, where blacks came to outnumber whites quite quickly.

However, in the Chocó, there was no period of numerical parity between black and white. The nature of mining is such that relatively large numbers of slaves were needed from the outset, and they were immediately engaged in work arrangements ensuring little contact with whites. One of the earliest *cuadrillas*, for example, was established with forty slaves and was increased to sixty-five later that year (Restrepo 1886: 77–8). Sharp disproportion of black to white was not only established at the outset, but also increased by leaps and bounds throughout the 1700s: there were 600 slaves in the Chocó in 1704, 2000 in 1724, and 7088 by 1782 (Sharp 1976: 21–2).

More to the point, the slaves never worked alongside whites as they would have in the English or French Caribbean, but instead alongside Native Americans, who were second-language speakers themselves. Furthermore, the Native Americans had neither lived in intimate domestic conditions with their masters nor been a long-term, stable presence as had the early slaves in Réunion. For one, they were used only for the first fifteen years or so (Sharp 1976: 119–20). In addition, Africans were imported not to supplement and be trained by the Native Americans but to replace them, the Indians tending to die of European disease or escape. In sum, the Indians were second-language Spanish speakers, had had only distant and negative relations with the Spaniards, and had worked the mines for only a brief period during which they exhibited a high turnover rate. The Indians that Africans encountered were thus likely to be recent and miserable recruits unlikely to remain in service for long—they could have transmitted only fragments of Spanish to Africans at the very most.

Today, the descendants of the Chocó slaves live in the same lowlands where their ancestors toiled under the Spanish, subsisting via small-scale mining. Whites, having retreated to the urban centers after the slaves were emancipated, are a negligible presence in the lowlands (e.g., 8 percent by the 1950s; West 1957: 108–9). Relations between blacks and whites are, unsurprisingly, edgy and distant (Rout 1976: 243–9). In short, we could conceive of no situation more likely to yield a creole: vast numbers of Africans of groups ranging from Senegal down to Angola (Sharp 1976: 114–5), in massive disproportion to whites, with few blacks engaged outside of the trade at hand, all in a difficult-to-access region which the blacks still inhabit in virtual isolation.

Yet the Spanish of black Chocoanos is essentially a typical Latin American dialect of Spanish, easily comprehensible to speakers of standard Spanish varieties:

(1) Esa gente som muy amoroso. Dijen que . . . dijeron que
    that people COP very nice they-say that they-say-PAST that

    volbían sí . . . cuando le de su gana a ello
    they-return-IMP yes when to-them give their desire to them

    vobe.
    return

    Those people are really nice. They say that . . . they said that they
        would come back . . . when they felt like it.

    (Schwegler 1991a: 99)

While displaying certain phonological and morphological reductions, as well as African lexical borrowings (not shown above), this dialect clearly lacks the radical grammatical restructuring in creoles such as Sranan Creole English, Haitian Creole French, and São Tomense Creole Portuguese.

To be sure, pidgins and creoles cannot be defined on the basis of specific *constructions*, since any commonly found in pidgins and creoles can also be found in regular languages, thus invalidating them as diagnostic of pidginization or creolization *per se*. However, it is uncontroversial that pidgins (and their creole descendants) can indeed be defined by two developmental *processes* in their past: marked structural reduction and heavy morphosyntactic interference from native languages (Hymes 1971: 70–1; see also Chapter 5, Section 5.5.3.2).

Along these lines, then, what is remarkable about Chocó Spanish is that, in contrast to Sranan or Haitian, inflectional morphology is robust, and structural transfer from African languages is minimal (but see Schwegler 1991a and 1996a for certain parallels). Thus there is no need to deny the African heritage of Chocó Spanish, nor that it displays a certain degree of paradigmatic leveling. However, this variety classifies more as a Spanish dialect, retaining some traces of second-language acquisition, than as an example of the extreme reduction and transfer typical of Sranan, Haitian, and others.

Such an assessment cannot be based upon a formal line of demarcation between "dialect" and "pidgin/creole": to require this would be to set up a straw man. Studies such as that of Thomason and Kaufman (1988) have long demonstrated that contact-induced restructuring operates on a cline. However, such clines do not invalidate the usefulness of a perceptual distinction between "dialect" and "creole," anymore than we would balk at distinguishing a puppy from a dog. The cline acknowledged, few would disagree that Chocó Spanish falls on the "dialect" end.

What is important is that creole theory predicts that the Chocó context would have generated not a second-language dialect diverging only slightly from the local standard, but a more radically reduced, pidginized register, with much higher levels of structural interference from West African languages. In short, the modern situation in the Chocó is a striking counterexample to current creole genesis theory, all strains of which would predict a Spanish creole in this region.

2.2.2 OTHER CHALLENGES FROM FORMER SPANISH COLONIES

Can we possibly ascribe the Chocó situation to a mere fluke, leaving the limited access hypothesis intact? If this were the only such situation, perhaps we could. In fact, however, the Chocó is nothing less than an unremarkable example of a regular pattern in Spanish America.

For example, when Jesuit missionaries settled in the Chota Valley of Ecuador in the seventeenth century, they established massive sugar plantations worked by Africans. Creolists have considered sugar plantations to be a prime context for the development of creole languages because of the vast manpower which sugar cultivation required. Significantly, then, La Concepción hacienda in the Chota Valley, for example, had no fewer than 380 slaves in 1776, the Cuajara 268, and so on (Coronel Feijóo 1991: 88). Slavery was not abolished until 1852. Today, descendants of these slaves live "a life apart" from the surrounding society, separated from the nearest city by a mountain, not marrying out, and considered an exotic local curiosity (Lipski 1986a: 156–9). Again, current genesis theory predicts a creole here.

Yet the black *Choteños* speak a dialect only marginally distinct from the local standard, typified by occasional, but by no means regular, lapses of gender and number concord (*haciendas vecino* "neighboring haciendas"), prepositional substitutions (*cerca con la Concepción* "near la Concepción" instead of *cercade*), article omissions (*porque ø próximo pueblo puede ser Salina* "because the next town may be Salina"; Lipski 1986a: 172). Such things leave the fundamental Spanish grammar intact, including, as in the Chocó, robust inflectional paradigms (see Schwegler 1996b, however, for some evidence of marginal West African structural transfer).

Once again, there was no initial period of parity between black and white which could explain the absence of a creole here. As in the Chocó, the original intention was to use Native Americans rather than Africans, but even they were brought to the plantations in large numbers at the outset. Unlike the English and French, who first devoted the small farms of their New World colonies exclusively to tobacco, coffee, or indigo, the Jesuits bought large swatches of land and devoted them to several products at a time: cotton, livestock, cacao, and plantains as well as sugar (Coronel Feijóo 1991: 63). Thus at one point two Jesuit haciendas were sharing some ninety Indian laborers (85)—clearly a different situation from the intimate interracial contact among a dozen or so whites and Malagasies on small farms in early Réunion. Even this phase, however, lasted a mere twenty years or so after the first haciendas were purchased in 1614. Consequently, when Africans were imported to gradually replace the Indians, it was immediately in the large numbers necessary to harvest and process sugar cane (e.g., a shipment of 114 in 1637 [86]), and by 1780, the eight Jesuit plantations were worked by no less than 2,615 slaves (88).

Two flukes? No—we find yet another example in vestigial, isolated Afro-Mexican communities in Veracruz, descended from African slaves who were imported at the transformation to sugar cultivation in the 1500s, Indian labor having proven unsuitable to the cultivation of other crops (Carroll 1991: 62–5). African labor forces were as enormous as elsewhere in the Caribbean, an example being the two hundred Africans working the Santísima Trinidad plantation in 1608 (65). Yet in the 1950s, the local speech in these Afro-Mexican enclaves was little different from vernacular dialects elsewhere in Mexico (Aguirre Beltrán 1958: 201), as shown in the following sample (with departures from standard indicated in parentheses):

(2) Ese plan tubo (<*estuvo*) bien hecho . . . pero si el gobierno
    that plan was   well done   but if the government

atiende (la) lej, ba a causá (<*causar*) gran doló (<*dolor*).
follows the law, go to cause   big pain

That plan was well done, but if the government follows the law it will cause a lot of pain.

(Aguirre Beltrán 1958: 208)

The examples continue. Large forces of African slaves also worked sugar plantations in Peru, in coastal valleys south of Lima (Bowser 1974). After emancipation, a large Afro-Peruvian community established itself in cities, retaining their cultural customs, and persisted until the turn of the twentieth century (Lipski 1994: 318). The African-born of this culture spoke a second-language ("bozal") Spanish, predictably, but blacks born in Peru simply spoke the local dialect of Spanish. More isolated Afro-Peruvian communities also survive on the coast today, who also preserve vigorous African influences in their culture. However, they speak nothing approaching a creole; their speech diverges only rather slightly in phonology from the local Spanish (Gálvez Ronceros 1975).

Venezuela is home to a vibrant, consciously Afro-Venezuelan culture of folklore, music and dance, heritage of the heavy importation of Africans to work mines and plantations. Once again, black-white disproportion reigned, such as the 230 blacks on the Mocundo hacienda (Acosta Saignes 1967: 179). Megenney (1988: 53) notes that "in this type of social situation we would have expected to see the formation of a genuine Spanish-based creole with heavy amounts of sub-Saharan influences," but once again, we find nothing of the sort. Megenney finds merely unremarkable phonological quirks and African lexical items (also in the more extensive Megenney 1985).

Thus we see that on a consistent basis, in Spanish plantation contexts, the sharp reduction and heavy morphosyntactic transfer diagnostic of creole languages failed to occur. Clearly this is no mere blip in the data: this is an important contradiction to any creole genesis model assuming limited access to a lexifier as a significant component.

The data above have played no part in the development of creole genesis theory. This is in part because much of the pertinent literature is in Spanish, and is not as copious as that on slavery under the other leading powers. There exists no general survey of Spanish slavery on the comprehensive, authoritative order of Curtin (1969) on the English, Debien (1974) on the French, or Postma (1990) on the Dutch slave trade. Furthermore, the Spanish-language literature often gives only cursory coverage to the African presence. One is continually struck by how many histories of individual Latin American nations—especially those written before the mid-1960s—scrupulously limn a five-century panorama with scarcely a mention of the tens of thousands of Africans forcibly imported into the country over centuries running (Indians, meanwhile, are generally accorded a full chapter or more).

Moreover, in their early stages, scientific investigations typically work from data most readily at hand (Kuhn 1970: 15). Thus it is natural that genesis theorists have more readily addressed the presence, rather than the absence, of creoles.

None of these things, however, belie two simple facts. One: a viable creole genesis theory must account for these Spanish contexts. Two: a limited access model simply cannot do so.

Of course, if scientists threw away their reigning framework every time puzzling evidence arose, then science would make little progress. Thus it is natural, and even advisable, that when confronted with challenging data, scientists attempt to defend the reigning theory rather than reformulate it. Along these lines, most creolists will prefer to suppose that the limited access conception is valid, and that the facts in Sections 2.1 and 2.2 must be due to some external factor.

On the basis of reactions to this data which I have received in the past, we can classify the responses into five groups. The first three will take issue with my basic claim about the scarcity of Spanish creoles by claiming either that there *are* Spanish creoles, *were* Spanish creoles, or that there *will turn out to be* Spanish creoles. The fourth group will accept my basic claim, but attempt to accommodate the reigning theory to it. The fifth group will claim that there is in fact nothing at issue at all. Below I address all five of these standpoints, and show that they leave our theoretical hole open.

2.3 "THERE *ARE* SPANISH CREOLES": PAPIAMENTU AND PALENQUERO

The most obvious response to my claim that no Spanish plantation creoles have emerged would be to point out that Papiamentu and Palenquero are, after all, Spanish-based creoles, and that therefore Spanish creoles *have* emerged in plantation-style systems under the Spanish. This would seem to suggest that the Chocó, the Chota Valley, Veracruz, Peru, and Venezuela are somehow "exceptions" for which explanations will eventually be found. As it happens, however, neither Papiamentu nor Palenquero contradict my assertion.

The reason for this is that while these creoles are clearly Spanish-based *synchronically*, both have been shown to have originated as Portuguese-based *diachronically*. Thus these creoles arose not via the pidginization of Spanish input, but via subsequent relexification of *Portuguese* creoles, which had themselves developed via the pidginization of Portuguese. Thus while unequivocally of Spanish-derived lexicon today, these two creoles leave intact our historical conundrum above: on plantations, Spanish itself

—unintermediated by a Portuguese creole predecessor—was never reconstituted into a stable pidginized variety and transmitted as such.

2.3.1 PAPIAMENTU

It is often forgotten that strictly speaking, Papiamentu is not a plantation creole at all. The soil in Curaçao was too dry for large-scale agriculture (Holm 1989: 313); thus this island was primarily used as a holding camp and entrepôt for slaves shipped from West Africa and destined for other Caribbean colonies. Therefore, Papiamentu emerged amidst Africans working within the slave trade itself and in domestic service, not as a plantation communication vehicle.

However, for many, it will perhaps seem *ad hoc* to dismiss Papiamentu on these grounds, since it was, after all, the product of interactions between African laborers and Europeans.[1] In this light, all evidence points to Papiamentu as the result of a gradual hispanicization of what began as a Portuguese-based pidgin.

This has been most conclusively demonstrated by Goodman (1987), who shows that it would have been simply impossible for Papiamentu to have begun as a Spanish-based pidgin. By the time slaves were brought to Curaçao in any significant numbers (the mid-1650s), there were no Spaniards on the island and only a few Spanish-speaking Indians (367–70). In the meantime, the first slaves were brought into the context by Jews from Brazil, who spoke Portuguese. In addition, for a period, Jews were the only people in Curaçao allowed to purchase slaves (369). Finally, many people running the slave depot in Curaçao had worked previously in Brazil. Thus the setting was ripe for the spread of a Portuguese-based contact language, and the motivation for the spread of a Spanish-based one was nonexistent.

The Spanish reentered the Curaçao context only later, when Spanish-speaking Jews from Holland emigrated there and became the majority among whites. The hispanicization of Papiamentu presumably began at this point, supplemented by the extensive business contacts between Curaçao and the Venezuelan coast. It is important to note that Spanish and Portuguese are so similar that no significant linguistic readjustment was necessary on the part of Papiamentu speakers during the relexification process: as Goodman points out, slaves were probably barely aware of Span-

---

1. For similar reasons, however, Philippine Creole Spanish will not be discussed, given its complete dissociation from slavery, having emerged via marriages between Iberian men and Philippine women. It, too, however, traces back to Portuguese rather than Spanish; see McWhorter (1995: 228–9).

ish as a distinct language (375). Even today, Spanish and Portuguese are partially mutually intelligible, and they were even closer four hundred years ago. Therefore, there was no need for a new Spanish-based creole to emerge at this point: the Jews from Holland could have adjusted easily to Portuguese-based early Papiamentu, especially since they spoke Portuguese as well (363).

The original status of Papiamentu as a Portuguese-based creole is strongly supported by the undeniably Portuguese items in its core lexicon. Table 2.1 is based on Grant 1996, the most exhaustive assessment and identification of Portuguese-derived items in Papiamentu. Grant's version of this list includes even items whose Portuguese derivation, proposed by other authors, he doubts; I have pared it down to what Grant believes to be the most plausible cases. I have further excised cases where the Papiamentu and Portuguese forms have /e/ where Spanish has /je/ (Papiamentu *téra*, Portuguese *terra*, Spanish *tierra*), as the monophthongization of /je/ would have been a plausible simplification of Spanish in a creole language. On the other hand, I have retained cases where Papiamentu and Portuguese have /o/ and Spanish /wɛ/, as /wɛ/-to-/o/ would be a possible, but much less natural, change. *Kabá* could technically come from Spanish, but its presence in other creoles with no Spanish influence (such as Saramaccan and Negerhollands) suggests that Portuguese was the source as well, especially in light of its use in West African Portuguese creoles possibly ancestral to Papiamentu. Similarly, Grant, citing Munteanu (1991: 65–85), notes that *vai* occurred in pre-1650 Spanish; however, its presence in Portuguese creoles like São Tomense tips the scale to Portuguese again. On the other hand, *antó*, *kaí*, and *lánda* are possibly attributable to nonstandard Spanish varieties, and thus I have omitted them (Armin Schwegler, p.c.).

Papiamentu also has some grammatical features linking it to Portuguese creoles still spoken on the West African coast, which emerged amidst the slave trade starting in the 1500s. For example, the plural morpheme *nan* is also found in Fa d'Ambu (Birmingham 1976: 22). Similarly, the parallel between the Cape Verdean Portuguese *el taba ta kanta* "he was singing" and Papiamentu *e tabata kanta* is striking (20), since this usage is impossible to derive from any Iberian construction and is only one of many possible reconceptualizations of the lexifier material.

Some might argue that Papiamentu could still have arisen from the pidginization of Spanish spoken by the Jews, and that this Portuguese element simply represents residual borrowings from some form of Portuguese now no longer spoken. However, as Megenney (1984) notes, these items are *core* lexical items. If they were tokens of a dead Portuguese variety largely

Table 2.1. Derivation of Papiamentu etyma with Spanish for comparison

Papiamentu	English	Portuguese	Spanish
afó	outside	(a)fora	(a)fuera
bai	go	vai (3S)	va
batí	to hit	bater	golpear
bing	come	vim	viene
bong	good	bom	bueno
brínga	to fight	bringar	pelear
dúna	to give	donar	dar
fórsa	force, strength	força	fuerza
fóya	leaf	folha	hoja
kachó	dog	cachorro	perro
kétu	quiet	queto	quieto
kobá	to dig	cova "hole"	cueva "hole"
lémbe	to lick	lamber	lamer
lo	(irrealis marker)	logo "soon"	luego "soon"
mai	mother	mãe	madre
mes	self	mesmo	mismo
mesté	to need	menester	necesitar
na	at, on, in	na	en (+ article)
nóbo	new	novo	nuevo
pai	father	pãe	padre
pápya	to speak	papear	hablar
pertá	to grip	apertar	apretar
prétu	black	preto	negro
pushá	to push	puxar	empujar
te	until	até	hasta
trese	carry, wear	trazer	traer
tur	all	tudo	todo

external to the development of Papiamentu itself, we would expect only concepts unique to Portuguese or African culture, in accordance with the lexical contributions typical of a displaced language.

The origin of Papiamentu as a Portuguese pidgin is strikingly supported by a little-known article by Martinus (1989), documenting a moribund secret language in Curaçao called Guene (<Guinea, i.e., the Guinea Coast of Africa). Guene has features tracing it to Portuguese-based contact lan-

guages of West Africa even beyond those in modern Papiamentu, most strikingly the third-person pronoun *ine*, a substrate borrowing also found in the Gulf of Guinea Portuguese creoles. Crucially, its speakers consider Guene to have been the language spoken by their slave ancestors, and it is particularly indicative that "Guiné" is still what some native speakers of Guinea-Bissau Creole Portuguese call their language (Birmingham 1976: 19). If Papiamentu truly emerged as a Spanish-based contact language, then we would expect any preserved "slave" language to be Spanish-based, like the *bozal* Spanish similarly preserved as a ritual language among Afro-Cubans (Cabrera 1954).

In previous presentations of this argument, I have occasionally been misinterpreted as stating that Papiamentu is not Spanish-based today. It must be clear that I mean no such thing: my point is strictly *historical*. While no one could possibly argue that Papiamentu is not Spanish-based today, synchronic, comparative, and historical evidence show that it did not emerge via an initial encounter with Spanish. Its *initial* lexifier was Portuguese; its subsequent *re*-lexifier was Spanish.

2.3.2 PALENQUERO

Palenquero is spoken in the rural community of El Palenque de San Basilio in Colombia by descendants of maroon slaves. Just as with Papiamentu, the evidence suggests that Palenquero has its roots in a Portuguese pidgin.

We are lucky enough in the case of Palenquero to have an unusually explicit statement from the seventeenth century which suggests that the language did not begin simply as a Spanish pidgin. In reference to his long-term residence in Cartagena, near where Palenquero is spoken, Sandoval noted in 1627 that there were many slaves who had lived in São Tomé who used a "highly corrupt and backwards" version of Portuguese "which they call the language of São Tomé" (*un género de lenguaje muy corrupto y revesado de la Portuguesa que llaman lengua de S. Thome;* cited in Schwegler 1998: 229). This passage suggests that many of the originators of Palenquero already spoke a form of what is today São Tomense Creole Portuguese.

The connection between São Tomense and Palenquero is supported by sociohistorical facts. There are core lexical items from Portuguese in the Palenquero lexicon. Since the slaves cannot have acquired these working under the Spanish who purchased them, this suggests that at least some of the original slaves already spoke some form of Portuguese upon arrival in the New World. Schwegler (1993a) notes the examples shown in Table 2.2.

Table 2.2. Derivation of Palenquero etyma with Spanish
for comparison

Palenquero	English	Portuguese	Spanish
ten	has	tem	tiene
ele	he, she	ele	él
bae	goes	vai	va
ele (pl.)	they	êles	ellos
ku	with	com+o	con

Another feature of Palenquero more specifically indicates a connection with São Tomense Portuguese Creole itself. The third-person plural subject pronoun is *iné* in São Tomense, while it is reflexes of standard *êles* in other Portuguese-based creoles (*élis* in Kriolu, for example [Kihm 1980: 44]). Palenquero has *ané*, rather than a reflex of Spanish *ellos* (see Schwegler 1993b on Palenquero pronouns). Schwegler (forthcoming) traces this to a Kikongo demonstrative meaning "those," such that technically the two creoles could have incorporated the Kikongo pronoun independently. This, however, is unlikely: why would both happen to choose an African etymon for the third-person plural specifically, and why would both happen to recruit a demonstrative rather than personal pronoun in the function?

Palenquero also has a postposed anterior marker *-ba* (*ele kelé ba* "he wanted") which is also found in the Upper Guinea Portuguese creoles. The most likely source for this *-ba* is *acabar* "to finish," found as *kabá* in other Caribbean creoles such as Sranan and Saramaccan. The particular elision to simply *ba* in both Palenquero and the Upper Guinea Portuguese creoles suggests yet another link between Palenquero and West African coastal Portuguese pidgins (although São Tomense lacks this particular feature). To be sure, Kihm (1989: 366) argues for Manjaku *ba* "to finish" as a reinforcing model for the construction in Guinea-Bissau creole. This analysis is unproblematic, but only reinforces the tracing of Palenquero back to a pidgin formed on the African coast—any Manjaku influence would have much more likely in their West African homeland than in Cartagena, where they would have been a subsidiary presence at best.

Indeed, the Palenques are firmly traceable to present-day Angola (Granda 1978; Schwegler 1993a, 1997). This is significant because Angola was one of the main sources for slaves shipped from none other than São

Tomé (Schwegler 1991b: 170), again tracing Palenquero to linguistic developments on this island. Kikongo is preponderantly represented in the African lexical retentions in Palenquero. Granda (1978: 455–62) notes that in funeral songs, there are Kikongo etyma for even core words such as "speak" (*bobo* from *vóva*). He also notes that their funeral songs include passages such as *Chi ma nkongo, chi ma ri Angola,* decodified by Schwegler (1996b) as Afro-Spanish dialect for "I am a Congolese, I am an Angolan."

The Angolan influence extends even to pronouns and core grammatical items. Not only the third-person plural *ané* but also the now archaic second-person plural *enú* are borrowings from Kikongo. Furthermore, Palenquero has even retained all three of the singular bound pronominal clitics of Kikongo, *i-*, *o-*, and *e-* (Schwegler 1996c).

Thus we see that Palenquero has Portuguese-derived core lexical items, idiosyncratic structural correspondences with São Tomense itself, and strong interference from African languages spoken by slaves who were shipped via the Portuguese-owned depot São Tomé. All of this is combined with an actual historical citation of the originators of the language having designated their language as related to the very creole of São Tomé. The connection between Palenquero and São Tomense thus seems virtually inescapable. Schwegler, who has most assiduously identified the Portuguese roots of Palenquero, deserves the last word (1991b: 170): "How could so many (clearly deep-rooted) phonological, morphosyntactic, and lexical features of Portuguese enter Palenquero, a creole which has not come into contact with Portuguese since its implantation on American soil?"

As it happens, Sandoval also mentions other African slaves speaking a pidginized Spanish (cited in Schwegler 1998: 229), opening up the possibility that Palenquero developed from this, with Portuguese pidgin as the subsidiary presence. However, this would beg the question as to why Spanish creoles did not develop from the first-generation African slaves' pidgin varieties in the Chocó, the Chota Valley, Mexico, Peru, or Venezuela. The Portuguese pidgin explanation resolves this question thus: it is unlikely to be an accident that the two places where a Spanish creole is spoken today are exactly the two countries where we have particularly explicit evidence —as opposed to marginal linguistic evidence—of a Portuguese contact language being a vital element in the context in which the creole was born. Only in Cartagena do we have a statement as explicit as Father Sandoval's; only in Curaçao have we encountered a register attributed to slave ancestors which reveals traits now alive in Portuguese creoles on the West African coast. This suggests that the Portuguese pidgin was the key to the emergence of creoles in these two places; otherwise we would find a Spanish creole today in at least one or two other places.

It should be said that the scholars who have traced Papiamentu and Palenquero back to Portuguese pidgins have had no investment in any contention such as mine that Spanish creoles have never arisen independently on plantations, and certainly not in my broader cross-creole contentions to be outlined in later chapters. They came to their conclusions independently of each other and independently of me. Thus their work reveals what will become an imposing mass of independently gathered evidence which has all pointed in the direction of the Afrogenesis Hypothesis for years.

2.4 "THERE *WERE* SPANISH CREOLES": *BOZAL* SPANISH AND THE "EXTINCT PAN-HISPANIC CREOLE"

My analysis of Papiamentu and Palenquero has been relatively uncontroversial in previous airings (McWhorter 1995). However, some Spanish dialectologists and creolists, aware that the absence of other Spanish creoles is anomalous amidst current genesis theory, subscribe to a hypothesis that Spanish creoles must have existed in earlier centuries. The cases for this, however, are problematic.

2.4.1 *BOZAL* SPANISH

Although the Chocó, Chota Valley, Veracruz, Peru, and Venezuela have been neglected by creole theorists, some scholars have indeed noted that the absence of Spanish-based creoles in Cuba and Puerto Rico requires address. One result has been an argument that the Spanish of African-born slaves (*bozales*) in these countries is evidence of a once-widespread creole.

2.4.1.1 LINGUISTIC EVIDENCE

The most influential *bozal* Spanish data was collected in Cuba by Cabrera (1954) from the descendants of African-born slaves, who could still speak the Spanish of their forebears as a ritual language.

We have noted that creole languages can be distinguished by showing sharp reduction in comparison to their lexifiers and extensive morphosyntactic transfer from substrate languages. According to this metric, the first thing to note about the *bozal* Spanish data is that paradigmatic *reduction* is only moderate. For example, in plantation creoles, the lexifier's inflectional system has been completely eliminated. However, *bozal* Spanish in Cuba displayed vigorous reflections of the local standard morphology, as in the following example:

(3) Cuch-**a**   canto. To nosotro brinc-**ó**   la mar.
    listen-IMP song   all we   cross-PAST the sea

Listen to the song. All of us crossed the sea.

(Otheguy 1973: 331)

Although the third-person singular preterit has apparently been overgeneralized to all contexts, the stressed *-o* nevertheless contrasts with the unstressed *-a* of the imperative *cucha*. Thus there is overt morphological past marking in *bozal* Spanish, a rare feature in creoles.

Moreover, what reduction there is in *bozal* Spanish is only variable, not regular. For example, Granda (1978: 481–91) was the first to note that *bozal* Spanish displayed many *reductions* in comparison to standard Spanish, such as lack of gender concord, omission of articles, occasional omission of copula, and omission of some prepositions and complementizers in favor of parataxis. The problem, however, is that many of these reductions are merely optional, as Otheguy (1973: 324–5) observed. In other words, the lexifier morphology appeared to have been basically acquired, although not expressed as consistently as by native speakers.

What this suggests is that *bozal* Spanish was merely a transient second-language register of Spanish, something we would expect of African-born learners. Significantly, no scholar arguing for *bozal* Spanish as a lost creole has explained how this data differs qualitatively from the Yiddish-inflected, second-language English spoken by Jewish immigrants to the United States in the late nineteenth century.

Meanwhile, *bozal* Spanish also lacks the *morphosyntactic transfer* from West African languages which we would expect of a plantation creole. The originators of *bozal* Spanish in Cuba were brought mostly from the West African coast, from an area extending from present-day Togo to Cameroon (Knight 1970: 48), with some from Mozambique. By the 1830s, slaves from the Slave Coast (modern-day Togo and Benin) and Mozambique predominated (Paquette 1988: 36). Plantation creoles whose originators came mostly from the Slave Coast area make extensive use of serial verbs, which are largely agreed to be calques on West African constructions (Boretzky 1983: 161–91; McWhorter 1992a). But where we would expect them, they are absent in *bozal* Spanish. Consider the following examples.

Saramaccan Creole English directional serial:

(4) A wáka gó a   dí opoláni.
he walk go LOC the airplane

He walked to the airplane.

(Byrne 1987: 204)

Bozal directional sentence:

(5) La mué   que fue   la río.
the woman that go-PAST the river

The woman who went to the river.

(Otheguy 1973: 329)

(*La mué que andó fue la río. [andó "walked"])

Sranan Creole English sequential action serial:

(6) Agu sidõ de   krei.
pig sit there cry

The pig sat down and cried.

(Herskovits and Herskovits 1936: 176)

Bozal sequential action serial:

(7) Obon Tanzé e rey muete que entrá   pecao y   pasá
Obon Tanze is king dead that enter-PAST fish and pass-PAST

bongó.
drum

Obon Tanze is the dead king who got into the fish and into the drum.

(ibid. 327)

(* . . . entrá pecao pasá bongó.)

Note that *bozal* used conjunctions between verbs denoting sequential action, rather than parataxis, as do classic creoles.

Another example is that in plantation creoles with West African substrates, the etymon derived from the comitative preposition also serves as a conjunction within the noun phrase; that is, "with" and "and" are the same word. This reflects a pan-Niger-Congo feature; for example,

Ewe:

(8) a. M-á- yì **kplé** wò.
I-FUT-go with you

I shall go with you.

b. dzí **kplé** anyígba
heaven with earth

Heaven and earth.

(Westermann 1928: 143)

Haitian Creole French:

(9) Papa-m **ak** mama-m te vini. (*ak* "with")
father-my with mother-my ANT come

My father and my mother came.

(Sylvain 1936: 156)

Principense Creole Portuguese:

(10) Mínu **ki** mwí sé (*ki* "with")
child with mother his

The child and his mother.

(Günther 1973: 80)

Bozal Spanish lacks this feature:

(11) Saya Coba, raya Mbele **y** cota Cambiriso (*y* "and")
tunic Coba stripe Mbele and coat Cambiriso

A Coba tunic, an Mbele stripe and a Cambiriso coat

(Cabrera 1954: 463)

Another example: all of the deep Atlantic creoles use unmarked verbs to express the past as well as the present in many cases. For example, Miskito Coast Creole English *Wi **liiv** from der an **kom** doun hiir fo stodi. Ai **staat** to pas mai gried-dem.* "We left that place and came down here so I could study. I started to pass from one grade to the next" (Holm 1978). This reflects a similar encoding of the past with unmarked verbs in the substrate languages:

(12) É-flè   só   ná-m.
      he-buy horse give-me

      He bought me a horse.

      (Westermann 1930: 50)

Meanwhile, note that in all of the *bozal* Spanish sentences treated here, the past is expressed with a morphological marker.

At risk of belaboring the point, one more example bears mentioning. Otheguy (1973: 327–8) takes the postposing of the demonstrative adjectives in *bozal* Spanish as evidence of West African calquing, as in the following:

(13) yo só **piera ese.**
      I   be stone that

      I am that stone.

However, he admits that standard Spanish does allow the construction *la pierra esa,* as opposed to the alternate *esa pierra,* and Lipski (1986: 182) notes that this is a common construction in colloquial Spanish. Otheguy claims that the omission of the definite article *la* identifies this as a radical restructuring of Spanish nonetheless. However, a more economical analysis is that the omitted article represents the effects of second-language acquisition on an otherwise fully acquired colloquial construction.

Otheguy (1973), however, while rightly taking issue with Granda (1978, but initially published before 1973), argues nevertheless that *bozal* Spanish signals an extinct creole, taking a different approach. Otheguy attempts to depict certain *bozal* Spanish features as radical reinterpretations of any Spanish dialect, and thus as diagnostic of creole status. However, as Chaudenson (1979, 1992) has demonstrated, in creoles, one must be careful to distinguish true restructurings of the lexifier from mere phonologically "evolved" inheritances from the regional varieties spoken by white colonials. None of Otheguy's arguments pass that test.

For example, Otheguy analyzes *tá* as a present-tense marker rather than a reflex of the verb *estar* "to be," and designates this a creole feature absent in any other Latin American Spanish dialect:

(14) cómo va sé máno   branco . . . ? ¡**Tá jugá!**
      how go be brother white   be   play

      How could I be a white man? You must be kidding!

      (326)

Table 2.3. Present tense and progressive aspect in standard
Spanish and *bozal* Spanish

	Standard	*Bozal*
Present tense	*júga*	*júga*
Present progressive	*está jugándo*	*tá jugá*

However, we note that when *tá* appears before verbs, the verbs always have
syllable-final stress. As it happens, the semantics and structure of this *tá* + V
construction correspond neatly with that of the present progressive construction in full varieties of Spanish (see Table 2.3). While the *-ando* ending is itself replaced by a simple stressed vowel (itself derived most likely
from an overgeneralized and phonologically eroded infinitive), the construction occurs precisely where the present progressive construction appears today. Furthermore, the *tá* + V construction is by no means the regular, obligatory way of expressing the present—it coexists with an equally
frequent simple present tense with no preceding marker:

(15) **Hace** saco pá sacá é   d'ahí.
   makes sack for take her of-there

   He makes a sack to take her out of there.

   (330)

Thus there is no more motivation to analyze *tá* as a "present marker" than
there would be to propose a similar analysis for *estar* in full varieties of
Spanish.

   In a similar vein, Otheguy proposes that *bozal* Spanish distinguished
between completivity, marked with verb-final stress, and noncompletivity,
marked with penultimate stress:

(16) Cuch-**a** canto. To nosotro brinc-**ó**   la mar.
   listen song all we   cross-PAST the sea

   Listen to the song. All of us crossed the sea.

   (331)

Otheguy proposes that since this system departs from any Latin American Spanish dialect, it is a structural innovation. However, we must note
that preterit endings are stressed in the standard, and the distribution of
the stressed ending in *bozal* Spanish corresponds perfectly with that of the

preterit in the standard. Thus we have merely the leveling of a morphological paradigm, not a semantactic departure from the standard system.

The above data are from *bozal* Spanish in Cuba; however, the same analysis applies to similar varieties across the Spanish Caribbean and Latin America. Here, for example, is a sample of *bozal* Spanish from Puerto Rico, from a play written in 1852 (taking place in the previous year) in which one character is an African-born slave and speaks in a particularly reduced variety of Spanish. Here is a representative selection:

(17) Tu siempre ta jablando a mí con grandísima rigó.
     you always be talking   to me with great   rigor

     yo ta queré mucho a ti; grande, grande así—
     I   be want much to you big   big   thus

     son mi sufrimienta . . . si tú   ta queré mi corazó . . .
     be   my suffering   if you be want my heart

     You are always talking to me with great harshness. I love you very much, greatly, greatly so—you make me suffer . . . if you want my heart . . .

     (Alvarez Nazario 1961: 388)

Of course, the writer most likely adapted the genuine register towards the standard somewhat in the interest of comprehensibility in the theater. However, the features shared with Cuban *bozal* Spanish indicate that the passage is relatively representative of the actual variety, and thus my analysis of the Cuban selections can be applied here as well.

Clearly, *bozal* Spanish departed from the local Spanish varieties in terms of paradigmatic levelings—no fully transmitted dialects of Spanish are known to be phonologically or inflectionally reduced to quite this extent. However, the linguistic evidence gives much reason to suppose that this was simply the incompletely acquired, second-language Spanish of an immigrant generation.

2.4.1.2 SOCIOHISTORICAL EVIDENCE

Sociohistorical depictions of *bozal* Spanish reinforce this analysis. For example, just as the moderateness of the reduction would lead us to expect, contemporary testimony depicts *bozal* Spanish as mutually intelligible with the Spanish of whites. Pichardo (1862: vii) notes in reference to *bozal* Spanish that "it can be understood by any Spaniard, except for some words known to all which need to be translated". Similarly, we encounter instances such as an instruction to priests in 1796, when working with *bozales*, to "talk to them in the kind of language they use, without cases, tenses, conjunctions, agreement, order" (Castellanos and Castellanos 1992: 349).

Although the language produced by someone following these instructions would certainly diverge considerably from actual *bozal* Spanish, the very fact that such an instruction was given implies a closer relationship between *bozal* and the local standard than between, for example, Sranan and English. Early written accounts of Sranan (Voorhoeve and Lichtveld 1975: 280–2) and Haitian (DuCoeurjoly 1802) treat them as separate languages and do not imply that the creoles are in any sense within the competence of Europeans through the application of some simple reductions. It is significant that while grammars were compiled of these two creoles, no such grammars were thought necessary for *bozal* Spanish. Instead, brief lists of *bozal* vocabulary items (Castellanos and Castellanos 1992: 350) were considered to suffice for the use of the Spaniard.

Furthermore, contemporary sources strongly support our suspicion that *bozal* Spanish was a transient second-language register, not a transmitted badge of ethnic identity. Pichardo (1862: iii) noted that "the Negroes born in Cuba talk like the local whites," and he was not the only person to make this observation (Bachiller and Morales 1883: 100–1; cited in Castellanos and Castellanos 1992: 353). Thus the claim that *bozal* Spanish is an extinct creole is supported neither by linguistic nor sociohistorical evidence.

Seen in perspective, the *bozal* Spanish literature typifies a tendency in creole studies to read moderate morphological reduction in a postcolonial language variety spoken by blacks as evidence of an extinct creole. In some cases, the evidence supports this. For example, Barbadian Creole English (Bajan) today is a highly metropolitanized dialect; its speakers do not generally consider themselves to speak a "patois." Nevertheless, sociohistorical plausibility long suggested that a more basilectal creole had once obtained (Cassidy 1980, 1986). In confirmation, field work has unearthed pockets of creole speakers (Roy 1986; Rickford 1992), and historical documentation has finally confirmed that a creole was once widespread (Rickford and Handler 1994; Fields 1995).

As often as not, however, the evidence suggests that the current situation is more or less the original. For example, a decades-long search just as diligent as the one on Bajan has failed to give any compelling evidence that Gullah itself was once spoken throughout the deep American South and that African-American Vernacular English is its decreolized descendant. Chaudenson's (1981a) case that Réunionnais French was previously as basilectal as Mauritian Creole French is a similar case (see Section 5.5.3.4), and despite top-quality research (e.g., Holm 1987, the work of Alan Baxter [De Mello et al. 1998]), Brazil has yielded only tentative evidence that a creole Portuguese was once spoken there.

These searches are eternally considered "open," however—usually less because the evidence suggests this than because the unearthing of a lost creole would be useful to general concerns. The discovery that Gullah was once spoken across the South would be advantageous to continuum-based models of decreolization, not to mention to the legitimization of Black English. For Chaudenson, a lost Réunionnais basilect would bolster his view of creoles like Mauritian as extensions of regional dialects, via proposing that Réunionnais, a clear derivant of Bourbonnais French, was once merely an intermediate step in a smooth progression of lects down to a Mauritian-like basilect. Meanwhile, the search for a Brazilian creole is motivated by the awkwardness of its absence in view of the limited access model.

However, we must always be open to the possibility that the object of such searches may not have existed. In this light, our question must be, Can it be said that the investigators of *bozal* Spanish have presented us with evidence as solid as the investigators of Barbados have? They have not: instead, the citations show not a creole but a second-language register, and contemporary observations depict it not as a new language in any sense, but as a variety understandable to local whites and spoken only by newcomer slaves. In other words, *bozal* Spanish was no more remarkable a phenomenon than Ellis Island English.

2.4.2 AN EXTINCT PAN-HISPANIC CREOLE?

Related to the *bozal* Spanish argument is a more general one claiming that a Spanish-based creole was once spoken throughout the Spanish Caribbean and Latin America, but that it now survives only in El Palenque as Palenquero, having everywhere else decreolized and disappeared in response to normative pressure from Spanish (Bickerton and Escalante 1970: 262; Granda 1978; Schwegler 1993a, 1996a). However, there is much reason to assume that no such creole ever existed.

The main problem with this argument is basic sociolinguistic implausibility. Sociolinguistics has taught us that vernacular dialects tend to be hardy in competition with dominant standards, and that it takes a great deal more than mere exposure to standard dialects in school to eliminate them from a speech community. In creolophone communities, authors such as Rickford (1986a) have shown that while the standard indeed has a definite prestige because of its association with advancement, basilectal and meso-lectal registers have just as powerful a covert prestige and are maintained as symbols of racial and social identity (see also Mufwene 1991b).

The "covert" aspect is important: we must not be misled by the notorious lack of fit between informants' statements to outsiders and their actual behavior—another lesson which the study of language attitudes and language planning has demonstrated repeatedly. Thus Schwegler (1991a: 90), for example, notes that in the Chocó, "constant influence from the schools . . . checks and corrects ancient local linguistic customs," and quotes an informant as saying that "everybody thinks that to speak well is to get ahead, and nobody wants to go back to the old way" [translation from Spanish mine]. To read this, however, as meaning that schoolroom chastisements and negative evaluation from outsiders would lead a long-established, isolated, vital community to shed the language expressing their very souls in warm, casual interactions is quite implausible. Creolophone speakers make similar devaluative comments about their speech across the English and French Caribbean, for instance, and yet the creoles persist, Belizean English Creole being a well-studied example (LePage and Tabouret-Keller 1985). Claims for an extinct pan-Hispanic creole are incomplete without an explanation for why the basic tenets of sociolinguistics were suspended in the Spanish Caribbean and Latin America.

To be sure, creoles *can* disappear via decreolization. However, this follows from the erosion of the social identity the creole expressed. Clearly, the isolation in which black Chocoanos or Ecuadoran *Choteños* live is hardly conducive to such an erosion. If schoolroom pressure were actually enough to erase a creole in the Chocó, then we would certainly not expect black urban Belizeans or Martiniquans to speak creoles, and yet they have, do, and by all indications, will.

Thus we must ask, Why would a Spanish creole in the Chocó vanish while African-American Vernacular English is vibrantly transmitted to generation after generation of even middle-class American blacks, despite its notorious devaluation in schools? A more likely interpretation of the Chocó and other former Spanish colonies is that a creole never was spoken, and that a community variety of Spanish itself has always served as the vernacular.

Furthermore, even if a case could be made for why local conditions did erase a Spanish creole in *one* Spanish colony, given the basic rarity of complete decreolization, how likely would it be that the pan-Hispanic creole would have vanished *everywhere* but El Palenque de San Basilio? Indeed, normative pressure is exterminating Palenquero today. However, we certainly would not expect this to occur so uniformly in Spanish America only.

Finally, the pan-Hispanic creole reconstruction is particularly implausible when viewed through a cross-colonial perspective. Namely, the hypothesis lacks an explanation as to why such normative pressure was so strong only under the Spanish. One creolist once argued to me that eloquence in standard registers is closely associated with manhood in Spanish-speaking cultures (the quote from the black Chocoano above could be seen as illustrating this). This acknowledged, the question simply is, What about the French? The French are notorious—more so than the Spanish, even—for their association of eloquence in the standard with status and legitimacy. Nevertheless, in Martinique, now officially even a *département* of France, French and the creole exist in a diglossic relationship in which French is treated as the hallowed vehicle of a noble culture while the creole is predictably stigmatized, to the point of being declared "dead" by some Martiniquan intellectuals. However, it is well known in creole studies and beyond that Martiniquais is a thriving language. Normative pressures are quite similar in the Spanish Caribbean and Latin America and thus cannot be seen as responsible for the "disappearance" of a former creole across the entire hemisphere (especially with such uncanny consistency). As Laurence (1974: 498) put it, "It seems inconceivable that if Spanish creoles did in fact exist, they should have disappeared so completely without leaving behind some residual traces."

Since Laurence's statement, Schwegler (1996a) has identified what he presents as just such traces of an original pan-Hispanic creole throughout the Spanish Caribbean and Latin America. However, he traces these clues back ultimately to the *Portuguese*-based pidgin of São Tomé; specifically, a double negation pattern and Portuguese lexical remnants.

I take no issue with slaves having imported a *Portuguese* pidgin to the New World; indeed, as noted in Section 2.3.2, the evidence allows no other interpretation. However, I cannot follow Schwegler in his subsequent conclusion that the pidgin was relexified into a *Spanish* pidgin or creole across the Spanish Caribbean and Latin America, rather than only in Cartagena (where Palenquero formed) and Curaçao. I maintain that it is extremely implausible that a widespread Spanish creole would have disappeared so completely, and that it is much more economical and theoretically sound to assume that a Spanish creole developed, via *relexification* of the *Portuguese* pidgin, only among the ancestors of today's Palenquero and Papiamentu speakers.

After all, traces of Portuguese pidgin in a variety of Spanish do not automatically imply that the Spanish itself was once a pidgin—other interpretations of this data are equally plausible. Pidgins and creoles can contribute lexical items and isolated grammatical influences to regular languages, just as regular languages do to each other. In other words, a more elegant interpretation of Schwegler's data is that the Portuguese pidgin traces were adstratal influences amidst the full acquisition of Spanish, with no necessary intermediate step of a Spanish creole.

My view hardly requires that there may not have been some Spanish-based creoles elsewhere in Spanish America in the past. Indeed, Granda (1978: 416–7) notes that a now-extinct creole was once spoken in the inner Colombian town of Uré by descendants of slaves who escaped from gold mines in the Antioquia province. It should be said that Granda gives no data and was unable to actually visit Uré. However, assuming that the creole existed, it is most likely that it, too, was based upon an imported Portuguese pidgin. If it were simply the result of a direct encounter with Spanish, then we would expect Spanish creoles in the other Spanish American locales where in fact, there are none.

Thus as noted, many scholars will respond to my interpretation of the Chocó, the Chota Valley, Veracruz, Peru, and Venezuela with the claims that either there *are* Spanish creoles elsewhere, or that there *were* Spanish creoles in the past. Both claims are highly questionable. The Spanish creoles which exist do not appear to have developed via the pidginization of Spanish itself: Palenquero and Papiamentu began as Portuguese pidgins, with Spanish lexicon a later overlay. The *bozal* Spanishes were mere second-language varieties spoken by first-generation arrivals, no more "creole" than the "Yiddishe dialect" of English in turn-of-the-century popular songs about the Lower East Side. The argument that there was once a Spanish creole spoken throughout Spanish America unduly strains sociolinguistic credibility, and the small amount of empirical evidence for it (Portuguese pidgin remnants) is easily accounted for as simply adstratal phenomena.

2.5 "THERE *WILL TURN OUT TO BE* SPANISH CREOLES"

Many creolists have long hoped that a Spanish-based creole would turn up spoken by a hitherto unstudied Afro-Hispanic group, with Cuba figuring especially large as a possibility. I am the last one to quarrel with hope. However, "they'll turn up" would have been a stronger counterargument in the 1960s, when less field work had been done. However, at this writing, we have seen thirty years of assiduous field work, during which travel has become easier, two new generations of creolists have been born, and a small army of linguists, anthropologists, and folklorists (mostly Spanish-speaking) have generated a considerable literature on Afro-Hispanic populations (as the bibliography of, for example, Lipski 1994 attests). Moreover, during all of this, a paradigm has coalesced which makes the scarcity of Spanish creoles a ringing anomaly, begging the discovery of one.

To be sure, work remains to be done. However, would not we expect that after all this time, given the obvious fact that the discovery of a new Spanish creole would make a career, that *someone* would have found a Spanish creole other than Papiamentu and Palenquero *somewhere* across the vast expanse of the Caribbean and Latin America?

2.6 ACCOMMODATING THE THEORY TO THE DATA: *SOCIÉTÉS D'HABITATIONS* VERSUS PLANTATIONS

There are scholars who have concurred that no plantation Spanish creole exists, ever has, or is likely to be found. However, instead of reading this as an indication that the limited access model is mistaken, they have attempted to explain it via extenuating circumstances. Successful though many of these arguments have been in themselves, they have all addressed an incomplete data set.

These treatments hinge upon a conception encapsulated in a classic study of Indian Ocean French creoles by Baker and Corne (1982). These authors argue that in plantation societies, disproportion of black to white transformed a European language into a creole only in cases where such disproportion set in soon after the establishment of the colony. If instead, there was a long period of demographic parity between whites and blacks, then by the time massive slave importations began, enough slaves in the society had been able to acquire a full enough register of the dominant language that subsequent arrivals were able to acquire a similar register from them, despite limited access to Europeans themselves. The test case for this hypothesis is Mauritius and Réunion. Slaves were imported to Mauritius in large numbers soon after its colonization, and a deep French-based creole emerged there. Réunion, however, became a sugar plantation society only in the nineteenth century after having begun as a society of small farms (*sociétés d'habitation* in Chaudenson's [1979, 1992] terminology) inhabited by whites and Malagasy spouses and servants in close interaction, followed by a long period of coffee cultivation, which required less slaves than sugar cultivation. Thus during the eighteenth century, slaves brought to Réunion had acquired a restructured, but hardly pidginized, variety of

French. Thus this variety was acquired even by the massive numbers of new slaves brought in at the transformation to sugar, because new slaves were able to acquire this register from older slaves.

Many have argued that the absence of Spanish creoles is due to conditions similar to those in Réunion. According to this argument, Spanish colonies were devoted to small farms, on which blacks and whites worked together in equal number, until conversion to sugar plantation economies in the nineteenth century (Mintz 1971: 481–5; Megenney 1985: 221; Chaudenson 1992: 124–8). This argument is indeed quite valid for Cuba, Puerto Rico, and the Dominican Republic, as even I myself (McWhorter 1995: 223–6) have argued.

In terms of Spanish colonization as a whole, however, this argument is fatally hobbled by addressing only the Spanish Caribbean islands, while neglecting the many similar Spanish plantation systems which the Spanish established in their mainland colonies. Crucially, these colonies did not follow the Réunion-style sociohistorical trajectory.

From treatments such as Chaudenson's and my own, a general impression has developed in creole studies that the late development of large plantations in the Spanish Caribbean was analogous to the delayed conversion to sugar plantations in English, French, and Dutch possessions, with the Spanish having simply taken 250 years (from the mid-1500s to about 1800) to make the conversion rather than a few decades (from the early to late 1600s) as did the other powers. In fact, the Spanish had the same expansionist bent as the other powers, and restricted their Caribbean islands to small-scale farming only because their mainland colonies offered richer opportunities for the establishment of large-scale plantation economies. In other words, the other powers began sugar cultivation by transforming their island colonies on site; the Spanish, however, moved to the mainland to accomplish this transformation.

One problem for the Spanish island colonies was that geographically, they were exposed to rampant piracy from the English and French, who in the 1500s and early 1600s had yet to establish footholds in the New World. In addition, the Spanish were not as committed to large-scale sugar production in the Caribbean as the other powers would be, out of a mercantilist commitment to avoid competing with the sugar grown in Spain itself (Guerra y Sanchez 1964: xv, Blackburn 1997: 138). The mainland colonies, on the other hand, offered two advantages. One was that, the Spanish colonies themselves needing a sugar supply, sugar could be grown in mainland colonies without interference from piracy. Second was that the Spanish were quite committed to mining gold and other metals, and these were in much greater abundance in the mainland colonies than in the islands. As a result, the Spanish concentrated their plantation-scale activities in New Spain (Mexico), New Granada (Colombia) and Peru (Blackburn 1997: 137–9, 142–4).

In these colonies, then, large-scale agriculture was an initial goal, small-scale farming having been established and found insufficient on the island colonies. The on-site farm-to-plantation development of the Spanish Caribbean islands in the 1800s was in no way a pan-Hispanic phenomenon. More specifically, the long period of intimate interracial contact—that is, the *société d'habitation* stage familiar to scholars of English and French creoles—simply did not exist in the mainland colonies.

For example, Africans indeed were not brought to the plantations immediately; the original Spanish intention was to use Native American labor. However, the Native Americans were in no sense stand-ins for the early Malagasy slaves in Réunion. They had not coexisted with Spaniards on the stable, long-term basis which would have led them to develop viable second-language varieties of Spanish to pass along to later African arrivals, as whites and older slaves passed on French to new slaves in Réunion. As we have seen, the Native Americans had been used by themselves only briefly, tending to either perish from European diseases or escape. Furthermore, they had not shared households with their masters, often even working under the *encomienda* arrangement which allowed them to live in surrounding villages.

Since the Native American population was waning via death and escape as the Africans came, the proper analogy is not with older slaves passing on French in Réunion, but with the white indentured servants in many early English and French colonies, who at the transformation to sugar were on the wane like the Spanish American Indians, serving limited terms of service and replaced, not supplemented, by slaves. Since creoles emerged in such societies, it is clear that input from the servants did not put a brake on the establishment of creoles once large influxes of slaves were imported. It would therefore be impossible to argue that Native Americans could have been responsible for preventing the emergence of creoles in Spanish America, especially since, unlike the English and French servants, they were second-language speakers of the lexifier.[2]

2. This is not to say that sociohistorical configurations in the mainland Spanish colonies were *always* of the type which would lead us to expect a creole. In Bolivia, for example, Africans were imported only in moderate number, often worked on small plantations in intimate contact with indigenized mulattoes and Indians, and upon emancipation intermarried with Aymarans and have identified culturally with

We also seek in vain for evidence that blacks ever coexisted in equal number with whites during or after the transition from Native American labor in the mainland Spanish colonies. As we saw in Section 2.2.1, in the mines of the Chocó there was no period of relative black-white parity which could have allowed relatively full acquisition by earlier slaves, nor was there in the Chota Valley, as we saw in Section 2.2.2. In Veracruz sugar was grown at the founding of the colony rather than after a later transition from less demanding crops (Carroll 1991: 42), and the plantations were begun on a large scale, rather than increasing gradually in size over the decades. A typical example is the Albornoz plantation, for which 150 slaves were purchased at the outset rather than accumulated gradually (63); Hernán Cortés himself is documented to have stocked his new sugar plantations with large single purchases of slaves (202). In Venezuela, as in the Chocó, the mines made a *société d'habitation* stage especially untenable: the Cocorote mine was founded in 1620, and after thirty short years, had 114 slaves, 50 Native Americans, and a mere 16 or so whites (Acosta Saignes 1967: 153–7). In Peru, as in the Chota Valley, a given estate usually cultivated a variety of crops at one time and thus immediately required much more than a handful of slaves. In the early 1600s, slave forces of more than 20 were typical, while some plantations had 40 or more slaves (Bowser 1974: 89, 94–5).

In sum, creolists have granted a great deal of useful attention to the social histories of colonies like Barbados, St. Kitts, Suriname, Martinique, and Cuba, their extended and sociologically intriguing *société d'habitation* periods having been widely discussed in the field. It must be clear, however, that one encounters nothing of the sort in the social histories of mainland Spanish colonies.

2.7 THE SPANISH AS KINDER, GENTLER COLONIZERS

Mintz (1971) is an example of an occasionally encountered claim that the scarcity of Spanish creoles was due to Iberians having presumably been more racially tolerant than other Europeans, leading to interracial relations more conducive to full acquisition of the lexifier than elsewhere. It is specifically often noted that manumission of slaves was common in Spanish colonies (Mintz 1971: 488; Laurence 1974: 492) and that the dedication of

---

them (Crespo 1977; Lipski 1994: 186–7). Thus the absence of a Spanish creole in Bolivia is quite predictable under current creole genesis models. However, this is not the case in the other colonies I have discussed.

Catholic Spain to religious instruction for its slaves led to richer language transmission (Chaudenson 1992: 124–5).

Once again, however, these arguments apply to only a sliver of the proper data set. Throughout Spanish America, it can indeed be argued that in certain contexts, Africans were not as sharply delineated as subhuman as they were under other powers. This appears partly to have followed from the fact that Iberians had imported large numbers of Africans to Portugal and Spain as house servants before beginning to utilize them in plantation colonies. Intimate contact inevitably made the basic humanity of a maid or footman more apparent than that of a fieldhand rarely encountered except in passing. This would also have been the case in many of the Iberian colonies themselves, where comparatively large proportions of Africans were used not in plantation gangs but as individual laborers for single urban households or in small groups on farms. As we have seen, in the slow-developing Spanish Caribbean islands, few Africans were even used as plantation laborers at all until the 1800s.

However, whatever fluidity in racial conceptions this situation conditioned, it predominated only in towns and on small farms. When it came to large-scale plantation agriculture, as Blackburn (1997: 237) succinctly puts it, "There was unpleasant work to be done, and even tender-hearted whites would be grateful for a system of slavery which gradually allowed them to be relieved of it," and all evidence demonstrates that the brutal exigencies of sugar cultivation obliterated any significant affection or clemency towards black slaves.

For example, the conversion to a sugar economy transformed Cuba into the same hell on earth for slaves that other powers' colonies were. Sugar plantations required more manpower, longer hours, and caused more injury and death, than any other plantation type. Life for slaves on Cuban sugar plantations was by all accounts as degraded and miserable, and relations between masters and slaves as negative, as on any New World plantation, if not more so. The death rate was as high as 10 percent per year, such that the slave population increased more through new purchases than births. At any given time, 20 percent to 40 percent of the slave force was in sick bay due to injuries (Paquette 1988). Sugar plantations were considered the worst possible lot for an African-born Cuban, and consignment to one was used as the direst disciplinary threat to slaves working in more benign contexts elsewhere in Cuba (Knight 1970: 82; Klein 1967: 150; Paquette 1988: 39). Finally, rates of manumission declined severely after the advent of sugar, due to the high demand for labor (Knight 1970: 93).

The same horrors are painfully apparent in the mainland colonies. For example, although in Colombia there was indeed a comprehensive slave code established in 1789 to protect slaves from abuse, most slaveowners in the Chocó had no access to it, and the small numbers of people involved in the mining operations did not justify the expense of traveling into the interior to enforce the code with any effective regularity (Sharp 1976: 128). Similarly, the oft-cited restraining influence the Catholic church had upon the treatment of slaves in certain periods of Spanish colonization held negligible force in the Chocó: clerics were in short supply and were often slaveowners themselves (Sharp 1976: 130–1). This also eliminated the possibility of slaves being taught Spanish during religious instruction. Thus slavery was a typically miserable experience: work proceeded from sunrise to sundown, often six days a week (136), and flogging was a regular punishment for any perceived offenses (139–40). The most unequivocal evidence of the misery of the slaves' lot is the simple fact that escapes and revolts were common (140).

Slavery was similarly oppressive in the Chota Valley where, for example, religious instruction was deliberately withheld, whites were notoriously cruel to slaves, and interactions between slave and white were strictly discouraged (Jaramillo Perez 1962: 52–3). Nor was Iberian racial tolerance evident in Veracruz, where slaves were regularly blinded, maimed, and infected with disease during their work (as they were on all Caribbean sugar plantations), and after emancipation were socially marginalized and disenfranchised (Carroll 1991: 82–5). In Peru, manumission of plantation slaves was rare (Bowser 1974: 298–300), corporal punishment was common (231), and religion was withheld even to the point of denying slaves their last rites (236). In Venezuela, blacks were actively maintained as the lowest caste, and their movements were restricted (Acosta Saignes 1967: 297–303). It appears almost unnecessary to state that racial harmony cannot be treated as the reason the descendants of slaves in mainland Spanish colonies speak no creoles.

2.8 "NOTHING IS AT ISSUE": THE "CASE-BY-CASE" ARGUMENT

A growing strain of creolist thought emphasizes that the genesis of each creole was a response to a different combination of factors in each colony, requiring thorough examination of the facts in each locale and a general wariness of universal formulas. This movement from the "lumping" tendency of earlier creolist thought (the source of monogenesis, the bioprogram and *Comparative Afro-American*) to a "splitting" one (the source of

Siegel's exhaustive 1987 study of Fiji, the work of Claire Lefebvre, and Speedy's 1995 proposal of two creoles in Louisiana), is partly a reaction to the sweeping orientation of Bickerton's (1981, 1984a) Language Bioprogram Hypothesis, fueled further by the discovery of quirky, taxonomy-straining creoles like Tayo Creole French and Berbice Creole Dutch.

However, it would be overgenerating this approach to claim, in response to this chapter, that it is unreasonable to see the absence of creoles in several mainland Spanish colonies as counterevidence to any "model" or "formula," and that the answer to the conundrum will be found via diligent sociohistorical research on each colony.

As I have noted, the limited access conception is so deeply rooted in creolist thought that it is barely considered a "point of view" at all. To be sure, limited access is not considered an absolute *sine qua non* in the emergence of a creole, Tayo Creole French of New Caledonia being a prime example. However, when it comes to New World and Indian Ocean plantation creoles, limited access, and when it set in, and at what rate it increased, is a pivotal concern in all creole genesis work. One way of illustrating this is to point how reluctant most creolists would be to concur explicitly with the following statement:

> Limited access to the lexifier was insignificant or irrelevant to the fact that creole languages emerged in Haiti, the Sea Islands, and Jamaica, and instead, creoles emerged in these colonies as the result of three sets of local circumstances between which no significant parallels could be drawn.

To the extent that this would seem an untenable statement to a creolist, it would appear that the limited access conception is indeed a model which they subscribe to. This is hardly to say that such people consider limited access the *only* factor in creole genesis. Quite simply, however, if a creolist cannot concur with the statement above, then this shows that limited access occupies an important place in their genesis model. My point in this chapter, then, is that the mainland Spanish colonies put in question a model which is crucial to current creole genesis theory.

Furthermore, the sociohistorical data on plantation colonies is usually so broad that it could be bent to "explain" either the presence or the absence of a creole. For example, we can use the surviving documentation of Suriname to account for why an English-based creole is spoken there despite the Dutch having taken it over from the English more than three hundred years ago. We can reasonably posit that Sranan-speaking slaves passed on their creole to new slaves imported by the Dutch; this is nicely supported by the documentation that the English withdrawal of their slaves took several years, during which English-bought and Dutch-bought slaves would have interacted extensively.

However, imagine that a Dutch-based creole *were* spoken in Suriname today. In that case, with the same sociohistorical data, we would imagine quite plausibly that the withdrawal of the English slaves kept them from affecting language acquisition among the new ones. We would certainly not be scratching our heads as to why no English-based creole was spoken in Suriname.

Similarly, we can quite plausibly attribute the absence of a creole in Brazil to retention of African languages or racial mixing (Holm 1987: 414–6), but if there *were* a creole in Brazil, no one would wonder how a creole had survived in a context of African language retentions and racial mixing (anymore than anyone has in, say, Jamaica). We would simply opine that the creole must have been more advantageous to interethnic communication than any single African language, and that racial mixing does not always eradicate the power of vernacular identity.

Thus there is an inevitable degree of *post hoc*-ness in tracing the emergence of a creole—it's the nature of the beast. Given how many interpretations the sociohistorical data in countries like Suriname or Brazil lend themselves to, even if we could concoct "reasons" that no creoles had arisen in the Chocó, the Chota Valley, Veracruz, Venezuela, and/or Peru, how conclusive could such accounts ever truly be? In this chapter, we have seen that these mysteriously absent creoles *cluster* under a single power. This suggests that something broader was at work than just unconnected, local demographic constellations.

2.9 CONCLUSION

To summarize what we have seen, I have brought to attention five mainland Spanish plantation colonies where, despite conditions considered perfect for creole genesis, no Spanish creoles are present. I claim that this data puts strongly into question the limited access conception of creole origin. I have shown the flaws in all of the likely objections to my assertion, as summarized below.

(1)   The claim that Papiamentu and Palenquero *are* Spanish creoles is true only synchronically; they began as Portuguese-based.

(2)   The claim that *bozal* Spanishes *were* Spanish creoles is false; they were transient immigrant varieties. The related claim that a Span-

ish creole like Palenquero was once spoken throughout Spanish America is extremely difficult to maintain in view of sociolinguistic plausibility.

(3) The claim that Spanish creoles will turn up is reminiscent of the hope many Western explorers have had of finding a living brontosaur in central Africa: one would have turned up by now.

(4) The claim that there are no Spanish creoles because Spanish colonies remained *sociétés d'habitation* long before importing Africans in large numbers is false; it applies only to the three Caribbean islands but flatly misdepicts the mainland colonies.

(5) The claim that creole genesis can be studied only on a case-by-case basis, and that there is thus no limited access "model" to be contradicted, would be belied by the crucial role that limited access plays in all genesis work on New World and Indian Ocean plantation creoles. Besides, sociohistorical data on creole genesis is so broad that it could always be use to "explain" either the presence or absence of a creole.

With all of these objections addressed, we stand faced with a massive contradiction to the limited access conception so deeply rooted in creolist thought. My aim in this chapter has been to show that under no analysis can these creoles and dialects be analyzed as supporting the limited access conception, and that Spanish America in general puts it quite starkly into question. In the next chapter, we encounter an even vaster body of data which further questions the limited access model, despite having served as one of its main demonstration cases: the English-based creoles of the Caribbean.

3 The Atlantic English-Based Creoles

Sisters Under the Skin

3.1 INTRODUCTION

The *modus operandi* in tracing the history of the Atlantic English-based creoles (henceforth AECs)[1] is to treat each major creole as a local development within its own colony. Mufwene (1992: 161) concludes that "the 1720–1740 period is most likely the time Gullah must have started as a creole"; Bickerton (1994b) considers Sranan to have emerged in Suriname in 1690; and so on.

Yet at the same time, it is common knowledge among creolists that the Anglophone Caribbean (other than Suriname) is essentially "a single speech community" (Holm 1989: 446). Intelligibility between many of the creoles is considerable, with speakers from various islands casually referring to the creoles as varieties of a single "patois." Literary sources demonstrate this in cases such as an edition of the poem "Buddy Quow," written in what its author called "Gullah-Jamaican dialect" (Cassidy 1994: 16). Even creolophone specialists, such as Winford (1985), treat most of them (again, minus the Suriname varieties) as a general "Caribbean English Creole" (CEC) to no complaint.

The question, then, is how plausible it could be that each, or even many, of these creoles arose independently if today they are varieties of the same language. In response to this, over the decades there have been a number of scholars who have argued that the English-based creoles of the Caribbean are traceable to a single English-based ancestor (Cassidy 1980, 1986; Carter

1. Atlantic English-based Creole (AEC) refers to the English-based creoles of the Caribbean, Central America, and South America, as well as the related creoles of West Africa (Krio, Ghanaian Pidgin English, Nigerian Pidgin English, Cameroonian Pidgin English, etc.).

1987; Smith 1987; Baker 1998; more briefly, Stewart 1971; Alleyne 1971: 179–80; and most comprehensively and vociferously, Hancock 1969, 1986, 1987). Hancock and Smith, in particular, have presented compelling evidence that the Caribbean English-based creoles (*including* those in Suriname) share an array of features diagnostic of a single common parent. And yet, in creole studies this work has received passing attention at most.

To the extent that the lack of fit between the data and the locally based genesis accounts has been addressed, creolists appear to suppose that the similarities between these creoles can be attributed to "diffusion" between colonies. However, only recently has Baker (1998) begun the spadework of investigating the intercolonial population movements which would have caused such "diffusion," and Ian Hancock has meanwhile left the field.

This demonstrates how powerfully the limited access model has affected creolist thinking, in a classic example of how a paradigm within a science can marginalize what later proves to be powerful counterevidence. The limited access model *requires* that each creole emerged independently within its colony. The dissemination of a single pidgin would restrict "genesis" proper to one location, invalidating the limited access mechanism in all of the subsequent colonies. Clearly, however, properly speaking, the polygenetic limited access model cannot coexist with the generic conception of a single "Caribbean English Creole." In a given colony, only one of these frameworks can be valid. The evidence suggests that in most colonies, it is the limited access conception which is invalid.

Specifically, if each creole were an independent development, we would expect the AECs to give the impression of having arisen via *independent encounters with English* in each colony. However, on the contrary, these creoles give every indication of having arisen via *a single encounter with English*. This makes it impossible for them to have arisen independently, and suggests that a single English-based pidgin formed in a single place and was subsequently disseminated. If true, this would eliminate the application of the limited access model to all colonies except the one where the pidgin would have first arisen. In the next chapter we will see that even there, the limited access model is extremely problematic.

However, the goal of this chapter is to make clear that local developments can have had only an adstratal, posterior impact on creoles like Jamaican, Gullah, and Guyanese, and that all of them must ultimately stem from a single ancestor. Thus while we have seen that the South American Spanish colonies contradict the limited access model outright, the AECs are inapplicable to it.

3.2 METHODOLOGY

One reason that arguments like Hancock's have been neglected is the impression that such similar creoles could indeed have emerged independently. Many creolists suppose that a common superstrate, similar substrates, and the operation of universals are responsible for the bracingly similar results across the English Caribbean. However, even the operation of these three factors could not have produced certain traits the AECs share. There is an array of idiosyncratic correspondences between the AECs which are traceable neither to English, West African languages, nor universals. By the laws of comparative reconstruction, these traits indicate common origin.

My argument will be highly constrained, and must be sharply distinguished from earlier related arguments making cases based on less idiosyncratic features. For example, many features common to AECs can be attributed to *substrate* features, easily conceived as operating independently in more than one place. An example is serial verbs. Common in West African languages spoken from Ghana eastward through Nigeria, homelands of a great many slaves delivered throughout the Caribbean, serial verbs could plausibly have been transferred via independent geneses in each locale. Thus substrate features such as this are irrelevant to this particular argument.

Other features are traceable to the *superstrate* to which slaves in each English colony were exposed. For example, the habitual/progressive marker *do* found in many AECs need not be a common inheritance, since related usages are found in regional British dialects spoken by English settlers throughout the colonial Caribbean (e.g., Rickford 1986b). Thus superstrate-derived features like this are also irrelevant to this particular argument.

Many other features in AECs can be attributed to *universals*. A prime example would be the centrality of the anterior-nonpunctual-irrealis distinction in the tense-mood-aspect system, as Bickerton (1981, 1984a) has noted. Because universals, by definition, could possibly apply in any number of separate encounters with English, universal tendencies are also irrelevant to this particular argument.

The motivation for the argument, then, is strictly limited to a specific assembly of AEC features which reveal themselves after we have stripped away the features derivable from source languages or universals. I will present six such features, which I consider hidden but precious evidence of common ancestry.

3.3 THE FEATURES

3.3.1 LOCATIVE COPULA *DE*

In all of the AECs save the most acrolectal, the locative copula is the item *de*. In Table 3.1 we see this item in a representative sample of nine AECs, representing African varieties (Krio, Nigerian), Surinamese varieties (Sranan, Saramaccan), Eastern Caribbean varieties (Guyanese, Antiguan), Western Caribbean varieties (Jamaican, Belizean), and a North American variety (Gullah). This presentation, and corresponding ones throughout this section, would be impossible without the invaluable research of Hancock (1987).

The widespread distribution of *de* across the Caribbean and on the West African coast constitutes in itself one of the most powerful arguments for the common ancestry of these languages, for the simple reason that it is all but impossible that its incorporation into a pidgin English grammar occurred in more than one place. We must arrive at this conclusion no matter which account of its derivation we subscribe to.

The use of there *as locative copula is not a superstrate inheritance.* There *does not serve as a locative copula in any dialect of English.*

The use of there *as locative copula is not a substrate feature, nor is* de *a substrate borrowing.* Alleyne (1980a: 163–4) has suggested that *de* is a compromise between a copula *de* from the Twi dialect of Akan and the adverb *there* in English. The first problem we encounter is that *de* (which in the modern language is now *ne*) is actually a specialized *identificational equative* copula in Twi, used to indicate complete identity between two entities; the locative copula is *wo:*

(1) Mé nùá **ne** Kòfí.
    my brother COP Kofi

   My brother is Kofi.

   (Christaller 1875: 110)

(2) O-**wo** dán mù.
    he-COP house inside

   He is in the house.

   (ibid., 118)

Alleyne's hypothesis requires, then, that this Twi *identificational* copula was recast as a *locative* copula, presumably under the influence of the se-

Table 3.1. *Where is he?*

Krio	*Na usai i **de**?*
Nigerian	*I **de** husai?*
Sranan	*Na usai a **de**?*
Saramaccan	*Naásɛ a **dé**?*
Guyanese	*Wisaid am **de**?*
Antiguan	*We i **de**?*
Jamaican	*We im **de**?*
Belizean	*We i **de**?*
Gullah	*Wisai i **de**?*

Data from Hancock 1987: 285; in this and similar tables, I have selected sentences in the above nine creoles out of the thirty-three referred to by Hancock, and used a broad phonetic rendering rather than the extremely fine one Hancock uses, retaining the lax/tense distinction in Saramaccan only because it is phonemic in this creole.

mantics of English *there*. However, as Mufwene (1986a: 172–5) points out, we must ask why those originating these languages would have chosen a Twi morpheme out of the range of choices represented. Table 3.2 presents the locative copulas in languages spoken by the greatest number of slaves brought to the English Caribbean.[2] Alleyne (1971: 176, 1993) has elsewhere noted the social and cultural dominance of the Akan, which could be invoked as the motive for borrowing from Akan rather than from other languages represented. However, this dominance notwithstanding, how likely is it to have led to the *specific* recruitment of a locative copula, rather than any number of other items, in *several separate locations?* Meanwhile, what of the non-Twi speakers, who would have lacked a native phonetic model encouraging the recasting of *there* as a copula? If Twi *de* did somehow triumph in this fashion, surely it would not have happened in several

2. The languages are the substrate languages which research suggests had the strongest influence upon most of the Atlantic English-based creoles in general, based on lexical imprint (Mittelsdorf 1978; Cassidy 1983; Smith 1987; etc.), grammatical transfer (Alleyne 1980a; Boretzky 1983; McWhorter 1992a; etc.), historical evidence (LePage and DeCamp 1960; Curtin 1969; Hancock 1986; Rickford 1987; Postma 1990; etc.), and cultural evidence (Turner 1949; Price 1983; Alleyne 1993; etc.). Sources for substrate language data are as follows unless otherwise noted. Wolof: Fal, Santos, and Doneux 1990; Mandinka: Gamble 1987; Akan: Christaller 1875; Gbe: Westermann 1930; Igbo: Welmers and Welmers 1968; Yoruba: Ogunbowale 1970; Kikongo: Seidel and Struyf 1910.

Table 3.2. West African locative copulas

Wolof	*nekk*
Mandinka	*be*
Akan (Twi)	*wo*
Gbe (Ewe)	*le*
Igbo	*dì*
Yoruba	*wà*
Kikongo	*-ina*

separate places independently, as the limited access hypothesis requires, but only once in one place.

A final argument against the substrate-borrowing argument is that there is a very strong tendency for pidgins and creoles to recruit a superstrate positional verb as a locative copula, even when eschewing an expressed equative copula. Locative copulas thus fall outside of the range of items which are typically encoded with substrate borrowings. To account for *de* as a substrate borrowing requires that the AECs instead, with no exceptions, went against that tendency:

Guinea-Bissau Creole Portuguese:

(3) Tuga   i **sta** ba li.
    Portuguese CL COP ANT here

    The Portuguese were here.

    (Kihm 1980: 91)

Tok Pisin:

(4) Pik i   **stap** long banis.
    pig PM COP LOC enclosure

    The pigs are in the enclosure.

    (Mühlhäusler 1985a: 362)

Naga Pidgin:

(5) Moy yate əse
    I   here COP

    I am here.

    (Sreedhar 1985: 107)

Table 3.3. West African copulas and distal demonstratives

	Locative copula	*there*
Wolof	*nekk*	*fa*
Mandinka	*be*	*jèe*
Akan (Twi)	*wo*	*eho*
Gbe (Ewe)	*le*	*afíma*
Igbo	*dì*	*n'ébe ahù*
Yoruba	*wà*	*nibe nã*
Kikongo	*-ina*	*kuna*

In short, it is impossible that in West Africa, Suriname, Guyana, Antigua, Jamaica, Belize, and South Carolina separately, slaves (1) in each place bypassed the superstrate locative copula completely, counter to a strong opposite tendency in pidginization in general, and then *in each place* (2) borrowed one from the same single language represented in the learning community, despite the general objective being to forge a language of interethnic communication. Obviously, given the confluence of fortuitous circumstances which even one occurrence of such a borrowing would require, if it did happen, it indeed happened only once.

There is only one way in which substrate influence could possibly have had a uniform effect in several different locations. This would be if a homophony between *there* and a locative copula were a substrate-wide feature. However, the distal deictic adverb and the locative copula are not homophonous in any of the substrate languages (see Table 3.3).

The use of there *as a locative copula is not a universal.* On the contrary, it is a striking anomaly. In a survey of twenty-five languages from a wide sample of families (NSF project BNS-8913104) supervised by John Rickford, there were no copulas derivable from adverbs found; no such examples have been documented in other studies of copula derivation (e.g., Devitt 1990); and this author, long specializing in cross-linguistic study of the copula, has encountered none in any languages but the AECs.[3]

3. Languages studied under NSF project: Swahili, Nama, Hausa, Russian, Arabic, Mandarin Chinese, Hawaiian, Yagaria, Jacaltec, Irish, West Greenlandic Eskimo, Melanesian Pidgin English, Hungarian, Vietnamese, Tagalog, Finnish, Bengali, Hindi, Nahuatl, Twi, Ewe, Gã, Yoruba, Igbo, Haitian Creole, African-American Vernacular English. Other languages examined by Devitt (1990): Spanish, Portuguese,

Thus it becomes clear that *de* is a radical reinterpretation of the superstrate source *there*, not a simple borrowing from a superstrate dialect, not a common substrate feature, and not a universal. For the limited access model to account for *de*, then, its adherents would have to identify a mechanism for the transformation of *there* into a copula which could plausibly have occurred in several different places independently.

This, however, is impossible. To be sure, recategorialization of superstrate morphemes is a well-documented concomitant of pidginization (Miskito Coast Creole English *He advantage her* "He took advantage of her"; *He catch crazy* "He became psychotic" [Holm 1988: 103]). However, the extension of an adverb into a verbal domain of limited lexical content such as a locative copula is undocumented except in the AECs. The fact that the adverb *de* "there" exists alongside the copula in the creoles makes it even more of an intuitive stretch to view the copula as simply a reconceptualization of the adverb. It seems unlikely that learners of English would acquire the adverbial meaning of *there* and extend it to a copular function, especially given the typological anomalousness of such an extension:

	Subject	Copula	Predicate
Gbe	*Kofi*	*is*	*in the tree*
Creole	*Kofi*	***there (??)***	*in the tree*

In fact, the most plausible explanation of *de* as copula is one based on grammaticalization over time, rather than an immediate reconceptualization of *there*. We must at the outset, however, bypass the garden path of deriving copula *de* from the reanalysis of the progressive aspect marker *de*, coexistent with the adverb and the copula in many of the creoles in question, as in Krio *I de wok* "He is working." A progressive marker is further advanced along the cline of grammaticality than a locative verb, which retains a small degree of semantic content in the form of indicating being in a place rather than simple existence. Thus locative verb *de* evolving from the progressive marker *de* would contradict the very strong tendency for grammaticalization to proceed from the less to the more grammatical over time.

Thus we proceed to a more likely derivation. In Saramaccan, the deictic adverb *dé* is often optionally inserted into sentences in order to lend deictic emphasis. *Dé* in this usage is not integral to the grammaticality of the utterance; the usage is expressive in nature:

Mangarayi, Turkish, Alyawarra, Kiowa, Tamil, Zuni, Hebrew, Tigre, Kui, Kilba, Greek, Quechua, Shuswap, Lakhota, Karok.

(6) Nóiti fa   mi dé   a   Winikíi **dé,**   nóiti mi jéi   táa . . .
    never since I COP LOC Winikii there never I   hear talk

Never since I've been there at Winikii have I heard that . . .

(Glock 1986: 51)

(7) Dí Gaamá dí   Kófi gó lúku **dé**   dé   ku   suwáki **dé.**
    the chief REL Kofi go see   there COP with sickness there

The chief who Kofi went to look at is sick.

(Byrne 1990: 673)

(8) Dí bɛ wáta **dé**   wɛ hén dá   buúu.
    the red water there well it   COP blood

The red water is blood.

(Rountree and Glock 1977: 186)

It is from this expressive usage of the adverbial *dé* that the copula in Saramaccan is most plausibly derived. Presumably, at first, there was no expression of the locative copula; there is independent evidence for this in the fact that the equative copula *dá* also appears to have been absent in earliest Saramaccan and related creoles (McWhorter 1996d, 1997a: 93 – 103).

Reconstructed:

(9) Dí wómi ø   a   wósu.
    the man   COP LOC house.

The man is at home.

However, it would have been a common expressive strategy to insert a deictic *dé* between subject and predicate, similar to today's usage.

Reconstructed:

(10) Dí wómi **dé**   a   wósu.
     the man   there LOC house

The man is there at home.

Modern colloquial English retains a possible model for this usage in utterances such as *He's there in the garden,* or *She gets cranky when she's there at Tony's.*

In this position, "expressive" *dé* was ripe for reanalysis as a copula, because the originators of the language spoke languages in which a copula was obligatory between subject and predicate, such as the Ewe:

(11) É-lè   xɔ   me.
     he-COP house in

     He is in the house.

     (Westermann 1930: 91)

As a result, *dé* came to be interpreted, in this usage, as copular rather than adverbial:

(12) Dí wómi **dɛ**   a   wósu.
     the man   COP LOC house

     The man is at home.

(Migge 1995 proposes a similar pathway for Belizean *de*.) What is important about this account is that it describes a process which, while systematically plausible, hardly instantiates a strong tendency likely to be replicated in nine separate creoles. We are still faced with the typological anomaly of the homophony (and diachronic relationship) of adverb and copula cross-linguistically. The extensive literature on the diachronic origins of copular morphemes cross-linguistically (Li and Thompson 1977; Arends 1989; Devitt 1990; Luo 1991; Gildea 1993) clearly reveals a strong tendency for locative copulas to be derived from (1) positional verbs and (2) verbs "to be." Given this fact, the use of an adverb as a copula again appears as an interesting aberration which, when encountered in so wide and uniform a distribution, is most realistically designated an inherited trait, in line with the basic tenets of comparative reconstruction.

   Thus no matter how we analyze locative copula *de*, it would have been utterly impossible for it to emerge across the Caribbean in several separate creoles. The acceptance of the specific grammaticalization pathway I have proposed is much less important than the main aim, which is simply to demonstrate that *de* can be only a one-time creation and thus argues strongly for an ancestral pidgin. Thus we must ask, Whichever account of the origin of copula *de* one prefers, how plausible is it that the process occurred in West Africa, Suriname, Guyana, Antigua, Jamaica, Belize, and South Carolina separately?

3.3.2 EQUATIVE COPULA *DA*

Da, like *de*, is strong evidence that the AECs share a single ancestor. In AEC, the equative copula is realized variously as *da*, *na*, or *a*. I will treat the

Table 3.4. *He's my partner.*

Krio	*Na* mi padna.
Nigerian	*Na* ma fren.
Sranan	*Na* mi mati.
Saramaccan	Hén *da* mi kɔmpé.
Guyanese	I *a* mi kompe. (John Rickford, Jan. 1994 p.c.)
Antiguan	Hi *a* mi paadna.
Jamaican	Im *a* mi paadna.
Belizean	*Da* mi paadna.
Gullah	Hi *duh* mi paadnuh.

Adapted from Hancock 1987: 284.

latter two as derived from the first. For example, we can observe an evolution from *da* to *na* over time in Sranan (Arends 1989: 151); similarly, we find *da* in earlier documents of other varieties which now have *a* (e.g., Rickford 1980; Lalla and D'Costa 1990). Furthermore, this process instantiates a general phonological tendency for initial consonants to elide in monosyllabic grammatical morphemes undergoing heavy usage in such varieties (Rickford 1980). We also find *da* and *a* coexisting in some varieties (e.g., Escure 1983 on Belizean), while other varieties have preserved the original alveolar stop. Thus, over time,

na (Krio, Sranan)

da (Saramaccan, Belizean) >

a (Guyanese, Jamaican)

In this book, then, I will refer to these allomorphs collectively as *da* for convenience. *Da* is uniformly distributed among Atlantic English-based creoles (see Table 3.4).

Da is derived from the English *that* (see Arends 1989: 25–33; McWhorter 1996d, 1997a: 93–103 for details). Apparently no variety today preserves an exact homophony between the distal demonstrative and the copula, and the earliest historical documents available (such as of Sranan) show a copula *da* having already evolved. However, we can reconstruct this etymology from a comparative perspective. In Belizean, we find the item *dada*, a portmanteau morpheme which serves as a demonstrative pronoun while also overtly representing tense. As such, it is likely to have arisen from the adjacency of a demonstrative *da* and a copula *da*:

(13) **Dada** we a de   tel yu.
that-is what I PROG tell you

That's what I'm telling you.

(Escure 1983: 193)

We see support for the plausibility of the phonetic evolution in Krio, where the demonstrative is *dat* when the demonstrative is used as a pronoun, but *da* when it modifies a noun:

(14) a. **Dat** na   di tin.
that COP the thing

That's the thing.

(Fyle and Jones 1980: 66)

b. Tɛl **da** man se yu de šem.
tell that man say you be ashamed

Tell that man you're sorry.

(Hancock 1987: 308)

Like *de*, *da* is not derivable from any source likely to occur in several separate locations.

The use of that *as an equative copula is not a superstrate inheritance.* No English dialect uses *that*, or any morpheme resembling *da*, as a verb "to be." We can safely eliminate the possibility that *da* is a preserved regional British archaism.

The use of that *as an equative copula is not a substrate feature, nor is* da *a substrate borrowing.* Cross-linguistically, copulas are not always verbs. AEC is no exception, in that *da* in all varieties lacks verbal behaviors such as tense-aspect marking and clefting (e.g., Todd 1973: 10–2; Escure 1983: 194–6). However, in all of the pertinent West African substrate languages except one, Kikongo, the equative copula is rendered with a verb "to be"; for example, Ewe:

(15) Etso   a-**nye**   asigbe.
tomorrow FUT-COP market day

Tomorrow will be market day.

(Kozelka 1980: 55)

Table 3.5. West African equative copulas and distal demonstratives

	Equative copula	*that (pron.)*
Wolof	*la*	*bɔɔbu*
Mandinka	*mu*	*wò*
Akan (Twi)	*yɛ*	*no*
Gbe (Ewe)	*nye*	*má*
Igbo	*bù*	*áhù*
Yoruba	*se/jέ*	*eyi*
Kikongo	*i*	*kiokio*

Furthermore, none of the substrate languages have a remotely plausible candidate for a direct borrowing, as we see in Table 3.2. Nor is there a homophony between equative copulas and demonstratives in the substrate which would have led West Africans to immediately process a demonstrative like *that* as also copular; see Table 3.5.

The use of demonstratives as copulas is frequently encountered cross-linguistically. However, this acknowledged, it is still difficult to imagine Africans simply recruiting a demonstrative pronoun in the copular function when originating a contact language. Note the conceptual leap involved:

	Subject	Copula	Predicate
Ewe	*Kofi*	*Is*	*the chief*
SM	*Kofi*	**that (??)**	*the chief*

The reason we find this impossible to imagine is that demonstrative-copula homophony is not due to a synchronically processible meaning relationship, in the sense that, for example, the use of a verb "to go" to express the future is. The homophony is the synchronic result of a *diachronic* development. However, the diachronic development, like that which produced *de*, is not one we could realistically expect to have such uniform results across the Caribbean.

The diachronic development in question involves the semantic bleaching of demonstratives used resumptively in topic-comment constructions (Li and Thompson 1977; Luo 1991; McWhorter 1992a; Devitt 1990; Gildea 1993). For example, Li and Thompson (1977) show that such reanalysis is documented in several languages. For example, Archaic Mandarin Chinese did not express a copula in equational sentences. Thus,

(16) Wáng-Tái ø wù   zhě   yě
     Wang-Tai   outstanding person DECL

Wang-Tai is an outstanding person.

(Li and Thompson 1977: 421)

Meanwhile, the demonstrative pronoun *shì* was used in topic-comment sentences, as in

(17) Qíong yù jiàn,   **shì** rén   zhǐ   sǔo   wù   yě
     poverty and debasement this people GEN NOM dislike DECL

Poverty and debasement, this is what people dislike.

(ibid.)

By the first century A.D., however, *shì* can be seen used unequivocally as a copula:

(18) Yú **shì** sǔo   jià   fū-ren zhǐ   fù   yě.
     I   be   NOM marry woman GEN father DECL

I am the married woman's father.

(426)

And today this copula occurs regularly in equational sentences:

(19) nèi-ge   rén   **shì** xuéshēng.
     that-CLAS man be   student

That man is a student.

(422)

Li and Thompson describe similar processes in Hebrew, Palestinian Arabic, and Wappo, and Devitt (1991) in a host of others.

All evidence conspires to show that this was the process that produced *da*. For example, some evidence in early documents of Sranan appears to capture a stage at which the generalization of the copula *da* was not yet complete. Arends (1989) shows that in the oldest Sranan documents, although there are many sentences with overt *da*, the omission of the equative copula is grammatical at least in some contexts. For example,

Sranan c. 1770:

(20) Mi ø no   negeri   fo joe.
     I   NEG black-person for you

   I am not your slave.

   (Arends 1989: 160)

   (cf. modern *Mi ano negri fu ju; ano* =COP + NEG)

(21) Mi blibi   joe ø wan bon mattie fo dem.
     I   believe you a   good friend for them

   I believe you're a good friend of theirs.

   (ibid.)

   (cf. modern *Mi bribi taki ju de wan bon mati fu den.*)

The fact is that many of the zero-copula sentences Arends cites actually allow zero copula in the modern language as well; the sentences I cite are the only ones which contrast with their modern equivalents. Thus the sentences cannot be seen as clinching the case by themselves, but are highly suggestive nonetheless.

Another feature typical of more basilectal varieties is that negation, tense, and aspect markers may appear after *da* rather than before, as they do with main verbs.

Krio:

(22) Moussa **nà-bìn**   màràbú.
     Moussa COP-ANT Muslim

   Moussa was a Muslim.

   (Nylander 1983: 206)

Jamaican/Guyanese:

(23) Jan **a   no** di liida.
     John COP NEG the leader

   John is not the leader.

   (Winford 1993: 167)

As Arends (1989: 30–1) and Winford (1993) have pointed out, this is accounted for under an analysis deriving copula *da* from a demonstrative pronominal subject, as negation and TMA markers would naturally occur after the subject position. The current anomalous word order, then, is a fossilization reflecting the earlier demonstrative syntactic function of today's copula:

Early Krio:

[*Moussa*] [*dà   bìn   ø   Màràbú*]
topic   subject ANT COP predicate

Topic Comment

Modern Krio:

[*Moussa nà   bìn   Màràbú*]
subject   COP ANT predicate

Another piece of evidence is a quirk in the behavior of equative sentences in the Suriname creoles, Krio, and at least vestigially in Belizean (Escure 1983: 190) and Jamaican (David Sutcliffe, May 1996, p.c.), which makes it all the more likely that such sentences began as topic-comment constructions. For example, the third-person subject pronoun in Saramaccan is almost always *a:*

(24) **A** téi   fáka kóti dí gwámba.
      he take knife cut the meat

      He cut the meat with a knife.

However, in equative sentences, *hέn* must occur in subject position, and never *a:*

(25) **Hέn** da   dí Gaamá. (**A da dí Gaama.*)
      he   COP the chief

      He is the chief.

This is a crucial feature because elsewhere in the grammar, *hέn* serves as an independent, emphatic, or topic pronoun:

(26) **Hέn** lési εn.
      he   read it

      He read it.

      (Byrne and Caskey 1993: 218)

Yet in equative sentences *hén* has none of these functions; as stated, the simple subject pronoun *a* is ungrammatical in equative sentences: *hén da dí Gaamá* is the only way to say *He is the chief*.

It is highly probable that this anomaly in the distribution of *hén* represents the phonological fossilization of a construction which began as a topic-comment construction with zero copula. We would expect *hén*, as an independent pronoun, to be the form of the third-person pronominal used as a topic. A sentence like *hén da dí Gaamá*, then, began as

(a) [*hén*] [*da*]   ø   [*dí Gaamá*] (*Him, he's the leader.*)
    topic subject COP predicate

    Topic Comment

and became:

(b) [*hén*]   [*da*]   [*dí Gaamá*] (*He's the leader.*)
    subject COP predicate

Note that the zero copula is required; otherwise, there would be no position for the erstwhile subject demonstrative to move into. Thus the derivation of *hén* incidentally provides further evidence that zero copula was the original rule. It would be difficult to explain the categorical presence of *hén* rather than *a* in such sentences in any other systematic way. Note in addition that in the modern language we can still see *hén* used for focus, as in (26).

Thus we can conclude that *da* is an internal innovation in these creoles. Many will find this difficult to accept given the traditional argument that *da* and *de* are calques upon West African substrate languages, which all make a similar subdivision between the equative and the locative copular domains (Holm 1984; Taylor 1977; Baugh 1979; Alleyne 1980a: 165–6). This conclusion, however, appears more plausible from our Indo-European perspective than when we note that an equative/locative copula split is encountered quite commonly across the world, and is if anything the norm; see Table 3.6. Recall also that most West African copulas are verbs, while *da* does not exhibit verbal behaviors. The fact that AEC *da* shows so many signs of having evolved on its own strongly suggests that this is a case where a resemblance between a creole feature and its substrate equivalent is accidental.

The crucial aspect of the development of *da* is that, like the development of *de*, it would strain credulity to propose that just this process occurred, with such consistent results, in several separate locations. While indeed it is a common process of language change for copulas to develop out of deictic

Table 3.6. Languages other than West African with separate equative and locative copulas

	Equative	*Locative*	*Source*
Irish	*is*	*tá*	(Stenson 1981)
Vietnamese	*là*	*o*	(Thompson 1965)
Nama	*'a*	*hàa*	(Hagman 1977)
Hawaiian	*he*	*aia*	(Hawkins 1982)
Chinese	*shi*	*zai*	(Hashimoto 1969)
CiBemba	*ni*	*lì*	(Sadler 1964)

elements in topic-comment constructions, there is a wide range of alternatives as to which specific pathway this development will follow in a given language. This follows from the fact that historical syntax reveals tendencies, not predictive formulations. The creoles under discussion brought a distal demonstrative into the copula slot. However, as we have seen, in Mandarin Chinese it was the proximal demonstrative that underwent the reanalysis:

Archaic Mandarin Chinese:

(27) Qíong yù jiàn,   **shì** rén   zhi   suo   wù   ye.
     poverty and debasement this people GEN NOM dislike DECL

     Poverty and debasement, this is what people dislike.

     (Li and Thompson 1977: 421)

In Swahili, it was the existential presentative which was treated thus:

Early Modern Swahili (reconstructed):

(28) a. *Vita, **ni**   taabu.
        war   it-is trouble

     War, that's trouble.

Modern Swahili:

     b. Vita **ni**   taabu.
        war COP trouble

     War is trouble.

     (McWhorter 1992b)

In Panare, a Cariban Amerindian language, both the proximal and the distal demonstrative became copulas, and both copulas retain the proximal/distal distinction in their semantics:

(29) a. Maestro **këj** e'ñapa.
teacher COP-PROX Panare

The Panare (here) is a teacher.

b. Maestro **nëj** e'ñapa.
teacher COP-DIST Panare

The Panare (there) is a teacher.

(Gildea 1993: 55)

In Hebrew, it is the third-person subject pronominals that are undergoing such reanalysis:

(30) David **hu** ha-ganav.
David he/COP the-thief

David is the thief.

(Li and Thompson 1977: 429)

Pidgins and creoles chose their equative copulas from a similarly wide range of sources, Chinese Pidgin English even having utilized *belong* (Holm 1989: 516). Moreover, as we see, it is quite possible for zero copula to persist *despite* the availability of a demonstrative or pronoun for reanalysis; the equative copula in Tok Pisin (*Mi ø tisa* "I am a teacher") has been expressed with zero for well over a century despite the availability of a pronoun for reanalysis. Finally, and crucially, we find divergent outcomes even within language groups. For example, some dialects of Arabic are developing equative copulas in the present tense, while some are not, etc.

Given all of these alternative outcomes that cross-linguistic analysis presents, we would expect, if the creoles in question arose separately, to find a variety of the above strategies represented among them. Some creoles would indeed have a *da* copula; others would have a *di* copula resulting from the reanalysis of proximal demonstrative *disi;* others would have an *i, a,* or *im* copula from the third-person subject pronoun; others would certainly have no overt equative copula (note that none of the Melanesian English-based creoles do). Yet instead, we find *da* in every single AEC with anything approaching a basilectal register. This distribution argues strongly for the reconstruction of a common ancestor.

3.3.3 MODAL *FU*

There is a much-studied homophony in AECs between a benefactive, possessive, or directional preposition; a complementizer; and a modal verb
(Washabaugh 1975; Bickerton 1981; Boretzky 1983; Winford 1985). Note,
for example, Providencia Creole English (Washabaugh 1975):

(31) a. Preposition:

   Wan a di granson **fi** di daata . . .
   one of the grandson for the daughter

   One of the grandsons of the daughter . . .

   (116)

   b. Complementizer:

   Ai mek **fi** stan op.
   I   make for stand up

   I tried to stand up.

   (116)

   c. Modal:

   Dem **fi**   put im ina i   yaad . . .
   they should put him in the yard

   They should put him into the yard . . .

   (129)

We will be concerned exclusively with the *modal* usage. The prepositional
usage is obviously a superstrate feature, while the complementizer usage is
easily traceable to regional British dialects (Cornwall: *The wheelwright's
here for mend the cart* [Hancock 1994: 104]). Thus these usages are irrelevant to the argument. The modal usage appears in all of the more basilectal creoles of the type, although it gives way to superstrate constructions
such as "must" and "have to" in all but the varieties with the conservative
basilects; see Table 3.7.[4]

4. Regarding the last entry in Table 3.7, Sranan specialists, noting the apparent
marginality of this construction in the modern language, have been skeptical of
the Sranan sentence, supposing that *fo* is actually merely a preposition. They have
claimed that in another example, *a fo ta' dape{ . . .}*"He had to remain there{. . .}"
(Herskovits and Herskovits 1936: 166), the transcription must have omitted a truncated *abi* "to have" following the pronoun. However, in the citation given in Table 3.7
—*mi ben fu suku mi futbal-susu* "I had to look for my football shoes" (Sordam and

Table 3.7. *You have got to do it.*

Krio	*Una fo du am.*
Nigerian	*Una fo du am.*
Guyanese	*Mi fi go tumara.* "I ought to go tomorrow." (Bickerton 1981: 109)
Jamaican	*Unu fi dwiit.*
Gullah	*Hunnuh fuh du um.*
Sranan	*Mi ben fu suku mi futbal-susu.* "I had to look for my football shoes." (Sordam and Eersel 1985: 59; see note 4 in text)

Adapted from Hancock 1987: 295–6 unless otherwise noted.

The use of for *as a modal is not a superstrate inheritance.* I have found no English dialects where "I am for to go" or "I am for going" signifies an *obligation* to go. (It must be emphasized that the use of *for* as complementizer in some English dialects, as I noted above, is irrelevant to the argument, which is concerned exclusively with modal *fu*.)

The use of for *as a modal is not a substrate calque, nor was it borrowed from a substrate language.* Edwards (1974) suggested that the Caribbean *fi* was a borrowing from the Twi verb *fi* "to come from." This derivation has been widely quoted since, but fails upon examination.

First of all, Byrne's (1984) elegant demonstration that *fi* is actually derived from an earlier *fu* makes the Twi *fi* a less likely source. As Byrne states (106), Edwards' hypothesis was spurred in part by the unlikelihood of the phonological evolution of the mid-back vowel in English *for* into the high front vowel in *fi*. *Fu* as the original form eliminates this problem.

Eersel 1985: 59)—the vowel of the preceding pronoun is not homorganic with the initial vowel in *abi,* making a missed *abi,* or its truncated form *a,* unlikely. Adrienne Bruyn (March 1996, p.c.) proposes that in this sentence, *ben* is a reflex of the full English verb *been,* such that the sentence would translate roughly as "I was/have been to look for my football shoes." However, it is difficult to see why the authors of the sentence, black, Surinamese native speakers of Sranan whose primary European language is Dutch, would display interference from English in this fashion (the book the sentence is taken from is itself in Dutch, not English). The validity of the sentence is further supported by the unequivocal presence of modal *fu* in so many of the other creoles.

On the other hand, modal *fu* has been elicited in Saramaccan only by Byrne (1984: 101; *I fú nján dí njánjan.* "You must eat the food."). Other Saramaccan specialists including myself have been unable to elicit it from speakers in Holland, the United States, or Suriname. Apparently, this construction happens to have disappeared in Saramaccan. However, items and constructions randomly become obsolete here and there in all languages; this gap does not speak against the reconstruction of a single AEC ancestor, since Saramaccan parallels its sisters in most other cases.

Table 3.8. Meanings of f + V verbs in West African languages

	fi	*fo*	*fu*
Wolof	here	to play	where
Mandinka	*fìi:* to plant	*fó:* until; *fóo:* to say, to miss	*fúu:* to be stupid; *fùu:* to lend
Gbe	to steal, to bleed	to strike, to shake	to be white, to project, to be dry
Igbo		*ífó:* to uproot; *ífò:* to narrate	*ífù:* to get lost; *ífú:* to roll up; *ífú:* to hurt
Yoruba	*fì:* to swing, *fí:* to dry, to put	*fó:* to float, *fò:* to fly	

Mandinka: Gamble 1987; Yoruba: Wakeman 1979.

Second, we are again faced with the question as to why speakers across the Caribbean would choose an item from Twi specifically with such consistency, especially when the item is not of the "indigenous" semantics most likely to lead to a substrate retention. Finally, the semantics of Twi *fi* make it even more unlikely as a source of the modal verb *fu* in the modern creoles. In Twi, *fi* means "to come from," used as in

(32) Osafohéne yi **fi**   Akyém.
     captain   this come-from Akyem

This captain comes from Akyem.

(Christaller 1875: 120)

(33) Onípa yi a-bé-**fi**   mè mú.
     man   this PERF-INGR-come me unawares

This man has come to me unawares.

(ibid.)

There is no documented, nor even remotely intuitive, relationship between the obligative semantics of the modal usage of *fu* and this verb. Furthermore, no other substrate verb with the phonetic form *f* V has a meaning relatable to any of the functions of *fu* (Table 3.8).

Finally, not only do none of these languages have an item resembling *fu* phonetically in obligative constructions, but there is no homophony be-

tween the benefactive, complementizer and obligative constructions in any
of these languages:

(34) Wolof:

    a. **War**   naa ko defari.
       should I   it take-care-of

       I should take care of it.

       (WEC International 1992: 174)

    b. **Pur** xale   yi
       for children the

       For the children

       (Njie 1982: 239)

    c. Man damma géna ag   moom **ndax** ma gis ko.
       I   I   leave with him so-that I   see him

       I'm leaving with him to see him.

       (248)

(35) Mandinka:

    a. í   **si**   n kòntong.
       you should me greet

       You should greet me.

       (206)

    b. A sàng n **ye**.
       it buy me for

       Buy it for me.

       (36)

    c. Ali bambang, **fo**   bànku jiyo si   sìi.
       you hurry   so-that clay water should suffice

       Hurry so that there will be enough water for the clay.

       (50)

(36) Akan (Twi):

    a. E-**twà me** se me-ko.
       it-pass give-me say I-go

       I must go.

       (Christaller 1933: 546–7)

    b. Me-ye iyi **ma** wo.
       I-do   this give you

       I do this for you.

       (Balmer and Grant 1929: 121)

    c. O-ba-a   **ma** o-a-boa   me.
       he-come-PRET give he-PERF-help me

       He came in order to help me.

       (169)

(37) Gbe (Ewe):

    a. E-**dzè ná** wò bé n-à-vá.
       it-fall give you say OBL-FUT-come

       You have to come.

       (Rongier 1988: 156)

    b. É-wò-e **ná**-m.
       he-do-it give-me

       He did it for me.

       (Westermann 1928: 129)

    c. Tsó-è ná-m′ **né** m-á-ù.
       take-it give-me that I-FUT-eat

       Give it to me so that I can eat it.

       (174)

(38) Igbo:

    a. **Kà** ó gaa.
       HORT he go

       He should go.

       (345)

b. Sìé-**re** há   nri.
cook-for them food

Cook food for them.

(244–5)

c. Ó byà-ra   **ka**   ó wèé   rie nrí.
he come-PAST HORT he CONS eat food

He came in order to eat.

(307)

(39) Yoruba:

a. Bàbá **gbódò** lo.
father must go

Father must go.

(110)

b. Ó pè òjó **fún** un.
he call Ojo for him

He called Ojo for him.

(74)

c. Bádé jí   àjàyí **kí**   o jeun.
Bade awake Ajayi COMP he eat

Bade woke up Ajayi to eat.

(110)

(40) Kikongo:

a. Mbatu tu-**xinga** kwenda.
soon   we-must go

We must go presently.

(Bentley 1887: 142)

b. N-sumb-**ila**   emfumi embiji.
I-buy-APPLICATIVE chef   meat

I buy meat for the chief.

(28)

c. . . . **kimana** ke   ba-mona nzala.
   . . . so-that NEG they-see hunger

so that they are not hungry.

(82)

Only in Twi do we see the same item *ma* "to give" in all three constructions, but in the modal construction it occurs only as a highly grammaticalized member of a serial verb construction. Serials were readily transferred into AECs, and thus to trace modal *fu* to the Twi construction would
require explaining the capricious disappearance of the first verb "to pass."
And again, derivations from Twi alone are difficult to support in general.
In the other languages, we see scattered polysemies, but none distributed
with the uniformity necessary of a viable substrate attribution (Singler
1988; McWhorter 1992a).

The use of for *as a modal verb is not a universal.* This is too obvious to
need illustration. To be sure, *for* figures *within* various modal constructions,
but we are concerned with *for* serving as the modal *by itself.*

In accounting for this bizarre construction, some have proposed that *fu*
is a verb despite its prepositional etymology (e.g., Byrne 1984). However,
Washabaugh (1975: 130) suggests that modal *fu* is a reflex of the preposition which occurs after an underlying, but unexpressed, verb of obligation:

Im ___ fi kom op ya. "He should come up here."

While we may question the notion of "unexpressed verb," the intuition
that modal *fu* is indeed a preposition is supported by other facts. First, the
analysis of *fu* as verbal requires a source, either superstrate, substrate, or
universal, for such a drastic reinterpretation of a humble preposition like
for. None have been presented. Elegance alone suggests that we treat it as a
preposition.

Second, in Saramaccan, one of the most conservative of the AECs, *fu*,
while not used in the obligative construction, displays an important anomalous behavior in its use in a possessive construction. While in general,
copulas preceding Saramaccan prepositions are overt, *fu* is preceded by zero:

(41) Dí búku ø (f)u mi. (*Dí búku da u mi.*)
     the book for   me

The book is mine.

Fu here, in its possessive usage, is unequivocally a preposition, not a verb. If *fu* was indeed used as a modal in earlier Saramaccan—as the distribution of modal *fu* throughout AEC makes likely—then Saramaccan could be analyzed as providing a concrete motivation for treating modal *fu* as an extension of a grammatical quirk which eschews copula before all appearances of *fu* despite its prepositional status.

Under this analysis, we have a possible distant superstrate source for modal *fu*. Louden (1993) has noted that in earlier English dialects, there was a *to be for* construction which denoted futurity, and by extension, intention, as in *I'm for doing it* "I am going to do it" and *Are you for going?* "Do you intend to go?" (Patterson 1880: 39). This derivation is promising, since the semantic relationship between futurity and intention on the one hand, and obligation on the other is not implausibly distant.

At this point, however, we are brought to the same place as with *da* and *de:* the obligative construction was only one of many possible ways the future/intentional construction could have evolved. As in the case of *da*, we would expect an array of outcomes. Some AECs would simply preserve the future meaning. In some, the *fu* construction would have entered into competition with alternate future constructions (*go, sa*) and dropped out. In others, the availability of *go* or *sa* would have prevented the incorporation of the *fu* future at all. And to be sure, in yet others, the future construction would indeed evolve into an obligative.

Hardly would we expect, however, that so many creoles would separately incorporate or develop the dialectal *for* future into the exact same obligative construction. Semantic change is never this regular. It is more plausible that the reinterpretation of the *for* future happened once and was then diffused.

As with *de*, the point is that whatever derivation we propose for modal *fu*, be it mine or another, how likely is the process to have occurred separately in Sierra Leone, Nigeria, Suriname, Guyana, Providencia, Jamaica, Antigua, and South Carolina? A sentence like *Im fi kom op ya* "He should come up here," when grammatical in such a wide array of languages with such suggestive sociohistorical links, calls strongly for the reconstruction of a common ancestor.

3.3.4 SECOND-PERSON PLURAL PRONOUN *UNU*

The second-person plural pronoun takes a form impossible to derive from English in the more basilectal AECs (Table 3.9). To be sure, it would be quite plausible to argue that several separate creoles replace the English plural

Table 3.9. *you* (pl.)

Krio	*una*
Nigerian	*una*
Sranan	*unu*
Saramaccan	*ũ*
Providencia	*unu*
Jamaican	*ũunu*
Belizean	*unu*
Gullah	*hunnuh*

Adapted from Hancock 1987: 295.

Table 3.10. Second-person plural pronouns in AEC
substrate languages

	Subject	Independent
Wolof	*ngeen*	*yéen*
Mandinka	*ali*	*altolu*
Akan	*mo*	*mo*
Gbe	*mìe*	*mìawo*
Igbo	***unù***	***unù***
Yoruba	*è*	*ènyin*
Kikongo	*nu*	*yeno*

you with *some* substrate borrowing, since West African languages have separate pronouns for singular and plural in the second person. What is implausible is that they would all choose one from *the same language.*

Clearly *unu* is not a superstrate inheritance. The uniformity of its distribution would lead us to imagine that *unu* or cognates appear in a range of the substrate languages. However, as it happens, *unu* is neatly traceable to exactly one of these languages: Igbo (Table 3.10). Some have derived *unu* from the convergent influence of many of these pronouns (e.g., Cassidy and LePage 1980), but only Igbo presents an identical phonetic match, and of the other candidates, all but the Kikongo *nu* are at best only faintly plausible as models. Thus the purpose of attributing influence to these other etyma is unclear.

The presence of this little pronoun across the AECs is a thorn in the side of any genesis account purporting that each AEC arose because of limited access in its particular colony. The presence of the Igbo was nowhere so overwhelming as to account for the occurrence of *unu* in so many separate locations. Culturally, the Twi, Ewe, Kikongo, and other cultures are much more strongly represented in the areas where the creoles in question are spoken than the Igbo (Alleyne 1971, 1993; Smith 1987). Slavers even avoided Igbo slaves, given their tendency to commit suicide in response to the harshness of plantation life (LePage and DeCamp 1960: 79; Handler and Lange 1978: 26; Postma 1990: 107–8).

Furthermore, *unu* is highly unlikely as a "diffusion": core vocabulary items such as personal pronouns are traditionally most resistant to replacement and change in situations of language contact and change. Even if it "diffused" once, it was vastly unlikely to have done so with such alarming consistency.

Hancock has made special mention of *unu* for decades (e.g., 1993: 185), presumably supposing that its implications would be too obvious to bear illustration. Yet his point has attracted little attention, which is why I have attempted to spell out those implications here. The limited access approach cannot accommodate this bizarre likeness across AECs.

3.3.5 ANTERIOR MARKER *BIN*

The anterior marker *bin* occurs in all AECs with a basilectal register (Table 3.11). (The Jamaican form is derived via a rule deleting initial /b/ in heavily used items [Rickford 1980]; the Antiguan forms and the Belizean forms arise from assimilatory nasalization of the initial consonant.)

While there has been much debate about the *behavior* of the anterior markers in creoles and its implications for Derek Bickerton's bioprogram theory, the area concerning us is seemingly mundane, but ultimately revelatory: the simple etymology of *bin*. Put simply, we must ask why the anterior marker is encoded with *bin* in every single one of these creoles.

The choice of been *is not a substrate calque.* The AEC substrate uses a wide variety of strategies to encode various forms of the past tense. Importantly, the verb "to be" figures in none of them.

Wolof and Mandinka use postposed inflectional markers which appear unrelated to verbs "to be."

Table 3.11. *Three of his friends were there.*

Krio	*Tri i padi **bin** de de.*
Nigerian	*Tri fo hi fre **bin** de de.*
Sranan	*Dri fu e mati **ben** de de.*
Saramaccan	*Dií máti fɛɛn **bi** dé alá.*
Guyanese	*Tri a i mati **bin** de de.*
Antiguan	*Tri hi fren **min** de de.*
Jamaican	*Tri a fi-im fren **en** de de.*
Belizean	*Tri a fi-i fren **mi** di de.*
Gullah	*Tri uh hi fren **bin** de de.*

Adapted from Hancock 1987: 282.

Wolof terminative aspect:

(42) Bey **na** dugub.
cultivate TERM millet

He cultivated millet.

(25) (Verbs "to be": *la, nékk*)

Mandinka past:

(43) Dindingo bòri-**ta**.
child run off-PAST

The child ran off.

(17) (Verbs "to be": *mu, be*)

In Kwa and Nigerian languages, the category closest to the creole anterior is what most grammarians term the perfective. In Akan (Fante dialect), this is encoded with the infix -*á*-, as in *o-á-bà* he-PREF-come "He has come" (Balmer and Grant 1929: 106–7). This infix seems unrelated to the copula forms, *ye* and *wo*. Ewe has lost its cognate to this infix (Westermann 1930 cites it only in the Anlo dialect, and subsequent grammars do not mention it at all); the modern language extends the FINISH serial verb construction as in

(44) Me-wo do vo.
I-do work finish

I have finished working.

(Fiagã 1976: 38).

Igbo has a postposed inflectional marker -*le* (*O rie-le ji* "He has eaten yams"; Emenanjo 1978: 180); its verbs "to be" are *bu* and *dì*. Yoruba has the marker *ti*, derived from a verb "to come from" (*Moti jeun* "I have eaten"); copulas are *je, se* and *wa*. Kikongo has what the best grammar available to me calls a "perfective" inflection which is postposed; its morphological form varies according to phonological constraints: *ntond-ele* "I loved," *ngij-idi* "I came." The copulas are *i* and -*ina* (33).

Thus (1) none of these languages encode the past with a form of the verb "to be," (2) no other single strategy prevails, and (3) in that most of the substrate languages encode pastness inflectionally, they lacked models for a past marker derived from "to be." (Again, recall that we are concerned not with the *function*, but the *etymology*, of *bin*.)

On the other hand, the superstrate, English, clearly offers a model for *bin*, in the form of past-perfect progressive constructions such as *I've been working since yesterday*. The question is, however, whether we would expect the anterior marker in several separate creoles to be drawn from just this construction.

The data creolists consult most makes it appear as if the answer might be yes. For example, the Pacific English-based creoles, such as Tok Pisin, Bislama, Solomon Islands Pijin, Torres Strait Broken, and Aboriginal Australian Kriol all have *bin* as a past marker. However, scholars of these languages concur in treating them as descendants of a single original source (most informatively Keesing 1988; Baker 1993, although they differ as to the exact identity of that source). Thus Pacific creole *bin* represents, in the strict sense, one incorporation, not several. In this light, it must be said that *one* other incorporation of *bin* as a past marker is unremarkable: I do not claim that the recruitment of *been* is so idiosyncratic that we would expect it to happen only once, as is the case with *de* and *fu*. However, even if *been* is selected here and there outside of AEC, would we expect its selection into *every single AEC independently?*

In relation to this, it is relevant that other English-based contact languages, many less regularly consulted than the Pacific group, show that *been* is only one of various options available to encode pastness. Chinese Pidgin English used *have* (Baker 1995b: 10), even though there is no reason to suppose *been* was not available at its emergence. The interior variety of Liberian Pidgin English uses *was* (Singler 1981). Native Americans are documented to have used both *have* and *was*, rather than *been*, in the restructured registers of English which they acquired in the nineteenth century, as in *I **have** work, Columbus **was** discovered America*, and *I **was** feel* (Schuchardt 1980: 36). Some less basilectal English-based creoles use *did*, as in Barbadian *Hi **di** boi mi* "It bit me" (Le Page and Tabouret-Keller 1985: 93).

Thus if the AECs emerged separately in each colony, at least a *few* creoles would use *have, was, did,* or other superstrate items as past markers. The absolute uniformity of the *etymology* of *bin* across the creoles in question, then, is most plausibly ascribed to the creoles having descended from a parent creole which happened to have selected *been* as its anterior marker.

3.3.6 *SELF* AS AN ADVERBIAL

A final trait common to too many AECs to be a matter of chance is documented by Hancock (1987: 320): the semantic extension of the word *self* to the adverbial meaning of *even* (Table 3.12). *Self* as *even* is not a substrate calque. None of our substrate languages extend the word for *self* to the adverbial meaning of *even*. Since the adverbial usage is one of pragmatic highlighting, we can assume that it is an extension of *self* in its *intensificational* usage (*I myself am the father*) as opposed to its *reflexive* usage (*I washed myself*). Thus, we will refer to substrate equivalents of this intensificational usage, which are not always identical to the reflexive morpheme.

Note that the item used to intensify pronouns is not used adverbially in any of these languages.

Wolof:

(45) a. **Moom**   moo dem.
he (EMPH) he-be leave

It is he who left.

(Njie 1982: 107)

b. Lépp la   mën, woy **sax**.
all   DEF can   sing even

He knows everything, even singing.

(189)

Mandinka:

(46) a. **Nne** "I myself"

(Spears 1973: 36)

Table 3.12. *He even had another horse.*

Krio	*I bib get oda os **sef**.*
Nigerian	*I bin get wan oda hos **sef**.*
Sranan	*A ben abi wan tra asi **seefi**.*
Saramaccan	*A bi ábi wan óto hási **seéi**.*
Guyanese	*I gat wan neks haars **self**.*
Antiguan	*I gat wan neks haas **self**.*
Jamaican	*Im ha wan neks haas **self**.*
Belizean	*Im av a neks aas **self**.*
Gullah	*I haa noduh hoos **sef**.*

Adapted from Hancock 1987: 320.

b. **Hani** suutoo a   be yaayi   la.
   even night   he be wander PROG

Even at night he is wan

(41)

Akan (Twi):

(47) a. Mé-**ara** m-a-fà.
        I-same I-PERF-take

   I myself have taken it.

   (Christaller 1933: 42)

b. **Mpo** m-a-di   awu   a . . .
   even I-PERF-commit murder EMPH

   Even if I had committed a murder . . .

   (41)

Gbe (Ewe):

(48) a. Nye **nuto** me-wo-e.
        I   self   I-do-it

   I myself did it.

   (67)

b. . . . ya **gõ** hã mé-va   o.
he even also NEG-come NEG

Not even he came.

(116)

Igbo:

(49) a. ó bù **onwé** m mè-re   ya.
it be self   I   do-IND it

I myself did it.

(340)

b. **M'òbúlá di** nwatàkíri   nwère íke imé ya.
even   small-child can   do it

Even a child can do it.

(235)

Yoruba:

(50) a. èmi **tìkálára** mi lo síbè.
I   self   I   go there

I myself went there.

(67)

b. èmi **tilèé** mòn.
I   even know

Even I know it.

(Abraham 1958: 643)

Kikongo:

(51) a. Mònò **kibêni**.
I   myself.

(Swartenbroeckx 1973: 135)

b. Gâna **kána** fióti.
give   even a-little

Give even a little.

(117)

Self as *even* is not a universal. The absence of such a development in any literature on language universals consulted will be taken as confirming this intuitively plausible assumption.

In fact, *self* as *even* is traceable to the Irish English which would have been spoken by indentured servants working alongside slaves in the early English Caribbean. In Irish Gaelic there is a homophony between *self* and *even* in the form of the word *féin*, such that sentences such as *If I got it itself it would be of no use* for *Even if I got it would be of no use*, or *If I had that much itself* instead of *Even if I had that much*, are recorded from Irish English speakers (Joyce 1910: 37, cited in Allsopp 1996).

However, the uniform distribution of this usage in AEC cannot be explained simply by the Irish presence in the early Caribbean. For one, a conventionalized Hiberno-English did not exist in the 1600s; most Irish people spoke only, or predominantly, Irish until as late as the 1800s, and Hiberno-English arose in the mid-1700s at the earliest (Rickford 1986b: 253). This means that if slaves picked up the *self* as *even* usage from the Irish bond-servants, it would presumably have been from individual interlanguages rather than a uniform indigenous English. In this case, we must wonder how consistently individual Irish people transferred this usage of *féin* into their second-language English. The variability of first-language influence upon interlanguage has been widely observed and is even easily perceptible on an everyday level. Even in creoles, this inherent variability in transfer is observable: most New World French Creoles postpose the demonstrative, as in *tab-sa* "that table," but Mauritian Creole does not (*sa latab* "that table"), even though both the West and East African languages spoken by its originators postpose demonstratives to nouns.

Next, even if for some reason the semantics of *féin* were transferred by all or most Irish learners of English, it is unlikely that slaves would have in turn picked up this usage across the Caribbean. There would have been, after all, a number of Hiberno-Anglicisms available to adopt, and since no creole adopted all of them, we must wonder why all of them would adopt any particular one. It is much more likely that the construction was adopted by one creole and subsequently transmitted to other slave populations.

Finally, all of the above must be seen in view of the fact that the Irish, although well-represented among Caribbean bondservants, were not the majority: whites from England itself dominated in Barbados (Niles 1980: 22–54) and in St. Kitts and the Leewards (Dunn 1972: 134), and Jamaica was relatively poor in servants at all (ibid. 157; all cited in Rickford 1986b: 253–4). This would make it even less likely that slaves would have adopted one particular Gaelic-modeled construction across the Caribbean so consistently.

Thus *self* is one more piece of evidence extremely difficult to square with the idea of slave populations developing their creoles independently in each major colony. When Hancock solicits a translation of the sentence *He even had another horse* from three dozen creolist scholars, and their independent answers are as uniform as we have seen above, sisterhood becomes a compelling analysis to say the least.[5]

Thus these are six items distributed with a striking degree of uniformity amidst the AECs, which can have been incorporated, or can have developed, only once. Neither superstrate, substrate, nor universal sources can explain these features. Other AEC features can be attributed only tentatively to common descent, leaving the field open to polygenetic genesis scenarios. These six features, unamenable to any explanation other than common inheritance, are a precious key to the truth. As such, they will henceforth be designated SSG, the Six Smoking Guns.

3.3.7. INGREDIENT X

The source of AEC in a single ancestor is further supported by a list (see Table 3.13) of West African borrowings present in all or most of them, identified by Smith (1987: 104–7). The fact that these words generally appear in more than one West African language does not belie the import of the list. Most have restricted areal distributions, and thus leave the idiosyncrasy of the word's use in AEC impossible to ignore. For example, even if *bakra* is present in several Nigerian languages, would not we expect that some AECs would have incorporated a Twi word?

Furthermore, whether or not a creole selects a West African borrowing for a given item at all is unpredictable. As is well-documented, substrate borrowing is more likely in certain semantic fields than others. However, this finding is not predictive, merely explanatory: what "metric" could ex-

---

5. The tracing of *self* to Irish English is meant as a revision of the analysis of this construction in McWhorter (1995).

Baker (1998), who has tentatively traced the AECs to an ancestor on St. Kitts, has made the interesting suggestion that *self* as *even* was modeled on the French use of *même*, during the joint occupation of St. Kitts by the English and the French in the seventeenth century. Deft as this surmise is, the Irish English source appears much more likely in the final analysis. Even if not, however, Baker's idea would reinforce the reconstruction of a single AEC ancestor. French would have been a possible influence on very few other islands but St. Kitts, and only St. Kitts had the status of being both the first island settled by the English and a prime source of later migrations. Thus if *self* was modeled on *même*, then this was likely to have happened only on St. Kitts and subsequently transported to other colonies.

Table 3.13. Smith's "Ingredient X"

njam	"eat" (Wolof, other West African coastal languages [Smith, p.c.])
kokobe	"leprosy" (Twi)
kongkosa	"gossip" (Twi)
pinda	"peanut" (Kikongo)
mumu	"dumb" (Twi, Ewe, Mende)
djumbi	"ghost" (Kikongo)
fufu	(food type) (Twi, Ewe, Yoruba)
anansi	(spider in folktale) (Twi, Ewe)
okra	"okra" (Igbo)
soso	"only" (Igbo, Yoruba)
akara	"pancake" (Ewe, Yoruba, Igbo)
potopoto	"mud" (Igbo, Twi; also Bantu [Morris Goodman, p.c.])
bakra	"white person" (Igbo, Efik)

Adapted from Smith 1987: 104–7.

plain why Saramaccan borrows from Fongbe for *shoulder* (*awá*) but retains the English for *finger* (*fínga*)? The fact that the AECs all show the preceding exact same choices reinforces SSG in revealing a single common ancestor.

3.3.8 IDIOSYNCRASY AND CREOLE GENESIS

Idiosyncrasy, key to the understanding of SSG and Ingredient X, is in general rather underacknowledged in creole studies. Even without SSG and Ingredient X, and even if all of the features AECs had in common *were* traceable to superstrate, substrate, or universal features, a single parent pidgin would still be apparent. This would be because of the vital role that chance plays in language contact, expressing itself even within the broad constraints that source languages and universals impose. A creole usually has many possible choices to make in recruiting a construction from the superstrate or substrate, and one of many choices to make among universal strategies.

For example, it is uncontroversial that Tok Pisin English Creole is the result of an encounter with English completely separate from that which created AEC. Here we contrast equivalent sentences in Tok Pisin and Sranan:

(52) a. Tok Pisin:

Em mipela i   bin kirap-im   dispela wok.
it we   PRED ANT start-TRANS this   work

It is us who started this work.

(Mühlhäusler 1985a: 352)

b. Sranan:

Na wi di   ben bigi a   wroko disi.
it-is we REL ANT start the work this

It is us who started this work.

(53) a. Tok Pisin:

Mi stap long haus.
he COP LOC house

I am in the house.

b. Sranan:

Mi de   na   ini   a   oso.
he COP LOC inside the house

I am in the house.

Under the current creolist conception, the differences between these two creoles are attributed to differences in the superstrate, substrate, or timing of demographic developments (e.g., Mufwene's [1994a, 1996] "linguistic ecology" concept). This is definitely valid—but leaves a crucial realm of the evidence unaccounted for.

For example, substratal influence is clearly one factor in the differences between the two creoles. The predicate marker and transitive marker in the Tok Pisin example (52a) are undisputed calques on Melanesian languages (Keesing 1988: 119–27, 143–70), and the *-pela* marker is also traceable to substrate behaviors (ibid. 113, 137–9). Meanwhile, the choice of *di* (<*disi* "this") as a relativizer in Sranan is firmly traceable to West African patterns (Bruyn 1995a).

However, other things are more fortuitous. It is a universal tendency for positional verbs to serve as locative copulas, cross-linguistically and in pidgins and creoles (see Section 3.3.1). However, while Tok Pisin observes this universal, Sranan happens not to have, opting instead for an adverb. It would be difficult to ascribe this to any parseable factor; for example, it cannot be traced to the substrate, since Sranan's West African substrate languages use verbs, not adverbs, as locative copulas. The AEC choice of *de,* as we have seen in Section 3.3.1, was a matter of chance.

Similarly, there is a universal tendency in pidginization to utilize one or two items alone as prepositions. However, this universal allows a wide variety of etymological choices. What factor could "explain" the choice of *long* (<*along*) in Tok Pisin as opposed to *na* (either from Portuguese "in the" or the Igbo general preposition) in Sranan? Tok Pisin radically reinterpreted a preposition from English; Sranan chose a substrate item—one would search in vain for a "reason" for the difference in outcomes.

Another example, not shown above, is how *by and by* became a grammaticalized irrealis marker in Tok Pisin but, despite being present in early Sranan documents (Baker 1995b: 12), happens not to have been grammaticalized in that creole, *go* and *shall* having been chosen instead. This was not due to any predictive mechanism—*go* was certainly available to Melanesians just as *by and by* was to Africans in Suriname. Surely, if we could "roll the dice" again, the results would be different.

These factors demonstrate the vital role of chance in creole genesis. The point is that if the AECs were really separate developments, we would expect them to be much more different from each other than they are. To exercise the imagination a bit, consider the following:

(1) Some AECs, under heavy Kikongo influence, would have the double negator (NEG-verb-NEG) found in other Atlantic creoles where this and related languages were particularly well-represented, such as Palenquero and the Gulf of Guinea Portuguese creoles.

(2) Other AECs would have chosen *stop, stay,* or a form of *be* as a locative copula instead of *there.*

(3) Other AECs, under heavy Twi influence, would have specifically Twi features such as a serial verb construction *pass-give* in place of modal *fu.*

(4) Other AECs would have generalized *at,* a phonetically salient and easily semantically broadened morpheme, as a preposition instead of using *na,* etc.

Instead, however, what we have is one speech community, composed of partially intelligible creoles clearly cast from the same basic mold. A creole genesis model would ideally reflect this more explicitly.

3.4 A CLOSER LOOK

Many creolists, however, have trouble accepting the notion of a pidgin or creole being carried intact from one colony to another. This is largely because of a conviction widely shared in the field that in a new colony, creole-speaking slaves from an earlier colony would have been so numerically overwhelmed by the massive importation of new slaves as the colony developed that any contact language would have had to develop from scratch. We will call this the "obliteration" scenario.

Again, however, like all creole genesis scenarios, including my own, this is merely a guess—an intelligent one, but a guess nevertheless. We have no contemporary accounts describing such "obliteration" (e.g., "The Slaues bought from Barbadoes have their own Dialect but there are so many new Slaues that the bastard Creole amongst them sounds quite unlike to the one to which the older Slaues are accustom'd," etc.). As we have seen, the linguistic data are our first clue that the guess is mistaken: SSG and Ingredient X suggest that there was much more linguistic continuity from colony to colony than the obliteration scenario supposes. We gain further insight on this by comparing just two AECs at a time, in the cases where we have relatively substantial comparative data.

3.4.1 SURINAME AND JAMAICA

After leaving Suriname when the Dutch took over, the English are documented to have brought at least 891 slaves to Jamaica starting in 1671 (Bilby 1983: 60). Nevertheless, accounts of the birth of Jamaican patois tend to propose only that Sranan "may" have been an "influence" on Jamaican. The potency they sense this "influence" to have had is clear when such writers continue to surmise on "when Jamaican Creole emerged," which implies that Sranan had, at best, marginal influence.

The linguistic evidence, however, suggests a more direct link. We must at the outset recall that Sranan and Jamaican share SSG, plus most of Ingredient X. However, these two creoles also share a great deal of other idiosyncratic lexical borrowings, which—especially in combination with SSG and Ingredient X—draw an explicit genetic link between Sranan and Jamaican.

For example, Cassidy (1964: 274–5) presents Portuguese words occurring in Sranan and Jamaican, both creoles in which the Portuguese lexical element is marginal. Again, such evidence must be seen in light of the fact that the establishment of *any* non-English word for a given concept is a matter of chance, and the choice of one from any particular language, when

Table 3.14. Portuguese words in Sranan and Jamaican

Sranan	Jamaican	Portuguese	English
bruya	bru-bru	embrulho	confused, disorganized
kaba	kaba	acabar	finish, complete
sabi, sa'	sabi, savi	saber	to know
tempra	tempa	temprar	temper, mix
aranja	arinj	laranja	orange
bakyau	bakalo	bacalhau	dried (cod) fish
bolu	bula	bolo	cake, dumpling
gran	gran	grande	grand, large
mangri	maaga	magro	thin
mofina	mofiina	mofino	miserable, poor thing
pikien	pikini, pikni	pequeno	small, small child

Adapted from Cassidy 1964: 275.

shared by two or more creoles, is therefore particularly significant. (I have abbreviated Table 3.14 to include only words of unequivocal Portuguese derivation.) Indeed, it is well known that Portuguese-speaking planters settled throughout the Caribbean, with varying degrees of impact on the creoles there (Goodman 1987). However, what this list is meant to demonstrate is not that both creoles have Portuguese words, but that they have so many of *the same* Portuguese words.

Another indication that Sranan was the precursor to Jamaican and not just an "influence" upon the usage of *no* as a highlighter of topicalized constituents appears in the following examples:

(54) **No** Jan wi a taak bout.
NO John we PROG talk about

It's John we're talking about.

(Bailey 1966: 95)

(55) **No** tiif Kofi tiif di manggo!
NO steal Kofi steal the mango

Kofi *stole* the mango!

(ibid.)

In modern Jamaican this is processed as a quirky use of the negator *no*. Clearly, however, such a usage of a negator is highly unusual and semantically opaque. This is particularly clear when *no* is used without any topicalization, as in *No Jaaji!* "It's *George* (not John)!" where the semantic contribution of the negator is particularly obscure under a synchronic analysis. Why would a grammar squeeze a negator into such a usage? This mystery is solved when we tie it to the Sranan use of copula *na* as a highlighter in similar constructions:

Sranan:

(56) Na **lon** mi wani **lon** gowe.
      it   run I   want run go

      What I want to do is run away.

      (Taylor 1977: 183)

In Sranan, highlighter *na* is not homophonous with the negator (*no*) but with the equative copula (*Jan **na** a Gaanman* "John is the chief"). Such sentences present no semantic anomaly; the highlighter usage is simply an extension of the deictic function of the copula (cf. Holm 1980). Thus even the Sranan equivalents to Jamaican oddities like *No Jaaji!* "It's George!" are unremarkable in Sranan, since *na* simply means "it is": *Na Papa* "It's Papa."

The anomalousness of the Jamaican construction is neatly explainable as a development from the Sranan one. In Jamaican, the copular morpheme has evolved to simply *a* (*Samwel **a** tiela* "Samuel is a tailor" [Bailey 1966: 65]) obscuring its relationship to the "highlighter" morpheme. Once the copula had eroded to *a*, the phonetic similarity of highlighter *na* to the negator *no* apparently led speakers to reinterpret these items as reflexes of the same form. Historically, however, this highlighter *no* is most likely derived from the affirmative deictic *na* which is still on view in Sranan. Its current status in Jamaican as an opaque use of the negator *no* is a chance analogical development. Thus the Jamaican "quirky *no*" is actually a piece of integral grammar transmitted directly from Suriname to Jamaica, obscured in Jamaican only by internal reinterpretation driven by phonetic likeness.

Nevertheless, the genetic relationship between Jamaican and Sranan is today somewhat obscured by the fact that while Sranan, spoken in a former Dutch colony, has had little contact with English since the 1670s, Jamaican has taken its place in a continuum relationship with the standard, with even its basilect considerably closer to English than Sranan is. One senses that

Table 3.15. Irregular vowel epithesis

English	MSL	Sranan
knock	*naki*	*naki*
talk	*taki*	*taki*
ask	*ak(i)si*	*(h)akisi*
glass	*glasi*	*grasi*
call	*kali*	*kari*
dog	*dago*	*dagu (dago, 1783)*
hand	*(h)anu*	*anu*
hog	*hagu*	*hagu*
cut	*koti*	*koti*
love	*lobi*	*lobi*

Data from Smith 1987: 92–7; Bilby 1983: 2–3.

this has helped keep the path open to the idea that the two creoles are essentially independent developments related only by "influence."

This is what makes the discovery of Maroon Spirit Language so fortuitous. Bilby (1983, 1992) has documented a language spoken under possession by maroons of Eastern Jamaica, apparently spoken as an everyday language until the 1920s. What is crucial about Maroon Spirit Language (henceforth MSL), much more basilectal than the deepest Jamaican Creole and mutually unintelligible with it, is that it is so strikingly correspondent to Sranan on all levels that, as Smith (1987: 92) puts it, "It seems well-nigh impossible not to consider MSL (or rather Pre-MSL) and Proto-Sranan as two closely related languages."

For example, as Smith notes (1987: 92–3), correspondence in *regular* vowel harmony (*waka* "to walk") is not strictly diagnostic of relationship between Sranan and MSL, since this is commonly encountered crosslinguistically. What Smith notes as important about the correspondences between Sranan and MSL, however, is that even the idiosyncratic *departures* from regular vowel harmony are shared (Table 3.15).

Furthermore, MSL shares a tendency in Suriname creoles towards monophthongization of diphthongs; see Table 3.16, in which Belizean is included for comparison. We also have idiosyncratic correspondences between grammatical items, as shown in Table 3.17.

Sranan (and other Suriname creoles) have a unique interrogative para-

Table 3.16. Monophthongization of diphthongs

/ai/ to /e/

English	MSL	Sranan	Belizean
climb	*krem*	*kren*	*klaim*
time	*tem*	*ten*	*taim*
ride	*re*	*ree*	*raid*
white	*wete*	*weti*	*wait*
fight	*fete*	*feti*	*fait*
night	*net*	*neti*	*nait*

/ai/ to /ei/ (Bilby 1983: 5)

English	MSL	Sranan
fly	*frei*	*frei*
high	*hei*	*hei*
cry	*krei*	*krei*
tie	*titei*	*titei*

Adapted from Smith 1987: 94; Bilby 1992: 4. The Belizean data are from Dayley 1979a, 1979b.

Table 3.17. Idiosyncratic lexical correspondences between MSL and Sranan

English	MSL	Sranan	Belizean
in	*indi*	*ini*	*iina*
to be	*na*	*na*	*a*
you (sing.)	*i*	*i, yu*	*yu*
he, she, it	*a*	*a*	*hin*

Adapted from Bilby 1983, 1992; Hancock 1987: 277.

digm that combines a noun with an interrogative marker which, as a single rounded vowel, is idiosyncratic among Caribbean English-based creoles (see Table 3.18). The interrogative paradigm in MSL is a clear derivant of the Suriname one. It uses the same nouns; in one case it uses the same interrogative marker, whereas in other cases it appears to have analogized the

Table 3.18. Interrogative paradigms in MSL and Sranan

English	MSL	Sranan	Belizean
who	(h)uma	(o)suma	hu
person	suma	suma	person
what	(h)onti	(o)sani	we
thing	sonti	sani	ting
how	(h)ofa	(o)fa	hou
fashion	fa	fa	fashan

Data from Bilby 1983: 50–2; Smith 1987: 98.

Table 3.19. TMA markers

English	MSL	Sranan	Belizean
progressive	e, he	e<de	di
irrealis	sa, wi	sa	wan, gwain
anterior	bin	ben	mi

Data from Bilby 1983: 49–50; Smith 1987: 97–8.

word toward *who* or *how*, probably under influence from Jamaican patois itself. The kinship, however, is obvious. Finally, the TMA markers correspond quite well (Table 3.19).

One can even find MSL sentences which match Sranan morpheme for morpheme.

(57) a. Maroon Spirit Language:

Cha in go na da bigi pre, kya in go na indi.
carry him go LOC the big place carry him go LOC inside

Take him to that big place, put him inside.

(Bilby 1992: 9)

b. Sranan:

Tja en go na a bigi presi, tja en go na ini.
carry him go LOC the big place carry him go LOC inside

(Earlier attestations of Sranan show that *a<da*.)

(58) a. Maroon Spirit Language:

> U   sabi   se   da sonti a   no   gudu sonti.
> you know COMP the thing COP NEG good thing

> You know that thing is not a good thing.

> (70)

b. Sranan:

> Yu sabi   taki   a   sani ano   bun sani.
> you know COMP the thing COP-NEG good thing

MSL and Sranan are not identical. Crucially, however, the nature of the correspondences between them—in idiosyncratic departures from vowel harmony, in idiosyncratic etymological choices for grammatical items—make a direct relationship dazzlingly clear.

This evidence allows a conclusion that, put simply, a form of Sranan was transported to Jamaica. Furthermore, the evidence also suggests that MSL was the source for what has since become Jamaican patois. There is no documentation of this development, but the linguistic data tell the story. Even within the few paragraphs of MSL recorded, we find four of the six items in SSG (*da*, modal *fu*, *bin*, and *de*—the latter only in its progressive marker function, but since this is a grammaticalization of the copula function, it is likely that copular *de* simply has yet to be recorded in MSL or is obsolete). Proposing a direct line of descent between Sranan, MSL, Jamaican, and other AECs is more economical than proposing mere "influences" between these varieties. Thus we can hypothesize that MSL is the modern remnant of a creole variety which was retained by maroons, but elsewhere in Jamaica moved more towards English and became today's patois and its continuum.

In view of this data, we must question "obliterationist" assertions such as Plag's (1993: 31) that Sranan was "continually repidginized" over 150 years, even as late as the early 1800s. Plag's claim is based on deductions from slave headcounts, but the comparative evidence paints a different picture: MSL shows us that Sranan had stabilized considerably long before even 1700. MSL is precious evidence that the transplantation of Sranan was a direct source of what was to become Jamaican Creole.

3.4.2 SURINAME AND SIERRA LEONE

We can also confirm that a creole could survive in recognizable form even after more than one transplantation, and even into nonplantation conditions. Hancock (1987) considers Krio to have emerged in the early 1600s in the Senegambia region and to have been parent to Sranan (and other AECs). He supports this argument via a series of idiosyncratic correspondences between Krio and Sranan. On the other hand, I have argued (1997b) for the traditional hypothesis that Krio is traceable to the Jamaica Maroons and former American slaves brought to Sierra Leone starting in the 1790s (see Chapter 4, Section 4.9).

However, this difference in analysis hardly belies that Hancock has documented a striking body of idiosyncratic correspondences between Sranan and Krio which render a direct historical relationship virtually inescapable. Folded into the prose of a lengthy article generally consulted for its majestic comparison of fifty sentences in thirty-three AECs (Hancock 1987), the Sranan-Krio correspondences appear to have escaped notice in creole studies. For this reason, I present them again here.

Since Jamaican Maroons are widely agreed to have seeded Krio in 1800, we can reconstruct a pathway of transplantation. Sranan was brought first to Jamaica. What is today MSL was spoken as an everyday language by Jamaican Maroons until this century (Bilby 1983: 68), and thus it is plausible to suppose that the Jamaican émigrés to Sierra Leone in 1800 were still speaking this Sranan-derived register. This would neatly explain the correspondences between Sranan and Krio, which are otherwise nothing less than dumbfounding.

What could explain, for example, the recruitment of the particular West African etyma presented in Table 3.20 by separate populations? Note that the concepts expressed are hardly central to communication, which renders the correspondences all the more uncanny. It is the idiosyncrasy that makes this list significant.

In addition, Krio and Sranan share a number of idiosyncratic coinages which do not even appear in the other AECs (Tables 3.21 and 3.22). Belizean Creole is intended to represent English-based creoles other than the West African and Surinamese groups. Note also that Krio retains part of the same specific interrogative paradigm shared by Sranan and MSL (Table 3.23). Furthermore, Smith (1987: 73) notes that monophthongization of English diphthongs in closed syllables is shared by Krio and Sranan (as well as the other Suriname creoles), while negligible and irregular in other AECs (Table 3.24).

As a crowning indication of a direct line of development from Sranan to Jamaican to Krio, it is unlikely to be an accident that just as Sranan speakers call their language *takitaki*, both Jamaican patois and one register of Krio were called *talkee-talkee* in the early 1800s (Lalla and D'Costa 1990: 38; Hancock 1986: 95).

Table 3.20. West African borrowings in Krio and Sranan

Krio	Sranan	English
gongongong (Yoruba)	gorogoro	gullet
bomã (Bantu)	aboma	boa constrictor
degedege (Yoruba)	degedege	shaky
jonk;ato (Wolof)	jonko	nod head
lagajaga (Yoruba)	jagajaga	untidy
lawlaw (Kikongo)	lawlaw	foolish
fukfuk (Yoruba)	fukfuku	lungs
pima (Twi)	pima	vagina
sokisoki (Yoruba)	soki	copulate
ras (?Fula)	lasi	buttocks

Data from Hancock 1987: 278–9.

Table 3.21. Idiosyncratic coinages in Krio and Sranan

Krio	Sranan	Belizean	English
na-do	na-doro	outsaid	outside
na ya	d'ya>da ya	ya	here
doks	doksi	dok	duck
som-man	suma	sombadi	somebody
go (future)	go	wan, gwain	(future marker)

Data from Hancock 1987: 273–4.

Table 3.22. Idiosyncratic adverbs in Krio and Sranan

Krio	Sranan	Belizean	English
wantem	wanten	nou-nou	immediately
sontem	sonten	mebi	perhaps
oltem	alaten	aalweez	always
trade	trade	shat-taim	recently

Data from Hancock 1987: 278; Belizean data from G. Escure, Dec. 1996 p.c.

Table 3.23. Interrogative words in Krio and Sranan

Krio	Sranan	Belizean	English
us-tem	o-ten	wen	when
u-sai	u-sai	we	where
us-fashin	o-fa(si)	hou	how

Data from Hancock 1969, and p.c.

Table 3.24. Monophthongization of diphthongs in closed syllables

English	Sranan	Krio	Belizean
bite	beti	bet	bait
fight	feti	fet	fait
night	neti	net	nait
white	weti	wet	wait
house	oso	os	hous
louse	loso	los	lows
mouth	mofo	mot	mout

Data from Smith 1987: 73.

Thus, however difficult some writers may find it to imagine a creole surviving large waves of immigration, linguistic data such as the above make it clear that such things were quite possible. The linguistic data allow no other interpretation: demographic disproportion, no matter how sharp, did not obliterate imported creoles in the English Caribbean.

The Pacific English-based creoles, Tok Pisin, Bislama, and Solomon Islands Pijin, have long demonstrated this. Today, they are undeniably dialects of the same system. Yet their ancestor was disseminated onto large plantations on various separate islands. Under the framework popular among Atlantic creolists, we would expect such dissemination to have overwhelmed the pidgin in each place. In fact, we would expect it to have been even *more* thoroughly effaced than it would have been in the Caribbean: unlike Africans, who spoke AEC for life, the Melanesian plantation workers were generally serving contracts of a few years, after which they returned to their native islands and lived the rest of their lives in their native language, controlling the pidgin as a secondary badge of the plantation experience. Yet even with briefer use than the Caribbean creoles, and more extensive use alongside native languages, the descendants of Melanesian Pidgin English remain close sisters. In this light, we can see that an AEC could quite plausibly have retained a core structure during transplantation from colony to colony.

3.5 IMPLICATIONS

Since on a day-to-day basis good science proceeds by attempting to accommodate challenging data into the reigning theory, many creolists may attempt to classify SSG and Ingredient X as mere static, meriting further investigation but leaving the limited access conception intact. Bickerton (1998: 88), for example, has conceded that *da* and *de* are "a puzzle" but urges us to simply "put such puzzling items on the back burner".

However, it would be difficult to do this within the bounds of historical linguistics, especially in view of new developments in this area. This becomes clear when we attempt to explicitly outline the "diffusion" of isolated features from one AEC to another.

3.5.1 A MERE JARGON?

One way of preserving the limited access model despite SSG and Ingredient X would be to treat them as evidence of a mere unstructured, rudimentary jargon. According to this conception, a small collection of words would have been passed from colony to colony, but was hardly substantial enough to obviate the need for a brand-new grammar to develop in each, via a traditional limited-access-based process. Under this conception, SSG would be mere adstratal influence, marginal to substantial discussion.

However, not all collections of features can be treated as remnants of a simple, unstructured jargon. For example, Smith's Ingredient X is difficult to classify as "jargon": lexical items such as *gossip, muddy,* and *leprosy* are too specific and narrow to have served merely for barter-oriented communication on the fly between traders, and would seem to imply usage by an established community.

The conclusive proof, however, is in the grammatical items of SSG. *Da* and *de* are particularly problematic as "jargon" items because, as noted, they can have developed only via grammaticalization. Grammaticalization is a strategy of language expansion, occurring as a response to heavy usage over time *within a stabilized grammar*. Thus the very presence of *da* and *de* indicates that the system they developed in had long passed a "jargon" stage. The development of *self* would have required similar development over time. Indeed, in loosely structured, rudimentary jargons available for examination (e.g., Russenorsk, Chinese Pidgin English, Basque Nautical Pidgin), one does not encounter items such as these, which could have developed only via gradual reconception over time. A "jargon" argument is more convincing for the Portuguese items found in many creoles of the world, which include general, universal concepts such as *know, small,* and *very,* most of them lexical. We do not, however, find words for spicy social practices, meteorological phenomena, and arcane diseases.

What we see, then, is that the nature of SSG and Ingredient X entails nothing less than a surrounding stabilized grammar. It would have been impossible for these items to exist disconnected, as a mere "set of words used to communicate with natives," as the *sabi/pikin* Portuguese core is often appropriately described. Thus we must reject treating the above data as a mere marginal "jargon" transported from colony to colony.

3.5.2 "DIFFUSION"

Having established that the data presented can have existed only within a grammar, we can retain the limited access conception for each colony only by proposing that not a jargon, but a structured pidgin, left its mark on all of the AECs, via some kind of language contact process in each colony. Specifically, we would have to commit ourselves to the following scenario: each AEC formed in response to local conditions because of limited access to a lexifier, while SSG was simply borrowed into the emerging AEC from a *separate* AEC spoken by slaves brought from elsewhere. Again, however, examined closely this notion does not hold up because SSG consists of grammatical items, and it is an established axiom of language contact that grammatical items do not transfer readily from grammar to grammar in isolation.

Indeed, Thomason and Kaufman (1988: 78–109) call attention to the fact that borrowing of grammar is not as rare as was once traditionally thought. However, they note that borrowing of grammar occurs amidst widespread bilingualism: one does not borrow grammatical items in isolation. Therefore, if we claim that SSG was "borrowed," we hoist ourselves with our own petard: the borrowing of *da, de,* modal *fu, unu, bin,* and *self* would have *entailed* control of a whole grammar as well as these grammatical items. One would no more "borrow" *only da* and *de* from an AEC than one would "borrow" *only* the complementizer *que* and the second-person singular accusative pronominal *te* from French.

And with this clear, the flaw in the "borrowing" idea reveals itself. Specifically, to "borrow" SSG, slaves would have to have acquired the very AEC it was in—but if they had acquired it, then, what was the need of a new creole developing at the same time? Surely we do not suppose that slaves working from sunrise to sunset in brutal, foreign, spirit-breaking circumstances saddled themselves with the task of both learning one lingua franca and meanwhile creating another! And (at risk of monotony) even if something this bizarre happened once, it certainly could not have happened across the Caribbean. It is much more economical to suppose that the uniform presence of SSG signals that the new slaves simply learned the whole AEC spoken by the slaves brought from other colonies. This is reinforced by Smith's Ingredient X and finally by the open secret that the AECs are mostly varieties of a single basic language.

The sole recourse available for preserving the limited access conception for each colony would be to claim that pidginization, creolization, and the context of the Atlantic slave trade were such that the rules of language contact no longer applied, and that the creoles that emerged were the chance coalescences of myriad fragments of various lexicons and grammars in the air. This appeal to a "deviled egg" model is particularly easy to dismiss: why would these coalescences have come out so similarly so often? The very crucialness of SSG is that even under such oddly chaotic conditions, we would not expect them to appear in so *many* AECs. Thus SSG and Ingredient X ineluctably prove that the spread of AECs throughout the Caribbean was accomplished via the transplantation of one basic system from colony to colony.

Mufwene (1992: 161–2, 175) presents an example of the type of genesis argument upon which SSG and Ingredient X cast a new light. Mufwene argues that the early preponderance of Barbadian slaves in South Carolina would have had no appreciable impact on the development of Gullah. His argument is based on careful inductions from demographics, which lead him to the obliteration scenario: he presumes that the large numbers of Africans imported as plantations were expanded would have overwhelmed and diluted any influence from the speech of the earlier Barbadian slaves. *Plausible* though this idea be, the linguistic data tell otherwise. Gullah shares most of SSG with Bajan: Gullah has all six features, while Bajan has *de*, *bin* (Rickford 1992), *unu*, and *self* (Hancock 1987); as a highly mesolectal creole, the absence of *da* and particularly the modal *fu* is expected. Furthermore, Gullah and Bajan share much of Ingredient X. This suggests that a system was transplanted from Barbados to South Carolina, *tout court*.

Any limited-access-based genesis account is incomplete without (1) explicitly explaining why the laws of language contact do not apply to creoles (i.e., how slaves could have *so regularly* incorporated grammatical items from a creole without competence in it), (2) explicitly explaining why the laws of sociolinguistics do not apply to creoles (i.e., why slaves, if they had learned a creole, would need to create a new one), and (3) a coherent alternate contact model for creole genesis which can account for *da, de,* modal *fu, unu, bin,* and *self.* To instead reconstruct that a single system was transplanted from colony to colony surmounts these problems.

3.5.3 LANGUAGE CONTACT VERSUS OBLITERATION

It bears repeating that the grammatical nature of SSG makes it impossible for the contact language spoken by slaves from earlier colonies to have been a mere "element" in the birth of Jamaican, Gullah, Guyanese, or other AECs. If this is by any chance unclear to the reader, then I may have failed to get my point across, and the reader might want to quickly reread the previous few pages. The grammatical nature of SSG tells us that the imported pidgin was nothing less than the principal linguistic model in each colony, rather than merely "something in the air."

This is hardly to deny that in each colony, the imported pidgin was exposed to different superstrate dialects, different West African languages, and differing demographic ratios and timings of their development (Hancock 1987: 264–5). However, it is these language contacts which were adstratal, not the imported contact language. The contact-based differences between the AECs in no way license the conclusion that a new language, in any sense, formed from scratch in each colony. The linguistic data tell us that one central system survived a wide variety of sociolinguistic conditions intact.

Thus the various and obvious differences between the AECs do not belie common ancestry. Bickerton (1998: 88), for example, notes that Guyanese Creole English lacks *unu;* another creolist once pointed out to me that this same creole uses *da* as a nonpunctual marker rather than *de* as many other AECs do, with the implication that this was counterevidence to common ancestry. In fact, however, such things are quite unsurprising.

For genetically related languages to be identical is exactly what we would not expect. We do not prove genetic relationship between languages by showing them to be identical, since if they were identical they would be the same language. All related languages differ, often profoundly, because of separate evolution and differing language contacts. Relationship is demonstrated via correspondences of a sort which indicate common origin. This is what SSG signals. Claiming that the AECs are not related because "they're different" is exactly like claiming that penguins and ostriches are not related because "they're different."

Thus in Saramaccan, evolution has led to two predicate negator allomorphs *á* and *ná*, while Sranan retains the original single form *no* (McWhorter 1996a). As for language contact effects, in South Carolina, our basic AEC template took on a *blant* habitual marker from a regional British usage (Hancock 1994: 104), among other things, while elsewhere in the Caribbean, British dialectal usages of *do* led *doz/da* to replace *de* as a nonpunctual marker (Rickford 1986b) (although its locative copula usage, crucial to SSG, survived). None of these things speak against genetic relationship between the AECs anymore than lack of nominal declensions disqualifies Bulgarian as Slavic, or the French lexical component of English disqualifies it as Germanic.

This also applies to SSG itself. I am in no way claiming that every AEC has all six of these features, anymore than Smith (1987) claims that all AECs have all of Ingredient X. Some of the features, like modal *fu*, are particularly conservative, such that AECs without a true basilect tend to lack them. Other gaps are more fortuitous: Guyanese, Antiguan and other AECs have a derivant of "all you" instead of *unu*, for example. My argument is that in general, these six features are distributed too uniformly across AEC as a whole—some AECs have all six, some have five, all have at least three —to be attributable to chance.

The Pacific creoles again serve as a useful analogy. Bislama has a heavy French lexical overlay, and is also developing prepositions from serial verbs (Crowley 1989) and new copulas (Crowley 1990: 339–50) unknown to its sister dialects. Solomon Islands Pijin has modeled adverbs upon indigenous language equivalents (Keesing 1988: 213–5). Tok Pisin has German and Kuanua (Tolai) lexical components, and its well-known development of VP-internal *bai* (Sankoff and Laberge 1980) is a local phenomenon, foreign to the other two dialects (Romaine 1992: 244–75).

Yet no Pacific creolist would claim that these differences show that these creoles each developed in their own locale in response to local sociolinguistic conditions, with any common ancestor having been at best an unstructured "jargon." Scholars of these creoles have always agreed that the creoles traced back to a single ancestor. Even Peter Mühlhäusler, whose genesis work on Tok Pisin is the most localist of any Pacificist, works within a basic assumption that the language is directly traceable to developments outside of Papua New Guinea (e.g., 1976). The evidence we have seen suggests that a similar frame of reference should be status quo among AEC scholars.

3.6 SOCIOHISTORICAL EVIDENCE

Substantial study of intercolonial population movements in the English Caribbean has only just begun (Baker 1998), and the data are such that any but the broadest knowledge of the linguistic aspects of these migrations is forever lost to us. However, what we do know neatly supports the linguistic evidence that AEC was transported from colony to colony.

Some work has pointed to Barbados, one of the earliest settled (1626) islands in the English Caribbean, as the source of origin for AEC. Barbados was a significant distribution point for settlers and the slaves to other colonies (Cassidy 1980: 6–7). Suriname was settled by planters from Barbados (Rens 1953: 14); almost one thousand Barbadian planters moved to Jamaica in 1664 (LePage and DeCamp 1960: 16); Barbadian slaves dominated in early South Carolina (Wood 1974: 24); and so on.

Along these lines, an observer in Jamaica in the 1680s once noted:

> The inhabitants of Jamaica are for the most part Europeans, some Creolians, born and bred in the Island Barbados, the Windward Islands, or Surinam, who are the Masters; and Indians, Negros, Mulatos, Alcatrazes, Mestises, Quarterons, &c who are the Slaves. (Lalla and D'Costa 1990: 16)

There could be no better illustration of the thesis of this chapter. Blacks from earlier settled colonies were a prominent presence, and as "masters," would have served as prime linguistic models for the new arrivals, and would have also done so even as slaves themselves, their experience making them more likely to serve as domestics and artisans. Similar statements are available in reference to South Carolina and other colonies, and support the idea of slaves learning their creole from older slaves from previous colonies.

Baker (1998), on the other hand, suggests that St. Kitts was a more plausible starting point, as the earliest settled colony (1624) and one from which there was also a great deal of migration to other colonies. Whether the most likely point of origin proves to be St. Kitts or Barbados will depend on future research, but either choice would concur with the basic point that the AECs trace to a single ancestor in a single colony.

3.7 SUMMARY

I once had occasion to watch a speaker of Guyanese Creole English and a speaker of Gullah carry on a conversation. Neither was at all surprised that this was possible. On the contrary, upon learning of each other's origins, they launched into conversation with the same spirit of communal adventure as would a Swede and a Dane, or a Xhosa and a Zulu. Comprehension was not perfect, but they managed quite nicely.

Current creole genesis theory would have us believe that these two men were speaking languages of independent origin, whose mutual intelligibility was due merely to similar source languages, universal tendencies, and subsequent "diffusion." Yet recall the importance of chance in pidginization, and the illustration via Sranan and Tok Pisin of how different the results of two "spins of the wheel" can be. Now review Example (53), repeated here:

(59) a. Tok Pisin:

Mi stap long haus.
he COP LOC house

I am in the house.

b. Sranan:

Mi de   na   ini   a   oso.
I   COP LOC inside the house

I am in the house.

Neither of these sentences contain anything specifically derivable from the substrates of the respective creoles, and thus intelligibility between speakers of these two sentences would be unaffected by substrate differences. Whatever the differences between the superstrate dialects of New Guinea and Melanesia and those in Suriname, no difference between these two sentences is traceable to such things (e.g., no English dialect has used *stop* or *there* as a locative copula). Under the limited access conception, the absence of substrate-derived differences, the common superstrate, and the operation of "universals" should mean that a Tok Pisin speaker should be able to understand the Sranan sentence and vice versa. At the very least, they should be identifiable as closely related dialects when viewed on the page. Yet clearly, a speaker of one of these creoles would find the sentence in the other utterly baffling even if enunciated slowly at high volume, and on the page they look as different as French and Russian.

To be sure, AEC specialists also identify "diffusion" as a source of similarities between AECs. However, even if there had been "diffusions" between Sranan and Tok Pisin, they would remain vastly distinct languages. This is especially the case, given that while only lexical items would plausibly diffuse, grammatical items, which would have done so only rarely if ever, are as crucial to the dissimilarity here as lexical items.

This is but one more demonstration that the idea of a new creole emerging in each colony, under any conception, conflicts too sharply with the facts to be viable. Specifically, theoretical statements such as the following become extremely difficult to support:

- Sranan: The English settled Suriname in 1651, yet Bickerton (1995) claims that

  > Sranan could not have constituted a stable, accessible model prior to 1685{. . .}[after which demographics] thoroughly repidginised what was left of the original language and led to a macaronic pidgin that persisted well into the eighteenth century.

- Gullah: The English settled near Charleston in 1670, yet Mufwene (1992: 161–3) claims that

  > Even if by 1670 there was a creole population in Barbados, from where the first British colonists and their slaves came to South Carolina, the absence of large plantations in the new colony during the first fifty years and the intimate living conditions between masters and slaves were not conducive either to the preservation of the putative pidgin or creole or to the development of a new one{. . .}the 1720–1740 period is most likely the time Gullah must have started as a creole.

- Saramaccan: This language patterns very closely with Sranan on all levels and thus was a direct linguistic offshoot thereof (McWhorter 1996b), but Byrne (1987: 32) claims that

  > Saramaccan as a natural language must{. . .}have been a product of the children of the early escapees born in the bush{. . .}as to the approximate time of the formation of Saramaccan, Morris Goodman (p.c.) notes that it probably coalesced sometime after 1700.

- Jamaican: The British arrived in Jamaica in 1655, but LePage and DeCamp (1960: 18, 115) locate the birth of the creole in the 1700s, claiming that in the seventeenth century the population could have been divided linguistically as follows: Speakers of various African languages (slaves); speakers of regional dialects of English (white servants, etc.); speakers of upper-class English (many of them with regional accents). (ibid., 115)

In this chapter, I hope to have shown that the limited access model is inapplicable to almost all of the AECs, with only St. Kitts or Barbados as potential sites for a creole to form in response to demographic disproportion. In the next chapter we will see that the limited access model was just as inapplicable in those colonies as well, and the analysis will point the way towards a revised model of plantation creole genesis.

4 The Creationist at a Cocktail Party

Afrogenesis and the Atlantic English-Based Creoles

4.1 INTRODUCTION

As we have seen, the limited access model is impossible to uphold in any English colony save the first ones, since the likenesses between all of the AECs indicate that a single language was disseminated throughout the Caribbean. As it turns out, however, the limited access model fails even when we try to apply it to the early English colonies, leading to the conclusion that the model does not apply to AEC at all.

4.2 DATING THE EMERGENCE OF SRANAN

The inapplicability of the limited access model even to the early AECs is revealed, oddly enough, in as seemingly arcane an issue as the first appearance of Sranan Creole English. While Sranan, English-based, has been the lingua franca of Suriname for over three centuries now, the English controlled Suriname only for a mere sixteen years, from 1651 to 1667, when the Dutch took it over. More to the point, it was the Dutch who established a thriving sugar plantation system there. Under the English, Suriname was firmly ensconced in the *société d'habitation* stage. Africans were primarily distributed among small plantations of twenty people each on average (Voorhoeve 1964: 234–6). Furthermore, on these plantations, English indentured bondservants were as numerous as Africans, with whom they worked side by side (Rens 1953: 58–61). Since there was no demographic disproportion in such settings and European-African contact was rich, we would expect slaves during the English hegemony to have acquired a relatively full second-language variety of English (cf. Holm 1989: 434; Plag 1993: 28; Arends 1995: 236–7).

The limited access model stipulates that pidginization would have begun only after the Dutch established large plantations after their takeover in 1667. Furthermore, even under the Dutch, for over twenty years small plantations remained the norm (Price 1976: 16), meaning that strictly, most creolists should expect that Sranan emerged around 1690.

Crucially, however, three deductions indicate that Sranan existed long before this, having already existed in some relatively stabilized form by the time the Dutch arrived in 1667. Thus while we have seen that throughout South America, *no* creoles appeared despite sharp demographic disproportion, here is a case where a creole did appear despite *no* demographic disproportion. This is yet another indication that limited access to a target has nothing to do with plantation creole genesis.

4.2.1 SRANAN EXISTED BY 1667: FIRST CLUE

The first indication that Sranan existed when the Dutch arrived in 1667 is that Sranan is unlikely to have developed under Dutch hegemony. Indeed, Dutch colonists are known for having been linguistically accommodating, but this has been where contact languages were already established. Where Dutch has been the first dominant language on the ground, we have ample evidence that the Dutch had no qualms about imposing it, given the existence of Dutch-based creoles in Guyana (Berbice and Skepi Dutch Creole) and the Virgin Islands (Negerhollands). The Dutch adoption of Sranan thus strongly suggests that they encountered it on site.

However, on the basis of this by itself, some might propose that the Dutch encountered slaves speaking an L2 variety of English, and that subsequent large influxes of Africans pidginized that English, the Dutch learning the creole as it developed. Other evidence, however, suggests otherwise.

4.2.2 SRANAN EXISTED BY 1667: SECOND CLUE

While our first documentation of Sranan is from fifty-one years after the Dutch takeover (1718), Sranan did leave a concrete footprint in the seventeenth-century historical record: none other than Maroon Spirit Language. The reader is asked to review the discussion in Section 3.4.1, showing the idiosyncratic correspondences between Sranan and MSL. Now recall that the English shipped a massive contingent of slaves to Jamaica in 1671. This obscure datum is of vital significance, because it tells us that Sranan existed in recognizable form by that year. Otherwise, Sranan and MSL would have to have developed their correspondences independently.

Situated within the sequence of historical events in Suriname, the year

1671 was merely four years after the Dutch takeover. Given that Maroon Spirit Language already displays grammaticalized elements such as the copula *da,* progressive marker *de,* and a conventionalized paradigm of interrogatives, it is vastly improbable that it had existed for merely the four years between 1667 and 1671. This suggests that it had stabilized long before 1667, and that the Dutch therefore encountered a stabilized creole in 1667.

4.2.3 SRANAN EXISTED BY 1667: THIRD CLUE

A final indication that Sranan existed even long before 1667 comes from the history of its sister creole, Saramaccan Creole English. Saramaccan is spoken by descendants of maroons from plantations run by Portuguese planters, who had settled in Suriname two years before the Dutch takeover, in 1665. Byrne (1987: 28) considers Saramaccan to have arisen independently of Sranan, forming in the bush among a band of escapees from the Machado plantation in 1685. Bickerton (1984a: 178, 1994a, 1994b) concurs that Saramaccan emerged in the bush.

This, however, is a demographic deduction, at odds with linguistic data (Smith 1987) and sociohistorical data (Goodman 1987: 375–82) which uncontrovertibly place the birth of Saramaccan on the Portuguese plantations, not in the bush. There are contemporary references to a mixed English-Portuguese pidgin spoken on Portuguese plantations, called "Djutongo" in one (Goodman 1987: 377–82). A word list in this Djutongo (Smith 1987: 125–8) confirms that this was indeed the precursor to Saramaccan (see McWhorter 1996b: 469, 488 for further discussion). Meanwhile, Smith (1987) demonstrates that systematically, the Portuguese lexicon in Saramaccan has been phonologically reinterpreted according to different rules than the English-based component. If one group of slaves encountered both sets of words at the same time, as the bush scenario entails, we would expect patterns of reinterpretation to apply across the board. Smith's analysis therefore shows that the Saramaccan is indeed an encounter between two separately stabilized components. Taken together, Goodman's and Smith's research shows that Saramaccan was a relexification by Portuguese of early Sranan, as spoken by English-owned slaves bought by the Portuguese as the English withdrew (Goodman 1987: 379).

This means, simply, that Sranan existed before Djutongo. Since we can assume Djutongo began forming soon after Portuguese planters began buying English slaves, it follows that Sranan existed by 1665, when the Portuguese planters arrived. We can be sure that they did start buying English slaves quickly, since by ten years later, in 1675, there were only fifty aged English slaves left in Suriname, all others having been bought or withdrawn (Arends 1995: 238).

However, the depiction of Saramaccan as an independent rain forest emergence was crucial to the treatment of this creole as a direct reflection of Universal Grammar (Bickerton 1984b, Byrne 1987). Meanwhile, Smith's (1987) arguments, hidden in an unpublished dissertation, have been all but ignored. The truth about Saramaccan's origins is further shrouded by the fact that, for reasons outside of the Universal Grammar issue, the linkage of Saramaccan to Djutongo has been resisted (e.g., Ladhams 1999).

Luckily, however, the direct relationship between Sranan and Saramaccan is demonstrable via simple comparison. The two creoles share the same basic grammar down to almost uncanny details, as shown in the following examples.

(a) *Epenthetic [m]*. In both languages, a constrained set of verbs develop an epenthetic bilabial nasal before certain monosyllabic vowel-initial following elements.

Sranan:

(1) a. mi njan en [mi **ñam** e] "I ate it," but

 b. mi njan ala [mi ña ala] "I ate it all"

 (Voorhoeve 1985: 91)

Saramaccan:

(2) a. fón en [mi fo**m**ɛ̃ɛ̃] "I beat him," but

 b. fón u [a fõ u] "He beat us"

 (Kouwenberg 1987: 11)

Ndjuka exhibits the same trait (Huttar and Huttar 1995: 591–2); it is absent in any other AEC. Neither Wolof, Mandinka, Kru, Akan, Gbe, Yoruba, Igbo or Kikongo have the feature. The distribution of this /m/ resembles that of a transitive marker, although its generation is phonological. Thus one might expect that there might have been an African transitive marker which was reinterpreted as a phonological process in Suriname. However, again, there is no such model in any of the languages above.

(b) De *as equative copula*. In both creoles, *de*, a strictly locative verb in other AECs, can also be used in the equative. This feature has no viable candidate as a substrate antecedent (McWhorter 1997a).

Sranan:

(3) A **de**   wan bigi dagu.
    it COP a   big dog

It is a big dog.

Saramaccan:

(4) Dágu **dέ** wan mbéti ku fó fútu.
    dog COP a   animal with four foot

A dog is an animal with four feet.

Jamaican:

(5) Mi **a**   (*de) big uman.
    I COP   big woman

I am a grown woman.

(Bailey 1966: 32)

(c) *Reduplication for resultative.* In Saramaccan, verbs are converted into resultative participial adjectives via reduplication.

(6) Dí páu dέ **látjalátja**. (*Di páu dέ látja.*)
    the tree COP chop-chop

The tree is/has been chopped.

(Alleyne 1987: 83)

There is no intensification or iteration implied in such constructions.

This trait is absent from the literature on Sranan, but is indeed a feature of the grammar (L. Adamson, p.c.). It does exist in Ndjuka, however, which is a direct offshoot of Sranan.

Ndjuka:

(7) A boto de   **lailai**. (*A boto de lai.*)
    the boat COP load-load

The boat is/has been loaded.

(Huttar and Huttar 1992)

While reduplicated verbs do serve as attributive adjectives *within* NP in Akan and Gbe, they do not occur in reduplicated form predicatively after the copula (e.g., Twi *adéso adùrudúru* "a heavy load" but *adésoa no yèduru* load the COP heavy "the load is heavy" [Christaller 1875: 46]). This predi-

Table 4.1. Interrogative paradigms in the Suriname creoles

English	Sranan	Saramaccan	Ndjuka	Belizean
what (what something?)	*(o)san(i)*	*andí*	*san(i)*	*we*
who (what person?)	*suma*	*ambé*	*sama*	*huu*
how (what fashion?)	*(o)fa*	*(un)fá*	*on-fa*	*hou*
which (what this?)	*odi*	*undí*	*odi*	*wich*
when (what time?)	*oten*	*na-untén*	*onten*	*wen*
how many	*omeni*	*un-méni*	*on men*	*humoch*

Adapted from Smith 1987: 98, with extra data on "when" and "how many." Belizean data from Dayley 1979a, 1979b.

cative reduplication is thus not a substrate retention, but appears to be an innovation (perhaps via extension of the attributive usage) in Suriname creoles.

(d) *Interrogative paradigms.* The interrogative paradigms of both languages are based on the combination of a certain general questioning morpheme with a nominal; there are no derivants of the English or Portuguese interrogatives (see Table 4.1). A system eschewing the European equivalents completely is unknown elsewhere in the Anglophone Caribbean. The bimorphemic interrogative is, of course, commonly encountered cross-linguistically. However, what distinguishes the Suriname system is idiosyncrasies of lexical choice. The marker, and the precise correspondences in the choice of etymon for the nominals, are clearly derivants of a single original system (Saramaccan *andí* and *ambé* are Gbe borrowings). Belizean is included to highlight the idiosyncrasy of the Suriname patternings.

(e) *Ideophones.* There are a wide range of ideophones from, particularly, Fongbe and Kikongo that we could expect Saramaccan to derive its ideophones from. However, there is a rich band of correspondence between Sranan and Saramaccan ideophones, even extending to function. For example, in both, the domain of *pii* "quiet" includes that of color, as in Sranan *a blaka so pii* "he is so very

Table 4.2. Grammatical items in Sranan and Saramacan

English	Sranan	Saramaccan	Belizean
(a) then	*noo*	*nɔɔ*	*den*
(b) never	*nowante, noiti*	*na wan té, nóiti*	*neva*
(c) nothing	*nowansani*	*na wan saní*	*notn*
(d) plural marker	*den*	*déé*	*dem*
(e) irrealis marker	*sa, go*	*sa, (g)ó*	*wan, gwain*
(f) complementizer	*taki*	*táa (<táki)*	*se*

black" (Adamson and Smith 1994: 226) and Saramaccan *a guún píí* "he is very green" (Rountree and Glock 1977: 147).

(f) *Other identical grammatical items.* If Sranan and Saramaccan arose separately, then the numerous correspondences in various other etymological choices made for grammatical items are a truly uncanny example of convergent evolution; see Table 4.2.

The treatments of Saramaccan as an independent rain forest creation neither address nor even mention this comparative evidence, which shows that Sranan and Saramaccan share a common source, and that this source furthermore was stabilized, including complex and idiosyncratic features such as the epenthetic /m/ and unusual uses of reduplication, foreign to any "jargon." Clearly, any attempt to place the emergence or stabilization of Saramaccan in the bush is untenable.

These data furthermore allow us to push Sranan's emergence even further back than 1665. If on Portuguese plantations Sranan was stabilized enough to undergo such extensive relexification and retain its grammar in such fine detail, then it is clear that the language had been in use for the long time necessary for such conventionalization.

4.3 A THEORETICAL ANOMALY

Thus we see that Sranan had already emerged in Suriname at a time when slaves were working on small farms side by side with whites. Access to English would have been quite free in such settings. At this point, then, we must ask, What was Sranan doing on these little farms?

Naturally, one response will be to attempt to accommodate this to the reigning theory. Specifically, many will suppose that these small farms were indeed a suitable context for the birth of a deep creole. It must be clear, however, that this would directly contradict a theoretical construct which leading creolists have been propounding for years.

For example, Chaudenson (1979, 1992) has dedicated a career to treating Réunionnais French as a mere evolution of the regional French dialect of Bourbon, and attributing its failure to become a true creole to the long *société d'habitation* phase in Réunion. His *oeuvre* has ceaselessly drawn attention to the intimate interethnic interactions in early Réunion and the unimpeded language transmission this context would allow, and he makes clear (1992) that he considers this model applicable to creole genesis worldwide, extending it to Martinique, Louisiana, Cuba, and the Dominican Republic (but neglecting Suriname).

Baker and Corne (1982), analyzing the same context, conclude that the creole nature of Mauritian Creole French is due to the absence of such a *société d'habitation* phase on Mauritius, concurring with Chaudenson that the less "creole" nature of Réunionnais is due to the long duration there of that phase. Their 1982 book has been a landmark work, its model influencing the work of countless others since its publication.

In a similar vein, Mufwene (1992: 161–2) is quite explicit that slaves on small farms developed L2 varieties of the lexifier, not creoles:

> Even if by 1670 there was a creole population in Barbados, from where the first British colonists and their slaves came to South Carolina, the absence of large plantations in the new colony during the first fifty years and the intimate living conditions between masters and slaves were not conducive either to the preservation of the putative pidgin or creole or to the development of a new one. The conditions seem similar to those discussed by Chaudenson for French creoles, in which what developed first were second-language varieties of the lexifier.

Finally, recall that Suriname specialists themselves have casually assumed that English Suriname was not a setting where creole genesis would have been expected (Plag 1993: 28; Arends 1995: 236–7). We are now in a position to see what a hairpin turn it would be for creolists to propose that Sranan *was* born on the small English farms I have described. This about-face would flatly contradict an assumption crucial to works considered authoritative in creole studies.

We are also perhaps in a better position to consider a more constructive way of approaching our data. One way of extracting ourselves from this theoretical dilemma is to consider that Sranan did *not* emerge in Suriname, but was brought there by slaves from elsewhere. In truth, this was already apparent at the outset, since as we have seen, all of the AECs are too much alike for one pidgin not to have been transported from colony to colony (recall the crucial reasoning behind this in Section 3.5). Our sociohistorical data have thus only reinforced what the linguistic data already suggested.

4.4 BARBADOS?

The most promising candidate as a source for Sranan in terms of sociohistorical documentation is Barbados, which had been settled in 1626. The first permanent settlers in Suriname in 1651 came from Barbados, and others followed during the 1650s (Rens 1953: 14). There is no official documentation that they brought slaves with them, but the practicalities of wresting plantations out of untamed land would seem to have made slaves a ringingly practical necessity.

If we propose that Sranan was brought to Suriname as a pidgin spoken by slaves from Barbados, there also seems every reason to suppose that on the small farms of Suriname, where contact with whites was extensive, they were able to also begin acquiring a fuller register of English. However, if they had simply replaced their pidgin with L2 English, then we would lack an explanation for why Sranan is spoken in Suriname today.

We can accommodate *both* the existence of Sranan *and* the free access to English on the small farms by positing that the slaves retained the pidgin as a vernacular, marking African identity, while developing an L2 register of English for communication with whites. This would be a typical example of the diglossic relationship of European and creole varieties found in many creolophone locales today.

We must not make the mistake of supposing that the pidgin was merely a way-station on the path to full acquisition of English, casually shed as competence in English increased. People do not shed vernacular registers on exposure to standard ones the way American undergraduates shed their schoolroom French during a year in Paris, as was discussed in Section 2.4.2. In this vein, Mufwene (1992: 175) dismisses the influence of Barbadian Creole on Gullah on the basis of doubting "the motivation for such slaves to be *stuck with* such varieties when the living conditions gave them ample opportunities to develop varieties closer to those of their masters" [emphasis mine].

This perspective, however, supposes that there would have no place on such small farms for a specifically African identity, and that the social fabric was dominated by white-black interactions. More realistically, however, the sociological spectrum of these farms was a web, characterized by a wide variety of interactions and identities. In such a situation, blacks would plausibly nurture a vernacular register among themselves while developing an L2 variety for use with whites. Sociolinguistic research has richly illuminated the variable nature of language and dialect use across race and class lines.

Thus while early Suriname would not have *generated* a pidgin, it could plausibly have *nurtured* one. This would be an unremarkable example of the fact that pidgins and creoles, after having become markers of a social identity, can easily persist in a context in which access to the lexifier has become available, Pidgin Fijian in modern Fiji being one example (Siegel 1987). To claim that an imported pidgin could not have survived in early Suriname, one must also be able to explain why an African-American secretary who spends every workday immersed in conversation with mainstream standard English speakers nevertheless maintains her African-American Vernacular English and passes it on to her offspring; why middle class Cape Verdean bureaucrats retain their creole in an officially Lusophone society; or why Hawaiian Creole English survives among speakers who all live in an English-speaking society.

However, locating the birth of Sranan in Barbados, we run into a similar problem as the one in Suriname: plantations were small in Barbados as well until 1665, with Africans working side by side with white indentured bondservants (Rens 1953: 70; Handler and Lange 1978: 290; Hancock 1980: 22). Thus as in Suriname, it is more likely that a creole, while indeed spoken on the island, would not have been created there, but brought in from elsewhere. Like early Suriname, early Barbados would not have *generated* a pidgin, but could have *nurtured* one.

Some have argued that Barbados never harbored a pidgin or creole English, Barbadian blacks being well-known today for their particularly acrolectal English (Hancock 1980). However, recent research has shown that an AEC was indeed spoken in Barbados in the past, and a living variety has been unearthed (Roy 1986; Rickford 1992). Meanwhile, there are explicit citations of such a language as far back as the 1770s (Pinckard 1806; Cassidy 1986; Fields 1995; and esp. Rickford and Handler 1994).

Returning to our question, then, as to where the pidgin spoken by these Barbadian slaves had been brought from, we are now running out of colonies—there were only three others which the English had settled by the founding of Suriname in 1651. The least familiar of these is the Providence Island settlement of 1630, but this was a short-lived experiment destroyed by the Spanish long before the settlement of Suriname, in 1641 (Blackburn

1997: 225–6). Virginia had been first settled as far back as 1607, but re-
lied almost exclusively on white indentured servants until after 1661, black
slaves being extremely few and spread thin (Blackburn 1997: 240), unlikely
to have developed a creole variety.

Only St. Kitts, settled before Barbados in 1624, was a remotely possible
source of creole-speaking slaves who were transported to Barbados. There
is historical documentation of some settlement, with slaves, of Barbados
from St. Kitts (Baker 1998). Furthermore, some settlers from St. Kitts, and
its offshoot colonies Nevis and Montserrat, were among the early English
settlers of Suriname (Rens 1953: 14). Thus we must consider that AEC may
have originated on one of these islands, as Baker (1998) has. However, before 1665, St. Kitts and the other Leewards were no more likely a setting
than Barbados for the generation of a creole. The plantations, small as in
Barbados until 1665, were turned over to sugar even later than in Barbados
due to the particularly high quality of tobacco grown there, and white indentured servants constituted the bulk of the work force for an even longer
period (Watts 1987).

Thus the evidence from Suriname shows us that AEC already existed in
stabilized form by the 1660s at the very latest, and yet at this time, nowhere
in the English Caribbean had the conditions developed which we would expect to pidginize English. Again, one response might be to suppose that
small farms could create creoles. However, this would create awkward discrepancies with a great deal of work in which creolists have ruled this out
in places like Réunion, South Carolina, Cuba, and Puerto Rico. Another response, then, would be to investigate the possibility that AEC was imported
to the Caribbean from another location.

In the early seventeenth century there was but one context outside of
the New World where Englishmen and Africans were in sustained contact.
Furthermore, the contact was of a sort which would definitely have led to
the development of a pidgin. Moreover, there were population exchanges
between this context and the Caribbean.

This context was the trade settlements on the West African coast, where
the English made use of squadrons of African slaves to assist in trade and
upkeep. By a process of elimination, this becomes a compelling place to
search for the ultimate origin of AEC.

4.5 WEST AFRICAN TRADE SETTLEMENTS

Most of the major European powers established such trade settlements,
where Europeans obtained goods and slaves from local Africans. Most of

these settlements, particularly by the seventeenth century, were centered around castles which both housed a staff of European personnel and contained quarters where slaves were held before shipment overseas. These settlements also made use of large numbers of African *castle slaves*, some paid artisans but most in varying gradations of bondage, who served in a wide range of capacities at the settlement rather than being shipped overseas as *sale slaves*. Their duties included loading and unloading ships in harbor, maintaining the castle and surrounding grounds, and tending to sale slaves after capture.

We have seen that the emergence of a pidgin English on the small farms of the early English Caribbean would have been highly unlikely, given that blacks and whites were working side-by-side, and in equal proportion. However, in the trade settlements, the failure of a pidgin to emerge would have been most unexpected, given the conditions under which pidgins have emerged consistently through history.

The demographic ratios in these forts were hardly of the degree of disproportion typically thought to have generated the Caribbean creoles. However, castle slaves did usually outnumber the whites considerably. A typical ratio, for example, was 184 Africans to 84 whites at the Dutch Elmina fort owned by the Dutch (Lawrence 1969: 45). However, demographic disproportion has never been considered a vital factor in the development of trade-based and labor-based pidgins, as opposed to plantation creoles. For example, Melanesian Pidgin English developed amidst conditions of relative parity between Englishmen and Australian Aboriginals or Melanesians, in Australia, on whaling ships, and then at sea cucumber and sandalwood processing sites (Keesing 1988; Baker 1993); Pidgin Fijian developed as a foreigner talk strategy, where Fijians vastly outnumbered foreigners (Siegel 1987); and so on.

Cases such as Fiji have shown us that sociology is much more important than ratios in generating a pidgin. In this light, these trade settlements sharply differed from the small farms of the early English Caribbean. At the trade settlements, slaves were maintained at a physical distance from whites, residing in huts outside of the fort (Lawrence 1969: 51), and were often even expected to grow most of their own food (42). There is no documentation of an orientation on the part of these castle slaves to acculturate to European ways. On the contrary, their tendency was, unsurprisingly, to identify with the Africans in the surrounding community (61), and desertion was common (49). In addition, while slaves in the Caribbean had been condemned for eternity to an alien land, castle slaves were sometimes locals working for wages or on loan from a local king. Even when consigned to castle slavery for life, they were able to use their native language (documents suggest that in many cases, much or most of a castle slave force spoke the same native language), and were still on their own continent in a setting less foreign to them than a New World plantation would have been. It was not infrequent for castle slaves to eventually buy their freedom (Postma 1990: 72–3). Such situations would have rendered full acquisition of the superstrate as sociologically superfluous as it was among Melanesians working plantations on limited contracts alongside many men who spoke their native language. The castle setting, therefore, would have encouraged the development of a utilitarian pidgin.

Given that a pidgin English was likely to have emerged at West African trade settlements, but not on small Caribbean farms, one way of accounting for the presence of AEC in the early English Caribbean is to reconstruct that an English pidgin was brought to the early English Caribbean by castle slaves who had developed it on the West African coast. Since all of the AECs must trace to a single ancestor, it is most likely that the pidgin was brought to one of the *first* English colonies. Since St. Kitts and Barbados were the first colonies settled and were the source of settlers and slaves to subsequent colonies, it is to one of these colonies that the pidgin was most likely transported.

Thus far, I have presented mere speculation. Now, however, I will show evidence which specifically supports this very scenario, linking AECs specifically to a trade settlement on the Ghanaian coast.

4.6 THE CORMANTIN CASTLE

If an AEC variety was available in St. Kitts or Barbados to be taken to Suriname in the 1650s, then the crucial transportation of a pidgin English from West Africa to the Caribbean would have taken place sometime before the 1650s. In that period, the English had only one castle on the West African coast, the Cormantin castle near present-day Accra, founded in 1632 (Porter 1989: 128). By a process of elimination, then, this becomes the most likely site of origin for AEC. Most strikingly, however, other aspects of Cormantin specifically pinpoint it as the most likely source of a transported pidgin.

In reference to most West African trade settlements, the transportation of a pidgin to the Caribbean would be a highly tenuous proposition (which has been one source of the resistance to Hancock's work; cf. Rickford 1987:

53–6). This is because it is well documented that castle slaves were not to be sold to overseas plantations except as punishment for serious crimes (e.g., Rodney 1970: 267); original documents from these settlements are rife with this provision.

However, Cormantin was unique. In the initial decades of their settlement of the Caribbean, the English were only tentatively devoted to active slaving, supplying slaves to their colonies mostly via the Dutch, and meanwhile attempting to rely significantly upon indentured whites for labor. As a result, Cormantin was devoted not to slaving but to material trade, mostly in gold and elephant tusks.

What this meant, however, was that when the Cormantin staff sold slaves, it was often from the ranks of the castle slaves: a number of such instances are recorded (E/3/85: 114; E/3/87: 109; Makepeace 1989: 239).[1] The procurement of Africans expressly for sale was explicitly forbidden (E/3/85: 165). More to the point, Cormantin was even advised from London to send castle slaves to help found new English colonies and even serve in positions of authority such as overseer (e.g., E/3/86: 86; E/3/87: 109). The wisdom of such a policy is so intuitively clear that it would be surprising if it had not been the case. It was one manifestation of a general tendency in the European settlement of the Caribbean to rely as much as possible on earlier experiences in settling each new colony (e.g., Chaudenson 1992: 57–65).

Unfortunately, the only records from Cormantin that survive begin in the 1650s, by which time we can hypothesize that an English pidgin would already have been transported to the Caribbean. (That these documents stretch as unusually far back as the 1650s, but not just two crucial little decades more, seems almost a cruel joke!) However, there is no reason to suppose that Cormantin castle slaves were not being sent to help found colonies during the 1640s and 1650s, when Barbados and, to a lesser extent, St. Kitts began the transformation to sugar economies. As noted, Cormantin was the only castle the English had from which to send such seasoned slaves in the first half of the 1600s, and since ships were regularly traveling between Cormantin and Barbados in the 1650s (E/3/25), we can assume that they were doing so in earlier decades.

Huber (1999: 89–90) is skeptical that castle slaves could have been sent from Cormantin early enough to have an impact in the Caribbean, given

1. Numbers refer to documents held at the Oriental and India Office Collections, London.

that an actual castle was not completed on the site until 1647. However, his assumption that a pidgin could have formed only in a castle proper, and only amidst great numbers of slaves, is difficult to accept. Indeed, by 1637 the English had barely finished a lodge at Cormantin, but trade was nevertheless brisk (Porter 1989: 142–3). The lodge, once completed, burned down in 1639, but by this time a castle proper had been begun (188). It is unknown whether slaves had been used in the 1630s, but it is documented that by 1644, African slaves were being used to finish the castle (201). Thus during the 1640s, the English were indeed using slaves at Cormantin even before the castle itself was finished. As for the size of the slave force, theoretically, a relatively stabilized pidgin could emerge between two people, after all. More to the point, pidgins and creoles are documented as forming between quite small numbers of people, such as Unserdeutsch at a single orphanage and Pitcairnese on an island amidst about thirty people.

The question, of course, is whether or not these slaves spoke a pidgin English. As noted, sociolinguistic plausibility virtually requires that they did. This is also, however, supported—albeit indirectly—by the records. In 1662, the East India Company explicitly requested the Cormantin factors to send "12 of own blacks . . . such as can speak English" to the new colony of St. Helena (E/3/86: 85). It is highly unlikely that the slaves' "English" would have been fluent, and we must keep always in mind that "speaking English" was a much more general concept to these colonial businessmen than it is to modern linguists. Huber (1999: 93) has countered that the staff in London would have been too unfamiliar with conditions at the fort to know whether the castle slaves spoke a form of English. However, we have no concrete indications to this effect, and this speculation appears contradicted by the fact that in the Cormantin factors' reply (E/3/27: 195), justifying with great servility their inability to send any of their slaves away at that particular time, at no point do they mention that their slaves did not speak any form of English.

To be sure, in the 1660s, at least, the Cormantin castle slaves were all drawn from the surrounding locality, and thus would have all spoken a dialect of Akan. Bickerton (1998: 81) sees this as counterevidence to an English-based pidgin having formed, claiming that Akan would have served as the slaves' medium of communication. This, however, neglects the fact that Akan would have been of no use between the Englishmen and the Africans. As Thomason and Kaufman (1988: 197–8) make clear, Whinnom's (1971) tertiary hybridization model must not be taken to mean that the presence of at least two substrate groups is a *sine qua non* of the birth of a pidgin.

Pidgins, and stable ones, have formed between one superstrate and one substrate language quite often, Pidgin Yimas (Foley 1988) and Chinese Pidgin English being two examples.

Indeed, it is well documented that individuals at European castles often learned local African languages to use in trading with local inhabitants. There are also many citations of African traders using Portuguese pidgin with Europeans of various linguistic backgrounds. However, it is undocumented that (a) entire castle staffs of soldiers, workmen, and artisans learned the language of the slaves working under them, rather than the slaves learning a form of English, or that (b) entire castle staffs of soldiers, workmen, and artisans and the squadron of slaves working under them all communicated in a pidgin based on Portuguese, a language native to no one in the setting and spoken by no one in a position of leadership over white or slave. To propose so would contradict the sociolinguistic fundamentals of contact language birth—namely, that the language of those in power is the lexifier. While studies such as that of Siegel (1987) have shown us that "power" cannot be reduced simply to a matter of white skin and guns, clearly the castle slaves were in no sense the ones in power at the trade settlements. It is also unlikely that Englishmen simply made use of an interpreter in commanding the slaves. Interpreters were extensively used in West African coastal trade for interactions of relatively brief duration. However, this would have become extremely cumbersome in the castle setting. The realities of extended coexistence would surely have led to the development of some kind of general communication medium over time. The use of pidgins rather than interpreters across the world in such situations would seem to support this, and recall that the supervisors of Cormantin in London casually refer to slaves who could "speak English."

Finally, there is much evidence of Africans speaking reduced versions of European languages other than Portuguese. For example, in 1686 an African trader was recorded as saying,

> Blackman good freind and doe all Black man very good butt
> hee noe savee for wt hee noo love mee butt I love him and
> tell him to make all Pallavra succaba Ile give him a very good
> woeman and then hee send mee ye two Pawnes and then
> Umbra Cooshie yt is to say a finall conclusion.
> (The author thanks Magnus Huber for this citation.)

This passage gives no indication of being a direct ancestor to AEC; it was most likely a mere transient interlanguage used by a particular African trader, and undoubtedly highly distorted in transcription besides (*succaba* and *umbra cooshie* are most likely Twi). However, it is significant in showing that African languages and Portuguese pidgin were by no means the only languages used in interethnic contact on the West African coast during the slave trade.

The evidence licenses the following specific hypothesis. An English-based pidgin, which we will designate Lower Guinea Coast Pidgin English (LGPE), formed between the English staff at the Cormantin castle and the African castle slaves in their employ, most likely in the 1640s. A number of these castle slaves were transported to the English Caribbean, their presence seen as useful in the founding or expansion of a new colony given their work experience and their control of a form of English. Because to serve as models, they would have to have been in place as the slave population began to expand, the transportation of castle slaves most likely occurred at some point between 1645 and 1655.

Often serving in positions of authority, these slaves served as models and teachers for sale slaves brought to the colony. As such, LGPE was the model for the sale slaves, and developed into AEC. After learning AEC, some of the new slaves, taken with pioneer settlers to a second colony, in turn transmitted AEC to slaves subsequently brought to that second colony from Africa. In this fashion, AEC was disseminated throughout the Caribbean, transformed in each colony according to degree and timing of contact with various dialects of English and African languages, but everywhere maintaining its essential structure.

Because it was the first colony to be transformed to a sugar economy (Porter 1989: 243), Barbados would have been the most likely destination of castle slaves from Cormantin. It may have been transplanted to Suriname with the first migrants from Barbados in 1651, but may also have been transplanted with a later contingent later in the 1650s. If Baker's (1998) hypothesis that AEC traces to St. Kitts proves correct, then it could have been with settlers from there or its offshoot Leeward colonies that LGPE reached Suriname, during the 1650s. Transported to Sierra Leone by Jamaican maroons in 1800, it developed into Krio, which in turn was the source of the dialects of West African Pidgin English in Ghana, Nigeria, and Cameroon.

LGPE is preserved in its most conservative form in Suriname as Sranan and Ndjuka, where it has had the least contact with English. Although it reached St. Kitts or Barbados first, on these islands as well as the other colonies, LGPE would have had constant contact with English. As a result, even the most conservative varieties on these islands are quite mesolectal compared to Sranan, and are one end of a continuum of lects extending to the local standard. However, the most conservative layers of the continuum AECs retain a core of commonalities with the Suriname varieties, and the grammatical nature of these reveals the roots of all of these creoles in a single, relatively stabilized common ancestor.

It must be understood, however, that in placing the birth of AEC at Cormantin we would depart sharply from anything resembling the plantation context. The motivation for Cormantin castle slaves to gain competence in English was strictly functional: they needed a communication vehicle for use with the Englishmen, as well as with castle slaves who did not speak their native language, if there were any. In the meantime, they continued to live and think in their native languages. Thus AEC was born as a pidgin in the same fashion as classic pidgins like Russenorsk: the castle slaves were no more attempting to "acquire English" than were the Cantonese in developing Chinese Pidgin English (cf. Baker 1990 on the role of motivation in contact language genesis).

Thus no variation on the limited access model, conceiving of creole genesis as targeted acquisition of a language receding from direct engagement, applied here, anymore than it would for Tok Pisin. The acquisition was only wanly targeted, and the relatively slight demographic disproportion and physical compactness of the setting can hardly be thought to have denied the slaves access to the language. In the New World, this pidgin was thrust into a new role, as a Medium for Interethnic Communication (in Philip Baker's terminology) in a setting where African languages were marginalized. Here, the stage was set for an erstwhile pidgin to develop into a creole via the expansion that accompanies heavier, broader use. However, the groundwork of the language had been laid in a very different setting.

This hypothesis lends itself to possible misinterpretation in three main ways. First, I consider AEC to have been born solely between Englishmen and castle slaves, not between Englishmen and other Africans with whom they interacted. Thus the aforementioned documentation that some Europeans learned African languages is not counterevidence to my argument, because they used these languages in trade with local chieftains and African traders, not with castle slaves. Similarly, given the impracticality of Africans mastering pidgins of all the European languages they encountered, until well into the 1700s their lingua franca of choice with Europeans was based on Portuguese, the European language they encountered first (since the Portuguese were the first European settlers of Africa). However, we see this used, again, with free local Africans, not with castle slaves themselves. It is highly unlikely that Englishmen utilized Portuguese pidgin on a daily basis with slaves *in their own permanent employ in their own forts*. As noted above, innumerable contexts worldwide allow us to confidently reconstruct that a pidgin based on the dominant language would emerge in such settings. Finally, it is documented that local Africans sometimes acquired competence in languages other than Portuguese, such as English (Hancock 1986) and Dutch (Jones 1985: 34). However, since these Africans were not transported overseas, their competence can have been of little if any import to the emergence of AEC in the Caribbean.

Second, I have proposed that AEC owes its presence in the Caribbean solely to *one* transportation of a pidgin from Cormantin to the Caribbean by a crucial seed population of castle slaves in the 1630s or 1640s. I am not proposing that slaves regularly brought this pidgin to all of the Caribbean colonies throughout the slave trade era, as earlier related arguments have (Hancock 1969, 1986; Voorhoeve 1973; Smith 1987: 10). In my opinion, the documentation of sale slaves arriving in the New World with no competence in European languages (Wood 1974; Rickford 1987: 53–5; Baker and Corne 1982: 245) is too uniform for it to be plausible that any significant number of sale slaves spoke pidgin English. Thus the fact that most sale slaves were brought to a given colony not from Ghana but from other regions of Africa is irrelevant to the hypothesis: I am proposing that all of the AECs owe their structure to one initial transplantation, from Ghana to St. Kitts or Barbados.

Finally, I do not consider the *creoles* who were products of marriages between Europeans and local African women to have been of any particular importance to generating LGPE. Thus I must disassociate my hypothesis from the frequent association in the literature of West African parent pidgins with these *creoles* (Stoller 1985, Hancock 1986, Williams 1988). For one, these *creoles* formed a minor aristocracy in West African communities, with an identity intermediate between European and African, and as such were not transported overseas to do plantation work. Some were indeed transported to serve as special assistants to Europeans (Berlin's "Atlantic Creoles" [1996]), but these Africans, working singly or in small groups alongside whites and often on shipboard or in cities, appear to have had no bearing upon the sociolinguistic situation on plantations.

In addition, the conception of interracial Africans creating a creole language is problematic upon examination. Especially in her homeland, an African mother of an interracial child would have spoken to her child in her native language, not a pidginized register of a European language used with her husband. Meanwhile, the child would be likely to acquire a full register of the European language from the father, given that the father-son bond, despite the unusual circumstances, would have made it unlikely that the father would communicate with his progeny only in pidgin. Jobson (1626: 39) indicates as much in describing the creoles as "in a manner naturalized . . . still reserving carefully the use of the Portingall tongue." Such a child would be likely to acquire pidgin, if at all, in later childhood when taking a place in the trade which was the business of the settlement. This would have entailed acquiring a pidgin which had already been developed by native Africans.

The tracing of West African coastal pidgins to the *creoles* has always been tempting because they were indeed cultural intermediaries. Cultural intermediaries were certainly linguistic intermediaries as well, but this hardly entails their having been the *creators* of the linguistic media through which European-African interaction was conducted. The *creoles* can be assumed to have had a marginal role if any in interactions between Europeans and castle slaves, which is our sole concern. (See McWhorter 1996c for further discussion of the *creole* issue.)

4.7 LINGUISTIC EVIDENCE FOR THE CORMANTIN SCENARIO

To briefly review the argument up to this point, I have outlined a sequence of *sociohistorical* inductions suggesting that AEC was ultimately born in Africa:

(1) Evidence suggests that Sranan existed in Suriname in the 1660s, before any disproportion between black and white had set in.

(2) This suggests that Sranan may have been imported by slaves from elsewhere, but blacks had yet to outnumber whites in any English colony established by then either.

(3) Cormantin would have the only context connected to the Caribbean where blacks and the English existed in a social relationship conducive to the development of a pidgin.

(4) Historical evidence shows that castle slaves were sent from Cormantin to Barbados, the intent being to use them in positions of authority over sale slaves.

I will now present *linguistic* evidence which points in the same direction.

4.7.1 THE LOWER GUINEA COAST TRANSFER BIAS

Comparative, historical, and synchronic analyses have consistently pointed to the languages spoken on the coasts of present-day Ghana through Nigeria as the models for much of the structure of the AECs (e.g., Alleyne 1980a; Boretzky 1983; Holm 1988; McWhorter 1992a). The best-represented languages in question are Akan (including its varieties Twi and Fante), Gbe (including Fon[gbe] and Ewe), Yoruba, and Igbo. While Bickerton's (1981, 1984a) objections to the unconstrainedness of earlier substratist work were well taken, much subsequent work has drawn rather unequivocal links between African and New World creole structures (e.g., Lefebvre 1992; McWhorter 1992a; Schwegler 1993a), which could be deemed accidental only from an extreme pretheoretical bias. Yet as currently expressed, the substratist perspective has always suffered a certain taint, from the uncomfortable fact that slaves speaking Kwa and Nigerian languages simply were not a significant or consistent majority among slaves brought to the English Caribbean.

As we have seen, deductions from Suriname show that AEC existed in that colony by the mid-1660s at the latest, and had possibly been imported from Barbados in 1651. This would place AEC as existing in Barbados as early as the 1640s. Thus we are concerned with the origins of slaves imported during roughly the first two-thirds of the 1600s.

Until 1660, slaves were brought to English Caribbean colonies by both the English and the Dutch. The traditional assumption that the Dutch were the dominant force (e.g., Price 1976: 13–4) has been questioned in recent work (Gragg 1995), but their contribution was clearly significant. Unfortunately, however, slaving records of both powers are extremely sparse during the first half of the century (Gragg 1995: 66), but certain broad indications can be gleaned from what records survive. Importantly, they are out of step with the Kwa-Nigerian cast of AEC in general.

The English Guinea Company concentrated its earliest efforts, from the 1620s to the 1640s, on the Kru-speaking Windward Coast, not the Lower Guinea Coast. In fact, however, independent traders dominated the English slave trade in the linguistically crucial 1640s and 1650s, and surviving records of their exploits involve a healthy amount of slave procurement on the Gambia River, at nearby Cape Verde, and at Sierra Leone (Gragg 1995).

Meanwhile, records are slightly better for the Dutch in this period. From 1636 to 1650, the Dutch procured about half of their slaves not from the Lower Guinea coast but from the Congo region (Postma 1990: 111). From 1658–1674, the balance tipped towards the Slave Coast somewhat (40.8 percent), but Congo slaves were still 25 percent of the imports, and most important, the origins of fully 43.2 percent of the slaves imported at this time are lost to history (112).

A great deal will always remain unknown about slave extractions in the early English Caribbean. However, what we know simply does not square with the Kwa-Nigerian mold of AEC as a whole. Speakers of Akan languages, Gbe languages, Yoruba, and Igbo were at best a consistent presence, but consistency does not entail prevalence. The slaving records show that West Atlantic, Mande, and especially Bantu languages were also "consistent" presences. Indeed, if it were Bantu languages which had been disproportionately influential on AEC and not Kwa and Nigerian ones, this would long ago have been attributed to their "consistent" presence, with no objection. Whereas the structure of AEC would lead us to expect Twis, Fons, and perhaps Yorubas and Igbos to have held sway in, for example, early Barbados, in fact, the shipping data concur rather neatly with Ligon's contemporary observation (1657: 46) that Barbadian slaves were a mixture of slaves drawn from "Ginny and Binny," "Angola," and the "Gambia River."

Why, then, can it be solidly demonstrated that, for example, the serial verb constructions in Saramaccan, and by extension all AECs, are an inheritance from Kwa languages (McWhorter 1992a, 1996b, 1997a)? Wolof, Mandinka, Kru, and Kikongo, languages well represented among slaves brought to the English Caribbean in the 1600s and early 1700s, do not serialize (LePage and DeCamp 1960: 74–5; Postma 1990: 111). What blocked them, especially Kikongo, from making an imprint? Of course, if serial verb constructions were the only evidence of this kind, we might appeal, as many authors have, to the possibility that something inherent to serial verb constructions, such as their unbounded morpheme structure, renders them especially borrowable. However, for one, there are features in Kikongo and related languages which have transferred readily into other creoles, such as discontinuous negators in Palenquero. More to the point, serials are but one of a range of features restricted to Kwa and Nigerian languages which appear in AECs.

1. Predicate fronting is a classic AEC feature, in which a predicate, with or without a "highlighting" morpheme, is topicalized to connote emphasis, with a copy remaining in its original slot.

Sranan:

(8) (na) **lon** mi wani **lon** gowe.
    it   run I   want run go

What I want to do is run away.

(Taylor 1977: 183)

This specific behavior (fronting and copy left behind) is also found in Akan, Gbe, Yoruba, and Igbo, but apparently not in Wolof, Mandinka, Kru, or Kikongo.

2. Bickerton (1981: 56) stipulates that in the typical creole article system, nonspecific nouns are zero-marked while specifics are marked either with an indefinite article (asserted) or definite article (presupposed). Janson (1984) has convincingly questioned the universality of this configuration, but confirms its validity for AEC (specifically, Jamaican and Cameroonian). It is also valid for the Suriname creoles. Crucially, it is also found in Akan and Gbe, as in the following examples in Akan (Twi).

Asserted specific:

(9) ɔ-huni   ɔberɛmba **bi**.
    he-see-PAST man   a

He saw a man.

(Balmer and Grant 1929: 19)

Presupposed specific:

(10) ɔ-de   sékáng **no** mãã   me.
     he-take knife the give-PAST me

He gave me the knife.

(Christaller 1875: 118)

Table 4.3.   AEC features in West African substrate languages (filled cells = present in the language)

	AEC	Akan, Gbe	Yoruba, Igbo	Wolof	Mandinka	Kru	Kikongo
Serial verbs	▓	▓	▓				
Predicate fronting	▓	▓	▓				
"Creole" articles	▓	▓					
de+good=be fine	▓	▓					

Sources for the various languages are as follows. Wolof: Fal, Arame, and Santos 1990; Mandinka: Creissels 1983; Kru: Marchese 1986; Akan: Christaller 1875; Gbe: Westermann 1930; Yoruba: Rowlands 1969; Igbo: Emenanjo 1978; Kikongo: Bentley 1887.

Nonspecific:

(11) ɔ-yɛ   ø pon.
he-make table

He makes a table.

(Balmer and Grant 1929: 19)

3.   Most AECs distinguish between a verbal and adverbial usage of the word "good" with a particular semantic implication: Saramaccan *mi búnu* "I am good" (a good person) versus *mi dé búnu* "I am doing fine." This construction is also appears in Akan and Gbe.

The striking anomaly of this Lower Guinea Coast influence is illustrated below. Wolof, Mandinka, Kru, and Kikongo have precisely none of the features noted above; see Table 4.3. Under the limited access hypothesis, we would expect either that the AECs would show influence from all of these languages, or perhaps that the competition between so many languages would have led none to have any identifiable impact. Yet this is not what we see. Creole genesis scholars assiduously attempt to correlate West African transfer in a given AEC to the slaves imported directly into each colony, but the result is always painstakingly thorough tables and tallies all perplexingly pointing in the opposite direction from what the linguistic data indicate (e.g., Arends 1995). This has left the substratist hypothesis an eternal puzzle, eternally cast as a questionably defended bias rather than as a theory (e.g., Mufwene 1990: 5–10).

In various publications, Mufwene (e.g., 1991a) has suggested that it was markedness which favored the retention of Kwa features over those from other languages. While intuitively plausible, this idea is insufficient when actually applied to the data. For example, the *de* + *good* construction gives no indication of universal unmarkedness; on the contrary, we can safely consider it an areal idiosyncrasy. To be sure, Mufwene conceives markedness as applying to the languages within the context rather than universally, such that even idiosyncratic constructions might prevail if widespread among the languages in contact. But note that even this does not work here: neither English, Wolof, Mandinka, Kru, nor Kikongo have this construction. Similarly, while predicate fronting itself is conceivable as a universal (Bickerton 1981), it is unclear that predicate fronting *with copy* is. (See McWhorter 1996b, 1997a for further discussion of the markedness issue on Suriname creoles specifically.)

Under the Cormantin scenario, however, this problem melts away: the Kwa-Nigerian bias is the result of LGPE having been originated by speakers of those languages. This is hardly to say that substrate influence within individual colonies was insignificant—for example, the specific influence of Gbe on Sranan and Saramaccan is quite clear (McWhorter 1996b). However, each AEC retains a core heritage of Lower Guinea Coast language influence. The restriction of the article configuration and the *de* + good construction to Akan and Gbe confirms what we would suspect—that the primary influence would have been the Akan spoken by the Cormantin castle slaves.

4.7.2 INGREDIENT X

Table 4.4 repeats Smith's list of pan-AEC West African borrowings. The "markedness" explanation is further weakened by the fact that almost all of these words are derivable from the Lower Guinea Coast. If AEC had been developed by slaves from the length of the West African coast, from Senegal down to Angola, then we would expect a much more even distribution. If on the other hand, it was developed by castle slaves at Cormantin, then this distribution is quite unremarkable. In combination with the bias in structural transfer, this list makes the case for LGPE even stronger.

Smith has since disavowed his reconstruction of a West African AEC ancestor (1997a), ironically via an expansion of Ingredient X rather than a deconstruction. He considers it crucial that what we will call "Ingredient X-plus" includes as strong a contribution from Bantu languages as from ones spoken further north, purportedly showing that the impression

Table 4.4. Smith's "Ingredient X"

njam	"eat" (Wolof, other West African coastal languages [Smith, p.c.])
kokobe	"leprosy" (Twi)
kongkosa	"gossip" (Twi)
pinda	"peanut" (Kikongo)
mumu	"dumb" (Twi, Ewe, Mende)
djumbi	"ghost" (Kikongo)
fufu	(food type) (Twi, Ewe, Yoruba)
anansi	(spider in folktale) (Twi, Ewe)
okra	"okra" (Igbo)
soso	"only" (Igbo, Yoruba)
akara	"pancake" (Ewe, Yoruba, Igbo)
potopoto	"mud" (Igbo, Twi; also Bantu [Morris Goodman, p.c.])
bakra	"white person" (Igbo, Efik)

Adapted from Smith 1987: 104–7.

given by the original Ingredient X, of a Lower Guinea coast bias, was an illusion (Table 4.5).[2]

However, we must explicitly differentiate data which suggests ordinary lexical diffusion from data which suggests common ancestry. Specifically, it is nothing less than expected that several West African borrowings will be scattered randomly among a moderate number of AECs. Given the extensive sociohistorical connections between Anglophone Caribbean societies, it would be odd if this were not the case, especially regarding easily transportable cultural concepts such as games, musical instruments, and so on. On the other hand, it would not be expected that if the AECs arose separately, a large number of West African borrowings from a particular region would appear in virtually *all* of them, or especially that among these items would be core lexical or grammatical items, less likely to be borrowed than peripheral lexicon.

In his original Ingredient X, Smith identified exactly such an unexpected spread. On the other hand, the new items in Ingredient X-plus give all indication of being the result of ordinary lexical diffusion: they appear much less consistently across AEC than the originals, none are grammatical items,

2. The change in Smith's position is based on criticisms of the Cormantin hypothesis in Huber (1997), all of which are shown in this chapter to be unwarranted by the evidence.

Table 4.5. Smith's "Ingredient X-Plus"

unu	"you" (pl.) (Igbo)
djagadjaga	"untidy" (Ewe)
boma	"boa" (Kikongo)
gobogobo	"peanut" (Kimbundu)
njamsi	"yam" (Mende)
akata	"headpad" (Kikongo)
fukofuko	"lungs" (Yoruba, Mende)
obia	"magic" (Efik)
dopi	"ghost" (Gã)
gombi	(drum type) (Kikongo)
wari	(game type) (Twi)
bombo	"vagina" (Kikongo)
bubu	"monster" (Kikongo)
fom	"strike" (Eastern Ijo)
sakasaka	"rattle" (Efik)
dokunu	"dumpling" (Twi, Yoruba)
aki	(tree type) (Kru)

Data from Smith 1997a.

and the one which could be considered core lexicon (*fom* "strike") has the very narrowest distribution, easily explainable as a mere diffusion from Suriname to Jamaica and Sierra Leone according to the pathway outlined in Section 3.4. Table 4.6 shows the original Ingredient X and its distribution (with *kokobe* added for Ndjuka, which indeed has these words despite this information not being available to Smith in 1987).[3] Shaded areas indicate that the item is present in the language. For contrast, Table 4.7 shows the distribution of the additions in Ingredient X-plus.

The contrast between Table 4.6 and Table 4.7 is obvious and significant: the original is a field of gray, while the addendum is a patchwork, in which less than half of the cells are even filled. The thin distribution of the new items would be even clearer if we counted the Suriname creoles, so genet-

3. In a slight alteration of Smith (1997a), I have included *unu* in Table 4.6 rather than in the additions shown in Table 4.7, as Smith does. The wide distribution of *unu* had been discussed by Hancock when Smith wrote his dissertation in the mid-1980s, and he would surely not have objected to its inclusion in his original list; moreover, as discussed in this and the previous chapter, *unu* is in fact crucial evidence for common ancestry and West African origin of the AECs.

Table 4.6. Ingredient X-Plus: Distribution (Abbreviations: SR: Sranan; ND: Ndjuka; SM: Saramaccan; KR: Krio; JAM: Jamaica; GUY: Guyanese; MC: Miskito Coast; GUL: Gullah; BAH: Bahamian; CAM: Cameroonian; T: Twi; E: Ewe; F: Fongbe; Y: Yoruba; I: Igbo; Ij: Ijo; M: Mende; K: Kikongo; Km: Kimbundu; Ef: Efik; W: Wolof. Filled cells = present in the language.)

	SR	ND	SM	KR	JAM	GUY	MC	GUL	BAH	CAM	
soso	■	■	■	■	■	■	■	■	■	■	I, Y
potopoto	■	■	■	■	■		■		■	■	I, T, K
pinda	■	■		■		■	■	■		■	K
okra	■	■		■	■	■	■	■	■	■	I, Ij
njam	■	■	■	■	■	■	■	■	■		W, other
mumu	■	■		■	■	■	■		■	■	T, E, M
kokobe	■	■	■	■	■	■		■		■	T
konkasa	■	■	■	■	■		■	■	■	■	T
djumbi	■		■	■	■	■	■		■	■	Km
bakra	■	■	■		■	■	■	■	■	■	Ef, I
fufu	■	■	■	■	■	■	■	■	■	■	E, Y, T
anansi	■	■	■	■	■	■	■	■		■	E, T
akara	■		■	■	■		■	■	■	■	
unu	■	■	■	■	■		■	■	■	■	I, Y, F

ically and geographically close, as one; meanwhile, many of the empty cells in Table 4.6 are due to Gullah, which is both rather mesolectal and not as well documented as many of the other AECs. In being highly unpredictable and dominated by rather specific, peripheral concepts, the distribution in Table 4.7 is typical of lexical diffusions over centuries. It is the relative uniformity of the distribution of the original Ingredient X and the nature of its components which suggest more.

As we see, then, even "Ingredient X-plus" leaves our question intact: if AEC was developed by slaves from up and down the West African coast,

Table 4.7. Ingredient X-Plus: Distribution (filled cells = present in the language.)

	SR	ND	SM	KR	JAM	GUY	MC	GUL	BAH	CAM	
boma	■	■	■	■				■		■	K
gobogobo	■		■	■							Km
njamsi	■	■	■	■						■	M
akata	■	■	■	■	■	■	■		■		K
fukofuko	■	■	■	■				■			Y, M
djagadjaga	■		■								E
obia	■	■	■	■	■	■		■			Ef
dopi	■		■		■		■	■			Gã
gombi	■		■				■		■		K
wari	■		■					■			T
bombo	■	■	■				■				K
bubu	■		■		■						K
fom	■		■								Ij
sakasaka	■	■	■								Ef
dokunu	■	■	■	■	■					■	T, Y
aki	■							■		■	Kr

then why are the West African borrowings shared by most of them disproportionately from Lower Guinea coast languages? As we saw in Section 4.7.1, the evidence does not support the idea that speakers from this region were predominant during the founding stages of the English Caribbean. The original Ingredient X is by no means an argument for Cormantin in itself; however, amidst various other arguments, it is a compelling additional one. Henceforth, I will continue to refer to Ingredient X, which will be meant as indicating Smith's original thirteen items and not the 1997 addenda.

4.7.3 THE IGBO BIAS

Another thing notable about Ingredient X is the particular impact from Igbo. As it happens, in the most conservative AECs, this specific Igbo influence penetrates even to the grammatical level. We have already encountered the general AEC second-person plural pronoun *unu*. In fact, however, *half* of the conservative AEC subject pronouns are Igbo borrowings: The second-person and third-person subject pronouns in the Suriname creoles and Maroon Spirit Language are *i* and *a*, paralleling the Igbo second-person and indefinite third-person pronouns (the Igbo third-person pronoun is the phonetically close *ɔ*). Also, as we have seen, the locative copula *de* in the AECs is a striking typological anomaly in terms of etymological source. Although I prefer a grammaticalization account, the single possible source for a direct borrowing (matching both phonetically and semantically) is none other than the Igbo locative copula *dì*, which is even expressed as *de* in some dialects.

To be fair, the Cornwall English second- and third-person pronouns were *ee* and *aw* (Hancock 1994), and thus could be seen as equally plausible sources for the pronouns. Two things suggest that Igbo was the main force here, however. First, *i* and *a* must be seen alongside *unu*, which has no superstrate source and is only derivable from strong Igbo influence. Second, if *i* and *a* were widely used by whites across the Caribbean—i.e., if they were the true superstrate forms—then we would expect to see them in AECs across the Caribbean, and in at least mesolectal levels as well as basilectal. On the contrary, we see these two pronouns together only in the AECs most *removed* from superstrate influence, the Suriname creoles and Maroon Spirit Language (with *a* appearing in documents of conservative Jamaican [Veenstra 1994: 109–10]). In *receding* as speakers moved towards English, these pronouns thus appear to have been tokens of substrate influence, not superstrate.

This strong Igbo influence in AEC would lead us to suppose that Igbos were a dominant element in the early English Caribbean. Yet as many creolists and historians will readily note, this was by no means the case. Since they were forbidden to draw slaves from the Gold Coast area where their trade settlements were, the English indeed drew a significant number of slaves from the Igbo-speaking region (Ryder 1965: 207; Porter 1989: 323). However, this must be seen in light of two facts. First, as noted in Section 4.7.1, the English were drawing slaves from many other areas as well, especially the Slave Coast (Porter 1989: 323); moreover, while the castle officials were officially forbidden to draw slaves from the Gold Coast, independent English slavers appear to have done so quite regularly (Porter 1989: 244–5). Second, as also noted above, the Dutch were supplying many if not most of the slaves to the English, and their main slaving areas were the Slave Coast and Congo area; their minor slaving in the Igbo-speaking region was quite overshadowed by the English (Ryder 1965: 207).

Furthermore, accounts from the Caribbean colonies themselves never indicate that the Igbos were anything but a subsidiary element in the general mixture of slaves, dominated by explicit mentions by tradesmen and planters of "Coromantees" (Akan speakers) and "Angolans." Igbo slaves were even out of favor with seventeenth-century buyers—the historical record abounds with complaints that the Igbo were emotionally unsuited to plantation labor, uniquely prone to suicide after arrival (LePage and De-Camp 1960: 79; Handler and Lange 1978: 26; Postma 1990: 107–8). Significantly, this disposition would have made the Igbos even less likely to be sociologically dominant on plantations. Thus it is not surprising that while various groups made strong cultural imprints upon colonies—the Twi in Jamaica (Alleyne 1993), the Fon in Haiti, the Yoruba in Cuba (Cabrera 1954) and Brazil (Holm 1987)—nowhere are the Igbo documented to have made such an impact, especially not in St. Kitts, Barbados, or Suriname.

Under the Cormantin scenario, however, we can account for the Igbo bias within what the historical documentation tells us. It is clear that Igbos were one of many presences on English Caribbean plantations in the 1600s, but it is extremely difficult to conceive of how they could have exerted influence dominant enough to contribute pronouns there. We seek, therefore, a context in which the Igbo would have plausibly been not just *present*, but a *dominant* influence.

One such context would have existed if the Igbo served as castle slaves in English slave forts. There are a number of reasons that this would have been plausible. First, there was a general preference on the part of the English to draw castle slaves from distant areas, in order to discourage identification with local slaves and, thus, discourage escapes (Davies 1957: 243; Lawrence 1969: 48). To be sure, in the early 1660s, Cormantin castle slaves were drawn from the surrounding Akan-speaking area. However, conditions at West African trade settlements were in constant flux, and this included sources of castle slave procurement. For example, in 1730 the French were staffing their Slave Coast castle with Bambaras from Senegal (Labat 1730: 42), but by the 1760s they were staffing it with local Gbe speakers allied with the local king (Archives Nationales C/6/27). Thus the Cormantin situation visible in the early 1660s is plausibly seen as a snapshot of what was in fact an ever-changing crew which, in the 1640s or 1650s, may well have included Africans drawn from elsewhere. Along these lines, in 1662 the Cormantin factors were requesting permission to obtain new castle slaves from the Slave Coast (E/3/27: 41). Similarly, at the later-founded Cape Coast castle eastward on the Gold Coast, the castle slaves are documented to have been a mixture of locally drawn and Slave Coast Africans (T/70/366 ff.). Interestingly, the Dutch often specifically used the Igbo as castle slaves in their own forts (Postma 1990: 60, 72, 112). Given that the Igbo-speaking region was a major source of slaves for the English, it is quite possible that they themselves brought some castle slaves from there as well. They may have seen placing Igbos as castle slaves as a better investment, enhancing their likelihood of survival.

Indeed, if Igbos dominated the castle slave force for even a rather brief period, then if they happened to be the castle slaves sent later to the Caribbean, then this alone would have set their influence on the development of AEC. As Smith (1997b) notes in relation to another issue, chaos theory has shown us that the flapping of a butterfly's wing can be the ultimate cause of a hurricane on the other side of the world.

4.7.4 THE PORTUGUESE ELEMENT

Goodman (1987) has made a compelling argument that the varying elements of Portuguese that Caribbean creoles of various lexical bases share resulted from the migrations of Portuguese-speaking Jewish (as well as Dutch) slaveholders from Brazil in the late 1600s. However, there is a well-known, small core of Portuguese-derived words which, unlike the above-mentioned items, are distributed across the AECs, such as *pikin* "small," *sabi* "know," *palaba* "set-to," and *na* (locative preposition). (If one prefers to ascribe the latter to Igbo's preposition *na*, then this simply becomes more evidence for the Igbo argument in the previous section). This particular core is most plausibly accounted for as a remnant of the Portuguese-based pidgin which held sway on the West African coast until supplanted by English-based pidgin by the 1800s (Goodman 1987: 396–7 *passim*).

Supporting this hypothesis is that the first two items in the above list, as well as various other Portuguese etyma, also appear in the Melanesian Pidgin English dialects (Holm 1992), which are certain to have arisen from an English-based pidgin. Indeed, the Pacific pidgins formed over a century later. However, the fact that they contain some of the same Portuguese items—or for that matter any Portuguese at all—shows that an English pidgin with such Portuguese input was definitely used in English maritime contexts, since the Portuguese played no part in colonizing Melanesia.

Further support comes from simple facts about Caribbean plantations. It is natural to conceive of Portuguese pidgin, slave ships, and AECs in a general picture of the slave trade. This has led to the characterization of the Portuguese items as "influence" within polygenetic genesis scenarios, in which the principal business was the acquisition of English via direct, albeit limited, contact with local whites. Yet when we look more closely at this situation, it becomes difficult to accept.

We might suppose that the white settlers of the early English Caribbean introduced the Portuguese items into an emerging creole. But the men who settled these colonies were mostly farmers, not sailors—their previous occupations were much too multifarious (Watts 1987: 150) to lead to an even distribution of Portuguese pidgin terms across St. Kitts, or Barbados, or any colony for that matter. It is equally unlikely that they picked up these words from sailors during the voyage across the sea. Conditions for white émigrés to the Caribbean were little better than that for Africans (Watts 1987: 150), rendering unlikely the type of social relations encouraging lexical borrowing. Besides, even if a settler for some reason did pick up a few such words on shipboard, why would they continue to use them once settled on *terra firma*? The notion of hardscrabble white settlers in Barbados casually using foreign words like *sabi* and *pikin* is, frankly, rather comical.

To be sure, there is documentation of Portuguese-owned slaves brought to Barbados. A trickle of the Portuguese Jewish refugees documented by Goodman (1987) did reach Barbados in 1645. More important, at this same time the Dutch, after taking over Brazil from Portugal, sold their expertise in sugar cultivation to other powers, including the English in Barbados. This partly entailed exporting some slaves with expertise in sugar production to Barbadian plantations (Watts 1987: 188), presumably the source of Ligon's (1657: 52) passing mention of some slaves on one plantation who had been "bred up amongst the Portugals." Ligon's wording reinforces the common-sense assumption that such slaves spoke a form of Portuguese, even though technically owned by the Dutch at this point.

The question is, how likely were these slaves to have contributed the *sabi/pikin* core? If Bajan obtained its Portuguese words *in situ*, then probability dictates that the result would not have been the same particular core we see everywhere else, certainly not as far away as Melanesia—obviously nothing anoints words such as *sabi* and *pikin* as inevitable borrowings. Note, for example, the variety of results where Portuguese influenced various other creoles. The Portuguese-speaking Jewish émigrés left French Guyanais with *fika* "to be, stay"; *suku* (<*escuro*) "dark"; *kaba* (<*acabar* "finish") "already"; and others (Goodman 1987: 390–1; Taylor 1977: 166–8).

In the meantime, the Dutch imported slaves trained in sugar cultivation to the French Caribbean as well, leaving Lesser Antillean with *mélasse* "molasses," *bagasse* "husk," *kōbos* "sexual rival," and progressive marker *ka* (Goodman 1987: 391). These collections show that lexical contribution from a given source will be different at each spin of the wheel. Thus the presence of the *sabi/pikin* core in Melanesia suggests that it was brought to Barbados from elsewhere, just as it was to Melanesia.

It will be assumed that the proposition often found in the literature that slaves under all powers regularly came to the New World with a competence in Portuguese pidgin has been invalidated. Indeed, slaves brought by the Portuguese themselves sometimes brought Portuguese pidgin with them (e.g., Schwegler 1993b, 1996a). However, Goodman (1987) has convincingly explained the Portuguese words in English, French, or Dutch creoles as remnants of the Portuguese Jewish migrations mentioned above. There would have been no reason for many, or any, sale slaves other than ones from Portuguese posts to speak the Portuguese pidgin in any case. This was a language of trade with Europeans, a context foreign to all Africans except those involved with the trade settlements; most slaves were taken from areas far inland from such settlements, where lingua francas would have naturally been African, as Goodman points out (384).

We know of precisely one context where a pidginized register of English interlaced with this Portuguese core was likely to have been spoken in the 1600s, in a setting in which acquisition by Africans would have been unimpeded and efficacious. That is the West Coast of Africa where, at the very time that St. Kitts and Barbados were being supplied with their first shipments of slaves, Portuguese pidgin was used as a lingua franca with African traders and chieftains. It would have been unremarkable for English traders to introduce a few words from the Portuguese pidgin into the emerging English-based castle slave pidgin, treating them as "words to be used with natives" just as Englishmen in Melanesia would two centuries later. At the same time, at least some of the castle slaves engaged in loading and unloading ships would have gotten substantial exposure to this pidgin.

Meanwhile, however, exactly who was speaking Portuguese maritime pidgin on St. Kittitian or Barbadian plantations?

4.7.5 IMPLICATIONS

Thus we see an imposing number of indications all pointing in the direction of AEC emerging on the Ghanaian coast:

(1) Sranan's existence by the 1660s.

(2) No large plantations in the English Caribbean until later.

(3) Cormantin as a likely context for a pidgin to emerge.

(4) Castle slaves were sent to the Caribbean from Cormantin.

(5) AECs all reflect Lower Guinea languages like Akan rather than the many others present.

(6) AECs share a collection of West African borrowings in which the Lower Guinea coast is overrepresented.

(7) Igbos, Lower Guinea coast people, left a mysterious imprint on AEC.

(8) The Portuguese lexical core in AEC is traceable to the Portuguese pidgin used on the West African coast.

Alone, none of these things make a case for LGPE. *Taken together*, however, this evidence constitutes a message.

4.8 PRESERVING THE PARADIGM

In tracing the AECs to West Africa, I am merely the latest in a succession of creolists who have come to similar conclusions (Stewart 1971; Alleyne 1971: 179–80; Hancock 1969, 1986, 1987; Smith 1987; Carter 1987). However, statements and work in this vein have been marginalized amidst a concentration upon plantation-based, polygenetic theories. I have attempted to make the case as carefully as possible, but the limited access conception is so firmly entrenched that, if the history of creole studies thus far is any indication, the inclination will be to perhaps accept an AEC parent pidgin from West Africa as "a possible element" in the plantation mix. In practice, this will leave creole studies to business as usual.

Indeed, at this writing, a person tracing the AECs to a West African parent pidgin is received like a creation scientist at a cocktail party. Social propriety dictates polite acknowledgment, but privately almost no one considers the idea worth serious consideration, and the few who do keep it largely to themselves. This mindset is partly due to certain epistemological barriers which I will now address.

4.8.1 BARRIERS: THE OLD MONOGENESIS HYPOTHESIS

One obstacle to serious engagement with Afrogenetic work has been a tendency to associate it with the more general proposal of the 1960s that all creoles were traceable to an original Portuguese pidgin (Taylor 1956; Thompson 1961; Whinnom 1965). Although dutifully cited in textbooks, this "old monogenesis hypothesis" is no longer subscribed to by any working creolist, with Goodman (1987) having perhaps dealt the official *coup de grâce*. It has been discarded because the cross-creole similarities it was based on, such as serial verbs and multiple copulas, have since been suitably explained as the result of universals, substrate influence, and other factors.

However, this appears to have left a perception that any West African pidgin-based genesis scenario is a backwards endeavor, cross-creole similarities having been long since explained via more demonstrable, sophisticated mechanisms. The analogy with our feelings about creation science is obvious: one feels that attributing nature's variety to an unknowable creator was once understandable, but has been rendered unnecessary by scientific advances.

Properly speaking, however, the old monogenesis hypothesis died not because it was shown that genetic links between creoles were an absurdity, but because the notion of genetic links between *all* of the world's creoles did not hold up. Thus to sniff "that's just taking us back to monogenesis" to any theory involving genetic links between AECs is throwing the baby out with the bathwater. Imagine an urban planner speaking out against paved roads because "the Ancient Romans did it, and look what happened to them!"

In this light, the problems with the old monogenesis hypothesis must not be extended to the Cormantin scenario. The Cormantin scenario refers not to a Portuguese pidgin source, but an English-based one; it is based upon features *not* traceable to universals or source languages; and it is founded upon numerous sociohistorical and linguistic observations which point to a specific location where such a pidgin would have emerged.

4.8.2 BARRIERS: "THE DATA ARE NOT YET ALL IN"

Another opinion deflecting attention from Afrogenetic work is the claim that the issue could be suitably addressed only after further research on the sociolinguistic situation in the early Caribbean. While reasonable *per se,* there are times when claims of this sort are ultimately more obstructionist than constructive, reminiscent of the ban on Rearden Metal until "further tests" in Ayn Rand's *Atlas Shrugged.* This is because when it comes to the English Caribbean of the early to middle seventeenth century, short of a truly shocking archival find, our sociolinguistic picture is about as detailed as it is going to get.

Claims that "more research" is needed imply that masses of original documents await examination, and that current theories are hasty constructs built upon mere preliminary research. One suspects, however, that those making this claim have not spent long hours, days, and weeks poring through colonial archives in the capitals of Europe, finding with numbing regularity that as one goes backwards in time, a flood of records from the 1700s slows to a stream in the 1680s and dwindles to a trickle by the 1650s, with data on the early 1600s virtually nonexistent. The fine-grained analysis in works such as Baker and Corne (1982) on Mauritius and Réunion is possible because the crucial developments were in the eighteenth century. This would be impossible to reproduce for early Barbados or Suriname. The fact that the records in Curtin (1969), Price (1976), Postma (1990), Arends (1995), and others give little if any data until the late 1600s is not due to a mysterious lapse in the authors' research, but to simple absence of documentation.

Thus it would be unreasonable to require that in order to be a valid or useful hypothesis, the Cormantin scenario be founded upon a sociolinguistic portrait of early Barbados or Suriname as fine-grained as, say, Gal's (1978) study of language shift in Oberwart, Austria. This requirement would be as unreasonable as expecting a scholar to reconstruct a nuanced history of NATO with two decaying newsreels and four telegrams. I have attempted to show that the data—small farms in the early English Caribbean, the Kwa-Nigerian borrowing bias, policy on shipping castle slaves from Cormantin to help found colonies, and so on—allow us to draw conclusions *despite* these lacunae in the documentation.

Creolists find this inductive approach unproblematic when implications are less difficult for traditional theory. For example, there have been no urgent calls for more research on American plantations before the acceptance of the view that smaller plantations prevented the spread of Gullah inland and led instead to Black English (thus supporting the limited access model). This is despite the fact that we have yet to see a sustained engagement of Gullah documentation on the order of Lalla and D'Costa (1990) for Jamaican, or Rickford (1987) for Guyanese.

Since substantial "further research" on the sociology of the early English Caribbean would be impossible, to require this before even considering the other evidence would be simply assassinating the entire Afrogenetic investigation. Given the severe gaps in the explanatory power of the limited access conception which I have shown, this would be unduly hasty at this point in time.

4.8.3 BARRIERS: STRENGTH IN NUMBERS

One eminently reasonable objection to the Cormantin scenario, however, is that it would seem unlikely that a single shipment of castle slaves to St. Kitts or Barbados would provide linguistic models for an entire colony. It must first be recalled, however, that I am stipulating that these castle slaves would have been a seed population, arriving early in the colony's history, when sale slaves were few (indentured whites being preferred at first) and spread thin (cf. Gragg 1995: 70 on Barbados). At this point, a stabilized Afro-American speech repertoire would have yet to be established. Certainly, if the castle slaves had arrived later, after large slave influxes, we would not expect them to have had any effect upon black speech, since by then patterns would have been long set.

However, introduced early, a squadron of castle slaves, especially in positions of relative authority as advised from London (E/3/86: 86), would establish themselves as linguistic models for subsequent sale slave arrivals (see Alleyne 1971: 179–80 and Hancock 1980: 32 for related arguments). It is well documented that established slaves were generally entrusted with transmitting the local creole to new slaves on Caribbean plantations (Patterson 1967; Cauna 1987: 107; Hornby 1980: 166). Again, the castle slaves are likely to have also begun acquiring L2 registers of English in contact with the whites, but their pidgin register would have taken its place alongside the L2 register as an expression of African identity—just as Pidgin Fijian coexists with Fijian and Sierra Leone Krio with English. Indeed, however, this is mere speculation. Only with empirical demonstration can such a scenario be compelling. As it happens, we indeed have such demonstrations.

First of all, from a broad perspective, we have clear proof that a coastal African trade settlement pidgin could be transported to the New World and be established as a lingua franca among slaves there. This proof comes from Palenquero and Papiamentu, both of which were shown in Section 2.3 to have arisen as Portuguese pidgins that had developed on the West African coast. A substantial group of slaves in early Cartagena explicitly linked their language to a Portuguese called "the language of São Tomé," and this lineage is visible in Palenquero traits such as the third-person plural pronoun *ané* (<São Tomense *iné*), and a double negation pattern similarly local to the Gulf of Guinea. Importation from Africa is quite simply the only possible source. To resist this would be analogous, as Schwegler once mem-

orably put it in a conference talk, to finding a car on the moon and refusing to allow that it had been brought there from the Earth.

Similarly, recall the Curccaçaoan secret language Guene, which speakers consider ancestral to Papiamentu. Guene, too, has this idiosyncratic Bantu borrowing *iné* as the third-person plural pronoun. The fact that Bissauan creole speakers still sometimes call their language "Guiné" makes the path of influence even clearer. With both Palenquero and Papiamentu, as obscure as the mechanisms of transfer are to us, the linguistic evidence is incontrovertible that slaves could and did transport a trade settlement pidgin to plantation colonies, and disseminate it to slaves there.

In the Portuguese case, we even have evidence of how slaves would have been exposed to Portuguese before shipment to the New World. Slaves sent by the Portuguese from the Congo region were regularly submitted to the process of *ladinização*, which included not only baptism but explicit instruction in Portuguese (Garfield 1992: 61). This was also the practice at the Cape Verde slave depot further north (Meintel 1984: 37), which could explain the Cape Verdean element in Guene. (The author thanks Mikael Parkvall for the references.) In the Congo region at least, it is also documented that slaves were often assigned work for lengthy periods before the embarkation of a ship across the Atlantic (Carroll 1991: 47), which would have provided them with more possible exposure to a Portuguese-based contact language.

Admittedly, however, in these cases we cannot be certain that the transmission was effected by *small* numbers of slaves (although it is likely). However, there are other cases which specifically prove that small groups can have profound linguistic influence disproportionate to their number. Melanesian Pidgin English was transmitted to plantation laborers by foremen who were vastly outnumbered by the workers (Keesing 1988: 35–9). Uniquely illustrative is Hiri Motu. At the turn of the 1900s in Papua New Guinea, the British stationed a squadron of just over 400 Hiri Motu–speaking Papuan constables in inland villages, with at most just two constables per village (Dutton 1985: 72). Yet because of the prestige of these mere 400 constables, 150,000 people spoke Hiri Motu in 1971 and more do now (3).

The power of a few linguistic models is perhaps difficult to intuit for Western linguists: we are almost never immersed indefinitely in a foreign language with no intimates who speak our mother tongue, and our acquisition of a new language is usually filtered through the distancing effect of classrooms and the printed page. However, in a plantation situation, language learning was a pressing necessity, and was accomplished via round-the-clock exposure to vivid oral input. In such situations, it is quite plausible that a single model could have powerful impact upon several slaves' speech. Thus with Palenquero, Papiamentu, Melanesian Pidgin English, and Hiri Motu in mind, we are in a position to realize what a profound influence even a single gang of Cormantin castle slaves could have had early in a colony's history.

4.8.4 BARRIERS: "FOR WHICH NOT A SINGLE CITATION HAS BEEN PRESENTED"

Armin Schwegler's "car on the moon" analogy was in response to being told, after presenting an indisputable Afrogenetic argument, that his case was incomplete without citations from West Africa of the proto-pidgin in question. Plausibly this argument will meet with a similar response from some readers. However, it is hardly inevitable that every language or language variety be transcribed at all. The charge "Where are the citations?" is valid only to the extent that it is reasonable to expect there to have been any. Thus our first question must be, "How likely was castle slaves' pidgin English to be transcribed, and by whom?"

At European trade settlements, disease claimed white lives so regularly that assignment to a castle was virtually a death sentence, with letters from the castles regularly including long lists of the recent dead. As a result, the Englishmen posted to such settlements were mostly of lowly origin (like the indentured servants sent to the New World), the personnel was in constant flux, and those who survived stayed only as long as required. All of these things meant that there were few long-term veterans of the type to be moved to pen nostalgic memoirs of their stay and the Africans they met, either at the settlement or after their return to England. The goal of an Englishman at Cormantin was to earn a good bit of cash and go home—ethnographic and sociolinguistic observation were extremely low priorities.

In these settings, writing was a marginal activity, strictly functional in nature. Amidst the reams of inventories, bills of sale, and business letters to and from London, when we find any reference to the castle slaves at all, it is in reference to their number or their payment. Certainly there was no motivation for anyone to transcribe passages of their speech! A useful example of how a low-status contact language can thrive and yet escape written recording comes from Namibia. In thirty years of records of mines in the Windhoek Archives, covering 1920 to 1950, there is not a single mention of the pidgin Zulu Fanakalo, despite its having been the thriving lingua franca between blacks as well as between blacks and whites (Ferraz 1984: 110).

The written citations which Hancock (1986) presents of what he calls Guinea Coast Creole English were gathered by *travelers* to the West African coast. These travelers generally sailed a broad swath of the West African coast, with visits to trade settlements interspersed with trips to African royal courts and observations of barterings with tribes unaffiliated with castles. Unlike English castle employees, the travelers were naturally inclined to write of their experiences and to (very occasionally) transcribe exotic language fragments. However, they were no more likely a source for information on castle slave speech than the castle personnel. When such travelers visited trade settlements, what they were invariably moved to describe was trade practices and the customs of the indigenous free Africans, having unsurprisingly little interest in, or interaction with, the Africans quietly working for the castle.

Thus LGPE was spoken by socially despised preliterates working under transitory semiliterates, a nonstandard, reduced variety spoken by the lowest caste in a grim, semitropical outpost, where nothing was written down besides accounts and business letters. For the few travelers who passed through—when they published memoirs at all—the castle slaves were a marginal presence, paling in interest beside the local indigenes and burgeoning trade networks of interest to their readers in England. Clearly, then, "Where are the citations?" while surely the easiest criticism to level at Afrogenesis, is also the weakest.

An analogy: paleoanthropologists have yet to unearth a fossil of a creature intermediate between apes and man. Even finds such as "Lucy" and the even older *Ramadus* are well advanced along the human branch; the true "missing link" has yet to be found. The fact is that it may never be, because of simple facts about preservation: apes and monkeys live in dense forest, where chances for fossilization have always been slim because corpses are quickly consumed by scavengers. Early hominids lived out on dry plains where fossilization was more likely.

Yet we do not claim that the absence of a missing link fossil invalidates the paleoanthropological enterprise. Comparative data make it clear that such a missing link must have existed, and that in this case, negative evidence is not counterevidence. The only people who treat the absence of a missing link fossil as counterevidence to the descent of man from the apes are, well . . . creationists.

The citation issue with LGPE must be seen in this light. The crucial goal of this chapter has been to show that a preponderance of *other* kinds of evidence can be interpreted as a strong case for a single pidgin parent of AEC born on the Ghanaian coast.

4.9 HANCOCK'S DOMESTIC HYPOTHESIS

Finally, this argument owes an inestimable debt to previous proponents of a West African pidgin ancestor for the AECs. However, it is imperative that the argument be evaluated in full awareness of how it differs from previous ones, especially, given its prominence, that of Hancock (1969, 1986, 1987). I am in full agreement with Hancock's basic proposition that the AECs emerged as a single contact language between Europeans and Africans on the West Coast of Africa. However, I propose a revision of the specific mechanisms via which the pidgin arose.

Hancock traces the AECs to an ancestor of Sierra Leone Krio. However, since the first AECs existed by the end of the 1600s, this contradicts the traditional hypothesis that Krio was born around 1800 when Jamaican Maroons were transported to Freetown. Hancock surmounts this problem by tracing Krio further back to a hypothetical Senegambian pidgin emerging in the early 1600s, supporting this with citational and sociohistorical evidence. However, this account, in itself masterful and (obviously) inspirational, raises certain questions.

4.9.1 SENEGAMBIA VERSUS GHANA

The first problem is that the English shipped only a quarter of their slaves at most from the Senegambia region in the seventeenth century (LePage and DeCamp 1960: 74–5), and had no permanent trade settlement in this area until 1664 (59). Thus a pidgin would have to have stabilized amidst mere transitory interactions, or amidst European-African marriages in communities settled by English traders individually. As I have noted above, the problem with these sources is that neither African traders nor *creoles* were shipped overseas.

More to the point, during the foundations of St. Kitts, Barbados, and Suriname, the English were shipping most of their slaves from regions much farther down the coast, and their most sustained contact with Africans would have been at Cormantin on the Ghanaian coast.

In response to this problem, Smith (1987: 10) has Hancock's Guinea Coast Creole English spread down to the Lower Guinea coast, therefore in place to be transported from this region by the mid-1600s. However, it is difficult to conceive of a mechanism via which a pidgin could have been transported in this fashion. There were no permanent settlements in Senegambia from which castle slaves could have been transferred to the lower coast. The Kru canoemen serving the English along the West African coast seem at first a possible solution, but they did not come into such service until well into the 1700s (Singler 1988: 40). My account eliminates these problems by placing the emergence of the pidgin directly on the Ghanaian coast.

4.9.2 LINGUISTIC EVIDENCE

For Hancock's hypothesis to be correct, we would expect evidence of an AEC-like language on the West African coast in the 1600s or 1700s. Yet Hancock's samples of Guinea Coast Creole English do not, in the final analysis, resemble modern AEC to an extent which makes its status as an ancestor obvious. A typical example from c. 1787 (Hancock 1986: 76) follows:

> Well, my friend, you got trade to day, you got plenty of slaves? No, we no got trade yet. By and by, trade come . . . What, you go for catch people, you go for make war?

This passage is indeed pidginized English, but the question is, is it an ancestor to AEC? There would not seem to be any features in this passage idiosyncratic to AEC; for example, the use of *for* as a complementizer is not only found in British dialects spoken at the time (*Maister zend me down vor tell ee* [Hancock 1994: 104]), but also appears in other English-based pidgins such as Torres Strait Broken (Shnukal 1988: 184, cited by Holm 1992). Furthermore, the usage of *by and by* is reminiscent more of Pacific pidgin English than Atlantic, suggesting that this register was a general English nautical register, which accounts for the core of idiosyncratic lexical similarities found between these two groups today (see Holm 1992).

Data from Nigeria around the same time give the same impression. Efik chief Antera Duke's famous diary (written from 1785 to 1788) is written in a pidgin English, but one which resembles AEC only in aspects easily due to universals (Spencer 1971: 13):

> At 5 am in Aqua Bakassey Crik and with fine morning and I git for Aqua Bakassey Cril in 1 clock time so I find Arshbong Duke and I go longsider his canow so I tak bottle beer to drink with him . . .

Note the absence even of *for* as a complementizer, and the rich inventory of prepositions. If Guinea Coast Creole English was the ancestor to the AECs, then we would expect this sample to resemble AEC much more closely: AECs elsewhere are well documented to have taken their modern form long before the late 1700s, while modern Nigerian Pidgin English in turn resembles them closely.

The language in the Antera Duke diary, as well as the other citations of eighteenth-century Guinea Coast Creole English in Hancock (1986), seems most likely to have been a pidginized register of English unrelated to the LGPE which I propose had been transplanted from Ghana to the New World, and only later returned to Africa with the Jamaican émigrés to Sierra Leone in 1800.

Lexical evidence reinforces this impression. In Smith's Ingredient X, we have seen that the West African borrowings which AECs share are almost all from languages spoken on the Lower, not Upper, Guinea Coast and below. Hancock himself notes of Krio specifically that "the African languages which were probably best represented in the situation during [the emergence of Guinea Coast Creole English], viz. Wolof, Sherbro-Bullom, and Kru, have made little lexical impact upon modern Krio" (1986: 94). This minimal lexical contribution from these languages is exactly the opposite of what we would expect if the parent pidgin emerged in Senegambia.

The presence of a single item, our trusty *unu*, across the Caribbean as well as in Krio, Nigerian Pidgin English, and Cameroonian Pidgin English, is alone astonishing if we trace the pidgin to Senegambia. If Krio already existed in the 1600s, we are left with a puzzle as to how an Igbo grammatical item made its way up from Nigeria to Sierra Leone. To propose that the Jamaican immigrants encountered Krio already in place, but ousted its second-person plural pronoun in favor of *unu*, is highly arbitrary given the tendency against the borrowing of grammatical items. Meanwhile, to attribute it to the Nigerians brought to Sierra Leone as recaptured slaves in the 1800s would be equally arbitrary, since the Yoruba were vastly dominant in this group, not the Igbo (Fyfe 1962: 170). Furthermore, the slaves did not arrive speaking pidgin English (129), disallowing that they brought *unu* as part of some pidgin or creole. To place the origin of the parent pidgin on the Lower Guinea Coast, where Igbos were a plausible presence, allows *unu* to diffuse from there to the Caribbean, and subsequently to West Africa within a language which did not exist in Sierra Leone until the Jamaican émigrés brought it there.

4.9.3 THE ROLE OF THE JAMAICAN MAROONS

Finally, Hancock takes issue with the general assumption that Krio was brought to Sierra Leone by the Jamaican Maroons in 1800, arguing that the maroons were too small a presence in Sierra Leone to have created the language since "over half of the ca. 550 Maroons who arrived in 1800 died or left the colony by 1810" (1986: 97).

However, Sierra Leone history suggests otherwise. With the statement above, Hancock implies that the Maroons were a recessive element in a population dominated numerically and culturally by other groups. However, despite these deaths and departures, the fact is that by 1811, no fewer than 807 out of 1,917 persons in Freetown were Maroons (Fyfe 1962: 114), and they went on to become a key, thriving element in Sierra Leone society—politically involved, owning property, serving as soldiers, generals, and doctors. Thus the Maroons were a linguistically pivotal element in the context.

The role of the Maroons becomes even clearer when we look at Sierra Leone in the 1800s as a whole. In 1800, the colony was inhabited by four main groups: the Maroons, American slaves having emigrated via Nova Scotia ("settlers"), other free Africans, and Europeans. Starting in 1807, to this mix was added slaves the British recaptured from other powers, in enforcement of their having outlawed the importation of slaves into British colonies. These slaves were brought to Sierra Leone in massive numbers, such as 1,911 in 1811 alone (Fyfe 1962: 114); by 1848, there were no fewer than 11,000 (Jones 1983: 19). Thus charting the history of Krio crucially entails identifying what form of language these recaptured slaves learned, and in what fashion.

To portray the Maroons as linguistically unimportant in the development of Krio, we must propose that the English spoken by the free Africans living in Sierra Leone before the settlers and Maroons arrived was adopted by the colony as a whole, rather than that of the Maroons or settlers. Presumably, the first generation of Maroons and settlers would have retained their modes of speech, but their progeny would have acquired competence in the presumed older pidgin spoken by the original Africans.

However, this scenario would entail the Maroons encountering a populous colony where speech habits were already established; this is what Hancock's account implies. In fact, however, the Maroons were nothing less than one of the two principal founding components of the colony itself. The 807 Maroons and the 982 American slave settlers (who had arrived only eight years before the Maroons) together constituted 1,789 out of the 1,917 people in the colony before the arrival of the first significant contingent of recaptured slaves. Meanwhile, the original Africans were the people least likely to serve as linguistic models for the burgeoning community. In 1800, these included *gromettas* working in the coastal factories, and

Kru boatmen. They together numbered a mere 100 out of 3,000 at the end of 1811. More important, they were not only numerically but socially marginal. The Kru occupied the colony only in transient fashion, earning money with the intention of returning to their homeland. They were thus accused of taking wealth out of the colony, and were widely suspect as thieves (Fyfe 1962: 135); they resided in their own segregated quarter as well. Thus these were hardly people likely to be linguistic models to Maroons or settlers.

These original Africans are even less likely to have been models for the waves of recaptured slaves. There is no evidence of especial contact of any kind between the recaptured slaves and the original Africans, and their small numbers would have precluded much contact at all unless they had occupied some high position in the society from which they could exert wide-ranging linguistic influence. As we have seen, they did not. On the contrary, the recaptured slaves are documented to have had considerable contact with the Maroons and settlers, especially the earlier arrivals, who were regularly apprenticed to them (Fyfe 1962: 115, 119). Later, mission education and religious services were equally crucial to linguistic transmission to the recaptured slaves (130); again, original Africans were marginal to nonexistent in these contexts, and certainly not in control. Finally, the original Africans are equally unlikely to have exerted linguistic influence on the first creole generation, who looked down upon them as crude and uncivilized (455).

Thus the social history of Sierra Leone strongly supports a crucial role for the Maroons in determining the composition of modern Krio. It seems likely that whatever English-based pidgin the original Africans spoke would have been thoroughly overwhelmed, and eventually eliminated, by the varieties spoken by both the Maroons and the settlers. The role of the settlers' speech is evident in features shared specifically by Krio and Gullah, most strikingly the grammatical marker *blant* "used to," found only in these two AECs. However, it is clear that the Maroons' language was decisive, given that Krio patterns idiosyncratically with Maroon Spirit Language and the Suriname creoles to an extent which delineates the three as a directly related group (Smith 1987; Hancock 1987; also cf. Sections 3.4.1, 3.4.2), while Gullah, on the other hand, patterns with the Western Caribbean group typified by Jamaican. Most importantly, however, it would appear impossible to derive Krio from a pidgin spoken by the original resident Africans, a marginal and despised presence in the society.

4.9.4 SUMMARY

Thus I differ with Hancock's conception on the following points:

(1) I do not locate the origin of AEC in Senegambia, but on the Ghanaian coast.

(2) I consider Krio to have been brought to Sierra Leone by Jamaican Maroons.

(3) I take no issue with the existence of Guinea Coast Creole English, but consider this a designation for a range of varieties used in transitory English-African interactions, unrelated to LGPE and thus not ancestral to the AECs.

(4) I do not propose that castle slaves taught sale slaves a pidgin English while awaiting shipment, but that a seed population of castle slaves developed the pidgin and brought it overseas.

(5) I do not propose that the parent pidgin was brought across the Atlantic regularly or even more than once, but that it was brought to the Caribbean once, by this seed population of castle slaves from Cormantin.

4.10 CONCLUSION

In Chapter 2, we saw that Spanish America is a striking contradiction of the idea that plantation creoles emerged as the result of disproportion between Africans and whites. In Chapter 3, I showed that this limited access conception cannot be applied to most English Caribbean colonies, because the AECs are traceable to a single ancestor transplanted in stabilized form from colony to colony. In this chapter, we have seen that even in the earliest English colonies from which AEC was disseminated, the conditions for the limited access model were not met, and that a great deal of evidence locates the birth of AEC in West African trade settlements, where the limited access model would have been equally inapplicable.

Afrogenesis is sometimes dismissed as a "return to the past," but in fact, it is unclear that the present, dominated by the limited access conception, is preferable. In devoting ourselves to a core concept while neglecting striking contradictions, we again risk making the mistake of the creation scientist.

The last stand for the limited access model is the French creoles. In Chapter 5, we will see that once again, when we scratch the surface, we find more questions than answers.

5 Off the Plantation for Good
The French-Based Creoles

5.1 INTRODUCTION

While never given its due, among AEC scholars Afrogenesis has always at least had its quiet adherents. Among scholars of the French-based creoles, however, Afrogenesis has been completely beyond the pale for decades. Goodman (1964: 128–9) made a strong statement in its favor, but has since recanted. Otherwise, until recently the only other adherent has been Hull (1979), whose main concern is dialectal sources. At this writing, Parkvall (1995a) espouses Afrogenetic origin, but only in tandem with a concurrent genesis taking place on St. Kitts (1995b) as well.

Instead, plantation-based polygenesis of some extent is an unquestioned assumption in the work of all leading scholars of French creoles. Their philosophical underpinnings could not be more divergent—the strident superstratism of Robert Chaudenson, the painstaking Fongbe-Haitian comparisons by Claire Lefebvre's relexificationist school, the sober "creativist" perspective of Philip Baker. Yet all converge upon the limited access model.

This chapter will argue that all of the French-based plantation creoles of the Atlantic and Indian Oceans (hereafter simply FPCs) trace as ineluctably back to a single West African ancestor as do the AECs. As with the AECs, our first clue is the striking similarities within the Caribbean FPCs, which are so close that many authors have treated all of them as varieties of a single "le créole" (Valdman 1978; Bernabé 1987), and even as polygenetically oriented a scholar as Baker (1987) considers, for example, Haitian an extension of Lesser Antillean.

What is most indicative of a single parent pidgin, however, is that even the FPCs of opposite hemispheres correspond too closely to be independent emergences. Holm (1989: 354) summarizes this well:

> It has been claimed that the French-based creoles are more similar to one
> another than are the creoles based on other European languages. . . .
> On the level of typology this is clearly true; the differences between
> the Isle de France and the New World creoles are not as great as those
> between the Asian and Atlantic varieties of creole Portuguese and
> Spanish, or the Atlantic and the Australian varieties of creole English.

Specifically, as we will see, Mauritian Creole (and its offshoots such as
Seselwa) and Haitian Creole appear to stem from the *same* encounter with
French, not *separate* ones.

In this chapter I will argue that the FPC data deliver the *coup de grâce*
to the limited access model. The similarities within the Caribbean subset of
the FPCs can potentially be attributed to intercolonial movements, originating from an initial colony, such as St. Kitts, where a plantation-based
genesis could be posited (Alleyne 1971: 117; Hazaël-Massieux 1990: 97;
Goodman 1992: 355, Jennings 1995b; Parkvall 1995b). However, there have
been no remotely significant intercolonial movements between the French
Caribbean and Mauritius, on the other side of the globe. The only sociohistorical intersection these colonies share is that both were supplied with
slaves via West African trade settlements on the coast of Senegal. This indicates that the FPCs, like the AECs, arose as ordinary work pidgins, and
not along the lines of any of the limited access-based plantation models.

5.2 LINGUISTIC DATA

There are seven features shared by Haitian and Mauritian Creole which are
indicative of common origin in Senegal. Like SSG in the AECs, these features are crucial because they *cannot* be derived from the French superstrate, commonalities among substrate languages, or universals. The features that Goodman (1964) refers to in making his Afrogenetic argument,
for example, are not conclusive because they are traceable to such factors.
For example, both Haitian and Mauritian use *with* as a conjunction within
NP, as in:

Haitian:

(1) Papa-m **ak** mama-m te vini.
    father-my with mother-my ANT come

My father and my mother came.

(Sylvain 1936: 156)

Mauritian:

(2) Ière **av**   tourtie
    hare with tortoise

    The hare and the tortoise

    (Goodman 1964: 94)

However, this is a substrate commonality, a pan-Niger-Congo feature
found from Wolof down the Guinea Coast through to the Bantu languages,
including those in the Bantu substrate, Makhuwa (Castro 1933), Yao
(Northern Rhodesia and Nyasaland Joint Publications Bureau 1954), and
CiBemba (Sanderson 1954) (see Baker and Corne 1986: 176 on choice of
substrate languages). Since substrate influence could have lent this feature
to all of the FPCs separately, this and like features are *irrelevant to the argument* in this chapter.

Goodman also makes reference to resumptive pronouns, but this is a
universal feature, so commonly encountered in contact languages and colloquial registers that we cannot treat it as evidence of common ancestry:

Haitian:

(3) Corde la **li** pas bon.
    rope   the it NEG good

    The rope is not good.

Mauritian:

(4) Mon paye   **li** bon aussi.
    my country it good also

    My country is good as well.

    (Baker and Corne 1982: 213)

Universal features of this type are *irrelevant to this argument,* as are any
features potentially derivable from regional dialects of French. The evidence
specifically pointing to common origin of the FPCs is presented below.

5.2.1 PREVERBAL TENSE-MOOD-ASPECT MARKERS

The most striking confirmation of a genetic relationship between Haitian
and Mauritian is their TMA markers. Philip Baker, in the section of Baker
and Corne (1982) that this passage comes from, ultimately rejects an Afrogenetic origin for FPCs, but with bracing fair-mindedness presents even

Table 5.1. Tense-mood-aspect markers in Haitian and Mauritian

Function	French	Haitian	Mauritian
H: anterior, M: past	*était*	*te*	*ti*
future	*va*	*va*	*va*
progressive	*après*	*ap*	*pe*
completive	*fini*	*fin*	*(f)in*
immediate past	*fait que*	*fek*	*fek*
H: obligation, M: definite future	*pour*	*pu*	*pu*

the evidence in its favor. His comment on TMA markers puts the case so well that I will simply quote him in entirety:

> Every (preverbal) "marker" attested in MC has an etymon for which there is a corresponding marker in HC, without exception. The similarity between MC and HC extends, more significantly, to the combinations in which they are attested . . . that essentially the same combinations should be found in HC and nineteenth-century MC texts is the more remarkable in that several of these are either very rare or obsolete in MC today. (Baker and Corne 1982: 234)

The correspondences in question are illustrated in Table 5.1.

This correspondence is too close to be attributed to chance, and suggests common ancestry. Contrary to general belief, the fact that the functions of these markers can be traced to French precursors does not explain Table 5.1.

The superstratist emphasis on identifying regional French sources for seemingly "exotic" creole structures began as a response to earlier tendencies to compare creoles with standard varieties of their lexifiers. To the extent that this tendency led to claims that creole TMA systems were based on "generalized West African verbal systems" (Alleyne 1980b: 9), or universalist claims that creoles resulted from "catastrophic" breakdowns of their lexifiers, the point is well taken. For example, to treat the Mauritian *zot ti pe ale* "they were going" as a "reinterpretation" of French is inappropriate given the construction *eux autres étaient après aller*—pronounced roughly [zot te prɛ ale] in rapid speech—in regional French vernaculars today.

What this approach cannot explain is why two creoles would fulfill TMA functions with markers *all derived from the exact same etyma out of many possible.* This is because of the chance factor in creole genesis, as discussed in Section 3.3.8.

For example, the *après* construction is hardly the only choice in French for a progressive construction. The superstratist framework cannot tell us why an FPC did not choose the *être à V* construction (*je suis à manger* "I am eating"), the *en train de* construction (*je suis en train de manger* "I am [in the process of] eating"), or a completely different source, such as a verb of location like *stop* (like Tok Pisin) or even an adverb (like AEC). Similarly, what anointed *était* as the choice for the past marker? Surely, forms of *avoir* used as auxiliaries were just as perceivable and generalizable. To say that the superstratist framework cannot explain these choices is not a criticism, since the operations of chance fall outside any "framework." What creolists have often neglected is that the chance factor allows conclusions that fragmentary sociohistorical documentation cannot.

Along these lines, examining the choices made by other French-based contact languages is instructive. FPC specialists appear to suppose that it is plausible that Haitian and Mauritian would make the exact same TMA choices on opposite sides of the globe. This, however, begs the question as to why we do not see such parallel choices in French pidgins and creoles which unequivocally emerged separately, outside of the Caribbean or the Indian Ocean.

The Melanesian creation Tayo Creole of New Caledonia will serve as our "French Tok Pisin," as a full-blown French creole whose birth was completely separate from that of the FPCs (data from Ehrhart 1993: 160–7). Another source of comparison will be Tây Bôi of Vietnam (Phillips 1975: 128–45). It is unsurprising that these languages make some of the same choices as FPC does. However, neither make anywhere near *all* of the same choices; see Table 5.2.

Clearly, all of the markers are derivable from superstrate usages. However, there is a range of choices available for each marker, and the fact that Haitian and Mauritian made the exact same ones suggests that they arose via the *same* encounter with French, not *separate* ones. Finally, we must view this stunning convergence within the context of the fact that the other New World FPCs have virtually identical TMA marker choices, which suggests that they, too, trace back to the same pidgin which spawned Haitian, rather than having developed independently. Indeed, the TMA grids among the New World FPCs are not identical. Most notably, Lesser Antillean and Guianese replace *ape* with *ka* and *va* with *ke*. However, this kind of minor paradigmatic variation is not counterevidence to a common parent for the FPCs. Such departures are plausibly attributed to separate evolution

Table 5.2. TMA Markers in several French contact languages

Function	H	M	Tayo	Tây Bôi
past /anterior	*te*	*ti*	***dzha*** *(<déja)*	***ai, être*** forms, *(te)*
future	*va*	*va*	*va*	*va*
progressive	*ap*	*pe*	***atra de*** *(<en train de)*	***maintenant***
completive	*fin*	*(f)in*	*fini*	*fini*
immediate past	*fek*	*fek*	*vya de (<vient de)*	*ø*
obligation /def. future	*pu*	*pu*	*ø*	*ø*

and different language contacts. In fact, historical data support this: *va* rather than *ke*, for example, is attested in earlier varieties of Martiniquais (Jourdain 1956: 173), Guadeloupean (Gérmain 1976: 108–9) and Guianese (Fauquenoy-St. Jacques 1979; the author thanks Mikael Parkvall for the references). It is quite plausible that contact with Portuguese, either via the trade pidgin or via the Portuguese slave presence across the Caribbean in the late seventeenth century, lent *ka* to FPC, with *ke* a later development, from the combination of *ka* and *ale* (to go), eventually ousting *va* (Hull 1979). The main point is that *ka* and *ke* no more speak against a common ancestor to the FPCs than the use of Turkish *eyer* for "if" in Asia Minor Greek speaks against the existence of Proto-Indo-European.

5.2.2 "EXPOSED POSITION" COPULA

Haitian has a copula *ye* which appears only after movement of the predicate to the front:

(5) Mwẽ te ø nã   bulõžeri.
    I   ANT LOC bakery

   I was in the bakery.

   (Phillips 1982: 250)

(6) Kote li **ye**?
    place he COP

   Where is he?

   (274)

(7) Amerikē yo te   dwe **ye**.
    American they ANT must COP

Americans they must have been.

(270)

Mauritian has a copula with the same occurrence pattern, although the phonetic form is *ete:*

(8) Pyer ø labutik.
    Peter   shop

Peter is at the shop.

(Baker and Syea 1991: 159)

(9) Kot Pyer **ete**?
    side Peter COP

Where is Peter?

(ibid.)

(10) Ki   Pyer **ete**?
     what Peter COP

What is Peter?

(ibid.)

In other words, in both creoles (as well as all other FPCs), copular overtness is sharply restricted to sentence-final position. This is striking evidence of the true origin of the FPCs.

We can be sure that no dialect of French has ever restricted copular overtness to the sentence-final position. Furthermore, this is not found in any possible substrate language of either creole. According to the most reliable research, slaves brought to Haiti in the late seventeenth century, Haitian's formative period, were mostly from Senegambia and the Slave Coast (Singler 1993: 242–3). This would mean that the most important substrate languages would have been Wolof, Bambara, Mandinka, and dialects of Gbe (such as Ewe and Fongbe). The copula is always expressed in all of these languages (Wolof: Njie 1982; Bambara: Brauner 1974; Mandinka: Gamble 1987; Gbe: Westermann 1930). In Mauritius, substrate influence operated in three "passes." For the first six years of the colony's slaving history (1729–35), West Africans were the majority. From 1735 to 1762, Madagascar was the main source of slaves. From this point until emancipation, East Africans were the main source of slaves. We have seen that West African copulas are overt. Zero copula is possible in Malagasy, but copula-like items appear in various constructions (Rajemisa-Raolison 1969: 30), and in a VOS language, there could be no model for a sentence-final copula since the final position in the sentence is occupied by the subject. Bantu languages generally require a copula, and always in the locative.

Furthermore, the FPC configuration is typologically marked as well. There is indeed a strong tendency for all languages to fill the copula slot when sentence-final. However, NSF project #BNS-8913104 found that none out of twenty-five typologically disparate languages have a copula which appears *nowhere* in the grammar but sentence-finally (see Chapter 3, n. 3 for languages studied), nor has this author, concentrating for several years on the copula worldwide, ever encountered any. The evidence converges in suggesting that this behavior would have been highly unlikely to have arisen in two creoles independently, and certainly not in five or six.

What is especially telling is that even among creoles, this behavior appears only in the FPCs, not in other French contact languages. Overt copulas are optional but quite frequent in Tayo (Ehrhart 1993: 170–2). As in many contact languages, zero copula was possible in Tây Bôi, but it was by no means categorical, and there was nothing approaching the FPC system (Phillips 1975: 124–5). If the FPC copula scenario is in any way typical or predictable, then how can we explain its stark restriction to the FPCs? There probably exist some languages in the world with this copular behavior, but even so, its uniform distribution in FPC would remain as a pressing question. Simple logic dictates that something unique to FPCs is responsible. As we have seen, the source languages were not responsible, which leads us quite simply to common origin. The sentence-final copula was a chance reinterpretation of French by one set of learners. Their choice was then disseminated via what would become the various FPCs.

Baker and Syea (1991: 166), on the other hand, consider the Mauritian sentence-final copula, *ete,* to have been a latter-day innovation, and thus to have appeared too late to be evidence for a parent pidgin. Their contention is based on the fact that *ete* appears in Mauritian texts starting only in 1880. However, "absence" in such texts is especially difficult to interpret with *ete,* since even today, *ete* is optionally omissible. Only with the support of other lines of evidence can we interpret these early zero tokens as indicating that *ete* had yet to emerge, and such support appears to be lacking. The authors propose that *ete* began as a reflex of French *était,* i.e., a past-marked verb "to be" (11), but that in juxtaposition with anterior marker *ti,* its past-tense semantics began to be processed as redundant and dropped, leaving today's tenseless place filler (12):

Mauritian 1880:

(11) Kot   Pyer ti   ete?
      where Peter PAST **be-PAST**

      Where was Peter?

Modern Mauritian:

(12) Kot   Pyer ti   ete?
      where Peter PAST **COP**

      Where was Peter?

This account, however, is difficult to situate within conventional pathways of syntactic change and reanalysis. A proposal that a verb be drained of its semantics like this requires an explicit motivation—changes like this do not simply occur for no reason. *Ti* and *ete* sharing the same semantics is not plausible as such a motivation, because such a situation would not have been a flaw or an opacity ripe for erasure—grammars tolerate redundancy readily. Baker and Syea's pathway begs the question as to why *been* in *I don't know where you **have been*** has not been reanalyzed as a mere place filler. On the contrary, if anything, the model of the local standard French *était* would seem to have *retarded* the interpretation of *ete* as anything but past-marked.

It thus seems more likely that *ete* was incorporated into Mauritian at its origin, reinterpreted as tenseless from the start. The authors themselves pose a question which ultimately supports this (Baker and Syea 1991: 169): if *ete* did not exist until 1880, then how did earlier speakers ask "What was Peter?" Baker and Syea note that *Ki Pyer ti ø?* is disallowed by Mauritian intonation patterns.

Another possible objection might be to view the different etyma used by the two creoles (*ye* vs. *ete*) as evidence of separate origin. Indeed, I have argued that the TMA markers evidence common origin because of the parallel etymological choices. In the case of the copula, however, it is the *syntactic* behavior which is too uniform to attribute to chance. The difference in lexical choice suggests that there was a lexical variation in the parent pidgin, resolved differently on opposite sides of the world. Such lexical variation is typical of all languages, and most certainly of pidgins and creoles (see also Section 5.5.1). For instance, both Tok Pisin and Solomon Islands Pijin have predicate markers, but it is *i* in the former (*wo i kam* "war came"), and *hemi* in the latter (*wo hemi kam;* Keesing 1988: 152). Thus the Guianese use of *fika* (from Portuguese *ficar* "to stay") as copula is easily explained as a result of the Portuguese presence in seventeenth century Cayenne (Goodman 1987: 389–91). What is important is that the lexical item was placed within a particular *syntactic* construction which cannot have arisen in French Guiana when it is also found in every other FPC.

5.2.3 NEGATOR *NAPA*

The next indication that Haitian and Mauritian stem from the same encounter with French is the negator *napa*, fossilized from *n'a pas* "does not have." Obsolescent in Mauritian but formerly prevalent, it is obsolete in modern Haitian, but attested in older documents:

Mauritian:

(13) Dokter napa ti   kapav   soy li.
     doctor NEG PAST be-able save him

    The doctor could not save him.

    (Baker and Corne 1982: 85)

Haitian:

(14) Mangé n'a pas dou   dan bouche.
     food   NEG   sweet in mouth

    No food pleases my mouth.

    (ibid.)

The source of *napa* in a reinterpretation of French is obvious: the negated auxiliary *avoir* before past participle (*il **n'a pas** mangé* "he hasn't eaten," "he didn't eat") was extended to use as a general predicate negator. However, the question is whether we would expect this particular reinterpretation in several independent encounters with French.

Other French contact languages indicate not. Tayo has simply *pa* as negator (although there is an item *napa* used as a negative existential, from French *il n'y a pas* [Ehrhart 1993: 191–2]). Tây Bôi did not use *napa* as a general negator (Phillips 1975: 157–60). Burundian Pidgin French has *apa*, not *napa* (Niedzielski 1989: 93).

Napa is also found in early Louisiana Creole (Parkvall 1995a) and pos-

sibly in early Lesser Antillean (Carden, Goodman, Posner and Stewart
1990). The distribution suggests that *napa* was prevalent in the parent pidgin but was quickly ousted in favor of *pa* in the Caribbean, while holding
on a bit longer in the Indian Ocean. This explanation is more economical
than attributing its prevalence to serendipity.

5.2.4 NP-MARKING *LA*

One of the most salient features of FPC is the postposition of determiner
-*la* to the noun (H *tab-la* table-the "the table"). Less well-known is that
Haitian, Mauritian, and all Caribbean FPCs as well (Bernabé 1987: 18) also
postpose *la* to relativized NP, as opposed to just nouns:

Haitian:

(15) Tab-la   [m te   ašte **(l)a**] bel.
     table-DET I   ANT buy DET pretty

     The table I bought is pretty.

     (Lefebvre and Massam 1988: 216)

Mauritian:

(16) Sa dile [(ki)   to   aste-**la**] in   kaye.
     that milk which you buy-DET COMP spoil

     That milk you bought has gone sour.

     (Baker 1972: 94)

The use of *là* as *a determiner of relativized NP* is unrecorded as a vernacular French feature. As Francophone superstratists have correctly noted,
vernacular Frenches indeed make rampant use of adverbial *là* "there" as an
expressive discourse particle often postposed to NPs, as in the Québecois:

(17) Mon char à moi **là**   i fait pus   ça.
     my car to me there it do no-more that

     That car of mine—it doesn't do that anymore.

     (Fournier 1987: 41)

However, *là* is not recorded in the specific usage of grammatically relativiz-
ing NP; for example, it does not serve this function in Québecois (Claire
Lefebvre, Sep. 1996 p.c.), as the literature on *là* in the *Revue Québecoise de
Linguistique* confirms.

One might suggest that the extension of *là* to mark relativized NP is a natural reinterpretation of French, and this may be true—but the question is, Is it natural enough to occur consistently throughout FPC? Tayo suggests not. In Tayo, influence from the colloquial usage of *là* is clear, in that *la* is extensively used as an expressive discourse particle (Ehrhart 1993: 125). However, Tayo has *not* made the particular choice of syntacticizing *là* as a marker of relativized NP as the FPCs have (152–3).

Tayo:

(18) Nu kõnta de rom sa   le   fe.
     we happy of dress REL they make

     We are happy with the dress they made.

     (Ehrhart 1993: 153)

However, this behavior of a determiner is a classic feature of Niger-Congo languages spoken on the Guinea Coast. Specifically, it is found in Wolof, likely to have been well-represented among castle slaves in Senegal (the determiner shape is *b* + V, the vowel varying according to semantic constraints).

Wolof:

(19) Xale bu   aay   **bi**   lool ci togga
     child DET strong DET very in kitchen

     The child who is good at cooking

     (Njie 1982: 229)

Taken alone, we could propose that Caribbean FPCs incorporated this usage locally, since Guinea Coast slaves were predominant in early imports to the French Caribbean (cf. Singler 1993).

However, we could do this only hesitantly in Mauritius. Of the three successive substrate components in Mauritius, West Africans, Malagasies, and then Bantus, West Africans had the advantage of being founders. However, the Bantus had the advantage of overwhelming numbers from 1762 onward, but Bantu languages have no articles *per se*, and the closest equivalents, demonstratives, do not figure in relative constructions (cf. Katupha 1983 for Makhuwa, for example). Meanwhile, Malagasy has no model for the construction either (Rajemisa-Raolison 1969: 67–8).

One approach might be to suppose that West African languages had a similar impact separately in the Caribbean and Mauritius. However, when we bring the three correspondences outlined above into the picture, we see a motivation for treating this behavior of *là* as one more piece of evidence that all of the FPCs stem from one ancestor. Below, we will see other features which further justify this approach.

5.2.5 TONELESSNESS

A final feature suggesting the common parentage of the FPCs is suggested by Mikael Parkvall (1999: 37–8). No plantation creole has inherited the lexically and syntactically contrastive tonal system typical of West African languages. However, some plantation creoles do reflect specific substrate tonal patterns (Kihm 1980: 37; Ham 1999). Furthermore, the pitch accent systems, intonational patterns, and occasional tonally contrasted lexical pairs often found in other creoles are clearly reflections of West African influence.

This leads to the question as to why tone does not play a significant role in any FPC (*pace* the marginal observations chronicled by Holm 1988: 140–1). The question is especially pressing in the case of Haitian, argued by Lefebvre (1993, et al.) to be a direct relexification of Fongbe. Since Saramaccan, heavily influenced by Gbe, reflects Gbe tonal patterns quite strongly (Ham 1999), would we not expect the same in Haitian?

One might object that the minor role played by stress on the sentential level in French discouraged the refashioning of stress as tone in the creoles. However, this first of all begs a question: Even if French largely confines stress to the final syllable of a sentence, what would have blocked Africans from transforming this into a high tone? After all, tone need not operate only on the lexical level in creoles; it operates on the sentential level as well in, for example, Saramaccan (Rountree 1972). Furthermore, the "musical" quality of the second-language French of modern Africans speaks against the resistance of French to tonality.

What feature could the FPCs share which would lead to this anomalous absence of tone? One answer is that Wolof is one of the few West African languages lacking tone. If the FPCs all stem from a pidgin with Wolof as the primary substrate, the puzzle is solved.

5.2.6 ABSENCE OF CV STRUCTURE

Pidgins and creoles are well-known for often exhibiting CVCV structure, and AECs are no exception (Sranan *luku* "look"). Less well known, however, is that this is rare in FCs. It is unlikely that this is due to French, because pidgins, creoles, and regular languages have readily applied CVCV patterning to French loanwords (e.g., Kituba *melesi*<*merci* "thanks"). If there were a Wolof-based parent pidgin, however, this problem would be solved, because consonant-final syllables are integral to Wolof phonology, but not in Lower Guinea coast languages like Twi and Yoruba, or Bantu languages like Kikongo. (See Parkvall 1999: 32–3 for details.)

5.2.7 OTHER FEATURES

Parkvall (1999) has also observed a variety of features shared by the FCs which, like the TMA choices, the sentence-final copula, *napa*, and relativizer *là*, are traceable neither to French nor substrate languages. If these creoles had truly emerged separately, we would expect the varying substrate compositions and lengths of exposure to French to have much more variegated results. These correspondences are therefore clues to a single common ancestor, especially given their number. I will note only the most striking examples; see Parkvall (1999) for a full discussion of this issue:

(a) All AECs with a relatively "deep" register substitute /b/ for /v/ frequently (Saramaccan *fébɛ* "fever"). However, FPCs never do. This substitution is not traceable to any particular West African language; some have /v/ and some do not. To ascribe this substitution to a general simplification tendency begs the question of why it is absent in the FPCs specifically. One explanation would be if the substitution happened, for any number of reasons, in one English pidgin which was then diffused, and did not happen, for any number of reasons, in one French pidgin which was then diffused. Smith (1987: 68) has already treated the /b/-for-/v/ trait as evidence for an AEC parent; the FPC evidence indirectly strengthens his case and points the way to a similar single-parent approach to the FPCs themselves.

(b) Many AECs have coarticulated and prenasalized stops (Saramaccan *gbóto* "boat"; *ndófu* "enough"), a sound class obviously inherited from West African languages since they are rare elsewhere in the world. However, even the most basilectal FCs lack these, even in West African borrowings which had them in the donor language (Haitian *bade* "God of wind" from Fongbe *gbade*). Why would Africans in Suriname retain their coarticulated and prenasalized stops, but not in Haiti? One economical explanation would be if in AEC, the stops were retained in an ancestral pidgin and then diffused to the Caribbean, while an original FPC parent pidgin omitted them and was then diffused.

(c) AECs have a complementizer derived from a verb meaning "to say" or, in the Suriname creoles, "to talk." FPCs, however, lack this, with the exception of a latter-day development, probably substrate-driven, in Seychellois, *pur-dir* (Corne 1977). If each FPC was developed by different groups of Africans, we would expect at least some of them to have a *dire-* or *parler*-complementizer. An elegant explanation would be that an FPC parent happened not have developed a *say*-complementizer, and that this was then diffused.

(d) The FPC bimorphemic interrogative markers are too similar to have emerged in several separate locations independently. Specifically, the FCs line up uncannily well in their choices of nominal components. Every FC has *ki sa* for "what"—why not *chose* "thing" in at least *one* FPC? If bimorphemic, "where" is never derived from *qui + lieu* or *qui + endroit*, but always *qui + coté*. Where "when" is bimorphemic, the rather singular *qui + l'heure* is always the choice, except the marginal Antillean alternate *qui + temps;* if each FC developed independently, *qui + temps* would be more widely distributed, being perhaps the most obvious candidate. (Note that I am not arguing that the choice of *qui* as the general interrogative marker is especially noteworthy, but the choices of following substantive.)

In sum, in having determiner-marked relativized NP, tonelessness, and consonant-final syllables, Mauritian Creole looks more like a Guinea Coast creation than a Malagasy or Bantu one. Only Wolof fulfills all of these qualifications.

Since West Africans dominated in Mauritius for the first six years, we might choose to attribute Mauritian's Guinea Coast bias to this period, and thereby sidestep tracing Mauritian to a Senegalese proto-pidgin directly. However, this decision would proceed upon an incomplete data set.

This is because the Guinea Coast bias must be viewed in tandem with the *first* three features, *not* traceable to substrate influence, and too idiosyncratic to have all emerged in five or six separate encounters with French. Even if Wolofs developed two French pidgins separately, we would hardly expect the exact same rare copula construction, the exact same TMA markers, and so on, especially since in neither the Caribbean nor the Indian Ocean were Wolofs the only Africans present, adding even more variation to the two mixes. Together, then, the Guinea Coast bias *plus* the idiosyncratic patternings elsewhere suggest that both Caribbean and Indian Ocean FPCs stem from a *single* ancestor in which Guinea Coast influence was strong.

5.2.8 THE WHEEL OF FORTUNE

It is paradoxical that Afrogenesis is considered even more heterodox among FPC specialists than among AEC specialists, despite the fact that the FPCs are even more similar to one another than the AECs. Again, one misses a full engagement with the role of chance in genesis work on FPCs. As I have shown, idiosyncrasy does not reveal itself only in common *innovations*, but also in common *selections*, out of many possible, from source languages. If an array of different creoles have all made the same several choices out of many from a superstrate, then this speaks against a model proposing them as separate emergences.

This becomes clear when we examine an unequivocally separate "spin of the wheel," Tayo. The common consensus, as noted in Section 3.3.8, is that creoles will differ on the basis of differences in source languages, the timings of their impact, and social relations, but that all these things being equal, results will be quite similar in separate locations. This consensus is sensible but incomplete: the mundane factor of chance also plays a crucial role in the outcome in each place.

For example, the second-person plural pronoun *zot* in FPC (also third-person in the Indian Ocean and Northern Haitian) is derived from regional French *vous autres*. However, this must be seen against the fact that in Tayo, the same item has evolved along a different phonetic route, as *uso* (Corne 1995a: 125). It would be difficult to find any predictive account for this, such as French or Melanesian influence, and it certainly has nothing to do with nature of social interactions. It is a simple demonstration of the fact that phonetic change is explanatory but not predictive. However, this casts the FPC data in a certain light. Since the phonetic reinterpretation and evolution of *vous autres* is identical in all of the FPCs, they reveal themselves as having arisen via a single encounter with French, not five or six.

A similar case is the postposed possessive markers in Tayo such as *pmwa* (from *pour moi*) and *puta* (from *pour toi*): *frer pu ta* "your brother" (Corne 1995a: 127, 134). Again, the source in French is clear. However, if the FPCs emerged separately, then is it not strange that *none* of them chose *pour* instead of *à* (Haitian *papa **a** m* "my father") or a zero marker for possessive marking within NP? (Caribbean FPCs indeed use *pu* in full sentences like *liv-la pu mwen* "the book is mine," but *not* in NPs like "my book.") Another example: Tayo has chosen *la* as its resumptive third-person pronoun: *Rok, la travaj o bato* "Rock works on the boats" (Ehrhart 1993: 220). Clearly, the third-person singular *il* was a ready candidate as well, having been incorporated into Seselwa in similar function (and note the Québecois model in [17]). *Elle, le, lui,* and so on were also possible choices. These things can be traced only to blind chance.

Some creolists dismiss such things with a shrug of the shoulders, supposing that enough evidence from elsewhere supports the limited access conception that these wrinkles will eventually iron themselves out. However, in this book we have seen that the limited access conception is much more problematic than conventionally thought when we attempt to apply it to Spanish colonies or English colonies. These problems in the French colonies merely take their place alongside the previously discussed ones as an increasingly dire gallery of demons.

More to the point, if the FPCs were separate encounters with French, among other things, we might expect the following to be true.

(1) Some FPCs, under heavy Gbe influence, would have extensive transfer from this language as does Saramaccan (McWhorter 1997a), such as the generation of adjectives via reduplication of verb stems, and postposed nominals to encode spatial relations like *behind* and *above*. If Gbe influence was as decisive in Haitian and Guianese as Lefebvre (1993) and Jennings (1995a) claim respectively, we would even expect more extreme cases of mixture akin to the inflections from Eastern Ijo in Berbice Dutch.

(2) Some FPCs would mark relativized NP with determiners, but just as many others would not.

(3) Some FPCs would have two categorically overt copulas, one equative and one locative, which is (a) cross-linguistically common, (b) common in creoles worldwide, and (c) a Niger-Congo feature.

(4) Some FPCs would overgeneralize a form of *avoir* as a past marker, others *être à* as a progressive; together the FPCs would present a smorgasbord of vastly different TMA grids, not a single one with one minor dialectal variation.

But this is not what we see.

There are two choices at this point. One would be to maintain that the correspondences between the FPCs are accidental. In this case, the FPCs constitute a minor revolution in historical linguistics, revealing an unsuspected determinism in language change, and refuting previously held conceptions about the meaning of idiosyncrasy in comparative reconstruction. Another approach, however, would be to investigate the possibility that the FPCs shared a single parent.

5.2.9 PROOF IN THE PUDDING

It is ironic that FPC specialists do not trace the creoles back to a single parent, given that the comparative current is much stronger among them than among AEC specialists. This is possibly the by-product of something beneficial. FPC scholars have excelled in substantial sociohistorical research, yielding studies such as Baker and Corne (1982) for the Indian Ocean, Speedy (1994) for Louisiana Creole, Jennings (1995a) for Guyanais, and Singler (1993, 1995) for Haitian. However, there is a tendency in this work to focus on local historical documentation to the detriment of the comparative data which complete the story.

5.2.9.1 LOUISIANA CREOLE

A prime example here is Speedy (1994, 1995), who reconstructs not one but *two* separate creole geneses in Louisiana, based on conclusions from the sociohistorical record. Only in the case of the second one, Tèche creole, does she acknowledge possible links with a pre-existent FPC, Haitian, on the basis of the incontrovertible fact that thousands of slaves were brought to Saint Martin Parish from Haiti after 1791 (Speedy 1995: 108). Even here, however, the prevalence of the "obliteration" scenario in creolist thought leads her to hedge:

> While it is not asserted that the Creole spoken today . . . in Saint Martin Parish is a direct "offshoot" of Haitian Creole, the input of this latter into the emergent community language must have been substantial. (109)

Speedy's sociohistorical research is laudable. However, her conclusions must be seen in the light of the linguistic evidence. Klingler (1997) shows that linguistic comparison reveals no grounds for deriving these two dialects from separate geneses. Meanwhile, it is also linguistic evidence which clearly demonstrates a direct relationship between Louisiana Creole and the other FPCs: it is, quite simply, impossible that even one creole, and certainly not two, emerged independently in Louisiana when both dialects have the common FPC features outlined in Sections 5.2.1 to 5.2.7.

The TMA grid by itself would virtually clinch the case; when it is combined with the following points, the facts are even clearer:

(a) Sentence-final copula

(b) *Napa* as negator

(c) *La* as relativized NP determiner

(d) Tonelessness

(e) Absence of CV structure

This is hardly to say that there are no differences between Haitian and Louisiana Creole—there are plenty, as we would naturally expect of any two different languages. The point is that what they share is diagnostically indicative of a genetic connection, rather than derivable from source language commonalities or universal tendencies.

No matter how detailed and reasoned, an analysis based on the sociohistorical evidence is incomplete without a full address of the comparative facts as well. Sociohistorical documentation is notoriously uneven, especially on the foundation of new plantations, before there was anything to visit or write about. Linguistic evidence, on the other hand, based on arbitrary phonetic and structural configurations which can evolve in any number of directions, can be conclusive when we find matches such as those among the FPCs.

Thus Speedy's conclusion (1995: 103) that the "first" Louisiana Creole, the Mississippi variety, "emerged and 'jelled' ca. 1720–1770" is faultless within the frame of the documentation, which gives no evidence of FPC being brought to Louisiana with the first slaves. However, that frame excludes the comparative linguistic data, which does not allow Louisiana Creole to have been born independently.

The linguistic data strongly suggest that an initial transportation of Caribbean slaves, speaking FPC, were crucial in transmitting language to Africans in Louisiana. We may never find concrete documentation of this, but the linguistic evidence demonstrates it as unequivocally as carved flint tools in a cave signal the presence of early hominids. This is especially compelling given that there is, after all, evidence that Haitian speakers emigrated to the region in large numbers (recent research suggesting that it was the Mississippi rather than the Tèche region where Haitians were most employed; Chris Corne, p.c.). What, in the linguistic data, licenses us to conclude that this massive influx of Haitians merely had an "impact" (Speedy 1995: 108)?

5.2.9.2 FRENCH GUIANESE

Based on stunningly detailed information on slave shipments and demographic compositions, Jennings (1995a) concludes that Guianese did not exist until the late 1680s or later. His conclusion is based on the fact that until
then, most of the slaves would have been Gbe speakers, and therefore would
have used Gbe among themselves, with a rudimentary pidgin serving for
usage with whites. The thoroughness of Jennings' research and the fresh-
ness of his sociolinguistic reconstructions are exemplary. However, again,
the linguistic data must be taken into account, and do not permit us to treat
Guianese as an independent phenomenon. Since Guianese corresponds so
idiosyncratically with the other FPCs, we are forced to assume that FPC
was imported there at an early phase, probably in the 1670s, and decisively
determined language patterns among the slaves.

One thing suggesting this indirectly is Berbice Dutch (Smith, Robertson,
and Williamson 1987), famous for reflecting Eastern Ijo influence even to
the level of borrowed inflectional morphology. Since this degree of transfer
resulted from the first slaves in Berbice apparently being all Ijo speakers, we
would expect similarly heavy Gbe transfer in Guianese. On the contrary,
however, there is nothing especially reminiscent of Gbe about Guianese.

One solution would be if the Gbe speakers were exposed to a preexistent
French-based pidgin imported from elsewhere, thereby obviating the need
for a new pidgin to develop. Indeed, this is what the linguistic data suggest,
since Guianese corresponds too closely to other FPCs to have arisen by itself, and meanwhile the pidgin can have had significant impact only if imported early.

When charting the histories of creoles, many creolists tend to see the
sociohistorical evidence as decisive, and as a welcome improvement upon
linguistic evidence considered merely tangential, capable only of "suggestion." In fact, one can argue that things are precisely the other way around.
No matter how thoroughly mined, the sociohistorical record of an early
plantation society is equivalent to a torn, stained photograph or a 78-rpm
record with a massive chunk missing. The linguistic evidence allows us
to transcend the omissions and losses inevitable in antique documentary
materials.

5.3 SOCIOHISTORICAL EVIDENCE

There are two indications that FPC had its origins on the coast of Senegal.
The first is that Haitian (and other Caribbean FPCs) and Mauritian are too

similar to have arisen independently, and have only one sociohistorical intersection: trade settlements in Senegal. The second, however, is similar to the AEC case. There is concrete evidence that FPC had already emerged in the French Caribbean before the onset of large-scale plantation agriculture, which is problematic for limited-access-based conceptions of their origin.

5.3.1 THE MARTINIQUE TEXT

In 1990, a text of unequivocal FPC, transcribed in Martinique in 1671, was discovered (Carden, Goodman, Posner, and Stewart 1990). The text, three parallel accounts of a mermaid sighting, has had mysteriously little impact on FPC genesis work. For this reason, I will cite the third account, the most striking, in its entirety:

(20) Moi miré bête   qui tini Zyeux, tini barbe, tini mains, tini
     I   see   animal REL have eyes   have beard have hands have

     Zépaules tout comme homme, tini cheveux et   barbe gris, noir
     shoulders all   like   man   have hair   and beard gray black

     et   puis blanc, moi na pas miré bas   li parce li té   dans
     and then white I   NEG   look underside his because he ANT in

     diau, li sembe pourtant poisson. Moi té   tini peur bete   là
     water he seem however fish   I   ANT have fear animal DET

     manger monde. Li regardé plusieurs fois, li   allé devant
     eat   person he look   many   time he go in-front-of

     savanne, puis li caché li   dans diau, puis moi pas   voir li
     meadow then he hide him in   water then I   NEG see him

     davantage.
     more

I saw an animal that had eyes, had a beard, had hands, had shoulders just like a man, had hair and a beard that were gray, black, and white. I didn't see the bottom part of it because it was in the water; however, it looked like a fish. I was afraid the animal ate people. It looked several times, it went in front of the meadow (part of the island), then it hid itself in the water, then I didn't see it anymore.

This text is indisputably FPC, based on features such as the following:

(a) Fossilized determiners: *Zyeux, Zépaules, diau*

(b) Postposed *là: bete là*

(c) Bare reflexive pronoun: *li caché li*

(d) Grammaticalization of *et puis* as conjunction (Note that literally, "and then" would be illogical in the context.)

(e) Postposed pronoun as possessive: *bas li*

(f) Conventionalization of *té* as anterior marker: *moi té tini peur*

The text differs slightly from modern Antillean Creole, because of three hundred years of change, transcription error, and possibly interference from French itself, the latter even more apparent in the other informants' depositions. What is important is that this variety, a radical reduction and reinterpretation of French, is clearly a creole and not an L2 variety. More to the point, it is clearly a variety of FPC specifically, full of features unique to FPC and absent in other encounters with French like Tayo and Tây Bôi.

Since this language presumably existed long before the text was recorded, this text confirms that Martiniquais existed in the 1660s at the latest. This document is thus a crushing blow to all claims that plantation creoles emerged with large slave influxes, because in the 1670s Martinique was just beginning its transformation to a sugar economy. We will explore this further shortly. First, however, it must be made clear how this document allows us to dismiss certain claims about the early French Caribbean made on the basis of priests' comments in the late 1600s.

5.3.1.1 THE PRIESTS' ACCOUNTS: L2 FRENCH INSTEAD OF FPC?

On Martinique in 1654, Pelleprat (1655: 50) noted in an oft-quoted passage:

> We accommodate ourselves to their (the new slaves') way of speaking, which is ordinarily by the infinitive of the verb, as for example: *moi prier Dieu, moi aller à l'église, moi point manger,* to say "I have prayed to God," "I have been to church," "I have not eaten." And adding a word which marks the time to come or the past, they say, *Demain moi manger, hier moi prier Dieu,* and so forth. One makes them understand in this way of speaking all that one teaches them.

Priests were still using this strategy in 1682, when Mongin (cited in Chatillon 1984: 134–5) made a similar comment about evangelization on St. Kitts. The Pelleprat data do not correspond in any meaningful way with FPC, and allow any number of interpretations. Chaudenson's is that slave speech in the early Caribbean was an L2 French, and he explicitly rules out that it could have been a pidgin (1992: 107). His approach stems from the fact that the presence of a creole in early Martinique would be problematic for his "approximation" genesis model, which claims that creoles developed via only gradual divergence from their lexifiers, and that this divergence would have been minimal until large numbers of slaves were imported into a colony. The case has merit in itself: for example, the French priests' comments are paralleled exactly by similar comments made by priests in Cuba in the 1800s (Section 2.4.1.2), and as we saw, the evidence suggests that Cuban slaves spoke a second-language Spanish, not a pidgin.

However, the 1671 text is conclusive proof that a creole did emerge before Martinique passed into the plantation stage. Priests may very well have continued using the register Pelleprat described even as the creole took hold. What Pelleprat is describing is nothing other than Foreigner Talk. This would have been both effective and even necessary in communicating not only with brand-new slaves, but also with more established ones who spoke only creole, which would have been as opaque to a French speaker as it is today. Nor would this accommodation have been one-way—slaves would have been quite capable of in turn accommodating their creole to ease communication with the priest.

If the priests were unaware that the slaves had developed a stabilized creole, it would not be surprising in the least. Creolists are familiar with laymen's tendency to dismiss creoles as simply incompetent command of a lexifier. However, the priests dropped hints suggesting that they were aware of a stabilized variety distinct from French spoken around them. In Martinique in 1679, Mongin notes that (Chaudenson 1992: 107):

> There is barely anyone among so many different nations who in little time hasn't learned enough to understand us and make themselves understood, *without the special jargon of the beginners presenting any considerable obstacle* (translation and italics mine).
>
> (Il n'est presque personne parmi tant de différentes nations qui en peu de tems n'en ait appris suffisament pour nous entendre et pour se faire entendre, sans que le jargon particulier des commençans y forme aucun obstacle considérable.)

In designating the language of the beginners as a distinct, perceptible "special" system (the French adjective is *particulier*), Mongin implies something perceived as a discrete, enduring variety. More importantly, Mongin assures us that the "jargon" is not a hindrance to the acquisition of French. In even considering this an issue, he reveals an awareness of a patterned system. It is patterned systems, "languages" in their own right, that teachers often fear as barriers to acquiring a related variety. While foreign language teachers do not worry that their students' transient interlanguage hinders them from progress, some American educators have indeed worried that African-American Vernacular English—a stabilized variety—might hinder black children from acquiring command of standard English.

5.3.1.2 THE PRIESTS' ACCOUNTS: INDIAN *BARRAGOUIN* AS THE SOURCE OF FPC?

Meanwhile, Wylie (1995) argues that Antillean FPC was a continuation of the pidgin the French used with the local Indians on Martinique, rather than an import from Africa. However, the 1671 text, in showing that FPC already existed in the early French Caribbean, allows us to conclude, as does Chaudenson (1992: 12–5) on different grounds, that there was no significant relationship between FPC and the Indian pidgin.

Our first clue to this has always been that the Indian pidgin has nothing in common with FPC other than typical features of simplification like zero copula and absence of morphology. More to the point, it is significantly different from FPC. FPC uses *pa* as a negator, the Indian pidgin *non: Non ça bon pour France* (Bouton 1640: 130). The Indian pidgin also has a considerable Spanish element (*magnane* "tomorrow," *mouche* [<*mucho*] "very," and so on), which FPC lacks. In general, there is little motivation for considering this sentence the precursor to FPC:

(21) Mouche manigat   mon compère, moy non   faché à toi.
     very   well-done my friend,   I   NEG angry to you

Very nicely done, my friend; I'm not mad at you.

(Bouton 1640: 107–17)

Previously, however, the field was open to the surmise that FPC had arisen as the Indian pidgin, and then diverged from it via changes now lost to history, as Wylie hypothesizes. However, now that we know that FPC stretches as far back as the *société d'habitation* phase in Martinique and *coexisted* with the Indian pidgin, we can let the differences between the Indian pidgin tokens and FPC speak for themselves and conclude that there was no link between them. Indeed, Du Tertre (1667: 510) attributes a "jargon," "made up of French, English, Spanish and Dutch words," to both blacks and Indians. However, this merely indicates the broad perspective on contact languages we would expect of a linguistically untrained observer.

The actual linguistic data suggest stark differences between the blacks' and the Indians' contact French.

5.3.2 TRACING THE BIRTHPLACE OF FPC

As noted, the date of the 1671 Martinique text is crucial because it was spoken by slaves in a *société d'habitation* society, just like those of early St. Kitts, Barbados, and Suriname. White *engagés* and blacks worked in relatively equal numbers on small farms in Martinique until the 1670s. For example, in 1664, 529 out of 684 farms had less than six slaves, and there were often fewer slaves than white family members (Chaudenson 1992: 95).

To nevertheless argue that a creole could have emerged in early Martinique would be a *trahison* of the many books and articles claiming the opposite (e.g., Chaudenson 1979, 1992; Baker 1990; Baker and Corne 1982, 1986; Bickerton 1983, 1996; Mufwene 1991b, 1992, 1996; Singler 1993, 1995). That this work has been approved through peer review and widely cited indicates that the assumption that *sociétés d'habitation* did not give birth to creoles is accepted in creole studies.

Thus it would be rather maladroit to trace FPC to these farms. Moreover, while the roots of FPC in regional French dialects are strong, there are certain FPC commonalities which cannot be traced to such dialects—no *engagés* omitted the copula or said *moi soif* "I'm thirsty." As with AEC, this leads us to examine whether we could trace the creole to a previous French Caribbean colony.

Before the settlement of Martinique in 1635, the French had occupied only two other islands, St. Kitts in 1628 and Tortuga in 1634. Agricultural activity was small-scale on Tortuga, vastly overshadowed by the meat-vending *boucaniers* and pirating *filibustiers*. On the eve of Martinique's settlement, in 1634, the Tortuga population was a mere 600 (Crouse 1940: 82, cited in Holm 1989: 382), and the African proportion of this was apparently minimal in itself (Singler 1995: 203). Finally, those leaving Tortuga went not to Martinique but, naturally, to nearby Haiti.

St. Kitts, on the other hand, played a similar role in the French Caribbean as it did in the English. It is established that Martinique was settled by a contingent from this island (Petit Jean Roget 1980: 6), and even among chroniclers of the period, St. Kitts had the status of "mother" of the French Caribbean colonies (Du Tertre 1667; De Chanvallon 1763: 68). In this light, recent work has investigated the possibility that an FPC arose on St. Kitts and was subsequently diffused to other colonies (Parkvall 1995b; Jennings 1995b).

In my view, the data speak against this. For one thing, early St. Kitts was, predictably, a quintessential *société d'habitation,* with blacks and white *engagés* working side by side on small farms until well into the 1670s (Jennings 1995b: 65–7). Furthermore, the French never managed to develop a truly large-scale plantation society there at all. As late as 1687, plantations had an average of a mere 27 slaves per plantation (hardly the hundreds-strong forces traditional genesis theory associates with creole genesis) (67). Not long afterward, the French had left St. Kitts permanently; most planters were gone by 1700, and the British takeover of 1713 was the *coup de grâce.* To argue that a plantation creole emerged here would, again, be a rather sharp *volte-face* in view of the general conviction that similar conditions prevented the appearance of creoles in Réunion, the American South, Cuba, Suriname, and so on.

Another problem is texts in slave speech from St. Kitts in 1654 and 1682, which give little indication of having been based on FPC. Jennings (1995b: 79) supposes that this text may have been a distortion of an FPC variety. Indeed, early creole texts must be analyzed with caution, having almost always been transcribed by Europeans with questionable, if any, competence in the creole. Nevertheless, in such texts, one always gleans the shibboleths of the actual creole despite the distortions. Early Melanesian Pidgin English citations, for example, are chockablock with mistranscriptions and English-influenced "corrections," but the essence of the language, such as *suppose* for *if,* transitive marker *-im,* and adjectival marker *-fela,* show that the transcribers were hearing the ancestor of Tok Pisin and its sister dialects (Keesing 1988: 26–50). Similarly, early citations of Bajan in sources such as Pinckard (1806) are clearly based on something we would recognize as AEC. Early attestations of Mauritian, Negerhollands, and Sranan are similar.

In contrast, there is not a single thing in the St. Kitts passages suggesting FPC, as opposed to merely a stereotypical depiction of L2 French. A typical passage follows:

(22) *Moi m'en aller où personne ne voir moi que le Bon Dieu et la Bonne Vierge; là moi me dépouiller et moi frapper et moi frapper toujours, toujours et partout, jusqu'à ce que mauvaise pensée quitter moi.*

I went where no one but God and the Virgin could see me; there, I undressed and hit myself everywhere very hard, again and again, until the evil thought had left me.

(Jennings 1995b: 73–4)

With its preposed object pronouns, and its retention of highly grammaticalized French constructions such as *ne . . . que* "only" and *jusqu'à ce que* "until (+ verb)," this passage is clearly in a different class than any FPC. One might argue that the transcriber (Père Mongin again) was accommodating to the reader. However, as noted above, in transcriptions of other creoles, such accommodation never completely disguised the creole in question. A postposed *là* here and a fossilized definite article there would hardly have made the text opaque to Francophone readers.

When we recall that by 1682, French St. Kitts had only a couple more decades before disintegration, these passages suggest that no FPC was ever spoken on St. Kitts. What Mongin was transcribing was "bozal" French, an L2 French similar to the Spanish of slaves in nineteenth-century Cuba. This conclusion is further reinforced by the 1654 sample, in which a fourteen-year-old slave boy is praying for his seriously ill younger brother and then speaks directly to him. As Jennings notes (1995b: 72), this event would surely be conducted in a native tongue—and yet the native tongue is the same stereotypical L2 French, achieved mostly via omitting articles and overgeneralizing the infinitive.

Once again, then, we have run out of colonies to derive a creole from. We need to know why an FPC existed in Martinique by the 1660s. Once again, in the 1660s the only place on earth where Africans and Frenchmen were involved in interaction likely to lead to a pidgin—rather than just L2 French—was the West African coast. Now recall that the similarities between Haitian and Mauritian alone have already pointed to this as the source of FPC.

5.4 THE BIRTH OF FPC AT ST. LOUIS

The French Caribbean was devoted to small farms for the first five decades of settlement. Thus as with the Cormantin scenario, in searching for a parent to the FPCs, we seek a pidgin which would have been imported to the French Caribbean as early as possible, before speech patterns would have had a chance to stabilize among blacks there.

For this reason, I concur with Parkvall (1995a) that Hull's (1979) location of a French parent pidgin at Ouidah, in present-day Benin, must be rejected. Ouidah was established in 1671, meaning that by the time a pidgin had developed to export, slave speech patterns in the Caribbean would have been long established. This would also disqualify Gorée Island, on the coast of Senegal, as a plausible site, since it was settled by the French in 1677.

It seems more plausible, then, to locate the birth of the pidgin further north on the Senegalese coast, where the French established a trade settlement on the Île de Bieurt in 1638. This settlement was moved to the nearby Île Bocos a couple of months thereafter, and finally settled in 1659 on an island christened St. Louis (Delafosse 1931: 11).

The conditions were in place here for the birth of a French-based pidgin. First, Africans working under the French are almost certain to have spoken a form of French. The argument from sociolinguistic plausibility, presented for Cormantin in Section 4.5, applied here as well. Certainly the local language, Wolof, was useful, and many travelers described and learned it. However, we can assume that Africans working under the French were expected to make an effort to speak French, rather than Frenchmen speaking to them in their native language. Visitors to St. Louis, typically, never describe castle slave speech. However, they make it clear that French was spoken by various free Africans around the settlement, which would make it particularly anomalous for the French to go to the effort of using local African languages with enslaved African underlings. Cultru (1910: 84, 87, cited in Parkvall 1995a) cites an account of a local tribe speaking a "français corrompu" in 1685, and chieftains with a better competence still. This shows that French was indeed the language of business and power, even with indigenes. Similarly, at the Gorée settlement, Isert (1793: 40–4, 141), in his account of Africans serving as soldiers under the French, occasionally quotes the Africans at fair length even including comments on phraseology, reporting no interpreter and never indicating that he is translating from an African language.

Furthermore, the Africans working under the French were more formally stratified than under the English, consisting of not only castle slaves but also the *laptots* or *gourmettes*, usually free but sometimes slaves, charged with transporting goods and slaves to and from the settlement (Parkvall 1995a). Importantly, castle slaves at St. Louis were mostly Bambaras, favored for industriousness and loyalty (Delcourt 1952: 130–1, cited in Parkvall 1995a). On the other hand, the *laptots* were mostly Wolof (Ly 1955: 277, cited in Parkvall 1995a). This may have led to a degree of tertiary hybridization, with Bambaras and Wolofs using French pidgin to communicate with each other and thus helping to expand and stabilize it.

While we lack any observations of castle slave speech habits at St. Louis, we have occasional glimpses of such speech at the Ouidah fort in the late 1700s. Although as noted above, a pidgin transported from Ouidah would have been too late to influence speech habits in the Caribbean, data from it can be seen as generalizable to St. Louis. Ouidah was home to three separate forts, owned by the French, the English, and the Portuguese respectively. As Isert (1793: 141) notes,

> It isn't at all unusual, walking through the town, to be greeted simultaneously in several different languages, each black in the city knowing at least enough of the language of the fort he is attached to to be able to make a greeting [trans. mine].

If castle slaves at Ouidah did speak pidgins of the language of their fort, then this description of their competence would be quite typical of a passing observer. We get even closer to castle slave competence in French with an observation by a former castle director in 1791 (C/6/27; Archives Nationales, Paris) that among the blacks "there are many who don't speak French on principle (*par politique*), but who understand it," and use this to "report well or badly what they hear" [trans. mine]. Again, this description would befit slaves with a strictly utilitarian competence in French, understanding more than they could produce, and thus possibly misreporting utterances in actual French on occasion.

The next question is whether Africans working under the French were transported to early plantation colonies. In the case of Mauritius, at least some were. Some boatmen were sent from Senegal to Port Louis in Mauritius at its founding in the late 1720s (Philip Baker, p.c.); 24 Wolofs from Gorée were also sent around the same time to serve as company slaves (Baker and Corne 1982: 142), and by 1761, there were 878 company slaves in the colony, most from West Africa. Baker and Corne (1982: 246–7) also conclude that these slaves would have been spoken to in French (or some form thereof). The records give no indication that these slaves had served under the French at Gorée before shipment to Mauritius. However, the advantage if they had is clear: more acculturated slaves with a better command of French would have been much more valuable than raw recruits. (It is possible that a French pidgin emerging at St. Louis could well have been carried to Gorée by the 1720s via exchanges of Africans in company service, a practice regular among, for example, English castles [Lawrence 1969: 47].)

The French Caribbean, on the other hand, was first settled a century before Mauritius, and the importation of a pidgin would have had to be in the 1660s at the latest to have significant impact. This puts us at the mercy of scanty seventeenth-century documentation, which unsurprisingly has not revealed a similar shipment of Africans in company service to the Atlantic. It is hardly implausible that this was done, however, especially given its intuitive plausibility, as discussed *with regard to* English colonization in Section 4.6.

There is indeed a hint that African company servants had been sent to the Atlantic—namely, the constant warnings against doing so in directives to the trade settlements from Paris. The St. Louis staff, for example, were forbidden in 1688 "to send any Christian blacks or *gourmettes* to the Americas . . . at pain of losing their wages" (C/6/1), while a Ouidah staff member dutifully records in 1763 (C/6/27) that the castle slaves are "in no way available to be bought by particular captains, nor to be transported to the Americas, except as punishment or for a serious misdeed" [trans. mine]. Emphasis upon a given rule often signifies lax observance thereof in the past, another example being the enslavement of local Indians in Martinique despite its official prohibition (Chaudenson 1992: 29).

Furthermore, at French slave posts, slaves meant for transportation were often kept not in dungeons, but put to work at the post until shipment, which was often not until a considerable period of time later (Cultru 1910: 266–7, cited in Parkvall 1995a). These slaves could have acquired some pidgin competence before shipment, and thus would have been another source of French pidgin in the plantation colonies.

The transfer bias in FPC matches Wolof better than Bambara: Bambara has tone and does not mark relativized NP with its determiner. Since the *laptots* were Wolofs, this suggests that erstwhile *laptots* may have been transported overseas more often than castle slaves, who were mostly Bambara. This would explain, for instance, the specific warning against transporting *gourmettes* above. This is supported by the fact that it was *laptots* whom the French brought from Senegal to assist in later colonization efforts such as of Gabon (Samarin 1989: 706). Perhaps *laptots*, as movers of materiel, were seen as more useful in the arduous work of taming land and building houses than the Bambaras, who had been engaged in gentler tasks of upkeep and artisanry.

Obviously, we are dealing in a great deal of speculation here. There is nothing in the historical documents themselves which would independently lead anyone to suppose that a French pidgin had emerged at St. Louis and been transported to the Caribbean. The motivation for these speculations, however, is the *linguistic* evidence, which reveals a group of creoles too alike not to have had a common ancestor. In examining the sociohistorical record, optimally we would find positive evidence of a parent pidgin. In the absence of this, however, if there is positive *linguistic* evidence, then it will still support our hypothesis if in the historical documents we find nothing *speaking against* the existence of a parent pidgin. Thus far, we have found nothing which would disallow a parent pidgin, which leaves the power of the linguistic evidence intact. The reconstruction of what will henceforth be called Senegalese Pidgin French (SPF) is a response to *linguistic* evidence which appears to allow no other explanation.

Afrogenesis is held in distinctly faint regard by some FPC specialists. However, in their addresses of the subject, one misses a sustained engagement with the crucial comparative linguistic evidence, which appears to at least suggest a broader perspective. One pictures a paleoanthropologist opining,

> The homologies between primate and hominid skeletons seem to suggest genetic relationship, but excavations at various African sites have failed to yield a skeleton of a creature intermediate between ape and man. Therefore we conclude that there is no such genetic link, and that the similarities between a human and a chimpanzee are traceable to similarities in environment, and other factors which ought be identified by further research. Thank you.

It is my view that the linguistic evidence among the FPCs—most usefully, Haitian and Mauritian—is as striking as that between a human and chimpanzee skeleton.

5.5 EXPLORING OTHER PERSPECTIVES

5.5.1 DEFINITE ARTICLE AGGLUTINATION

The fossilized determiners on many FPC nouns are well-known (Mauritian *lavi* "life" from *la vie* [*lavi-la* "the life"], *dilo* "water" from *de l'eau* [*dilo-la* "the water"]). Baker (1984, 1987), followed by Grant (1995), found that the percentage of nouns with fossilized determiners varies considerably from one FPC to another. In addition, the same noun can have a different fossilized determiner in one creole than another; for example, *man* is *nõm* in Antillean (<*un homme*) and *zom* (<*les hommes*) in Mauritian (Grant 1995: 154).

One thing which has deflected attention from Afrogenesis for the FPCs has been a conviction that these differences in determiner fossilizations indicate separate origins for the creoles. For example, Baker, again followed by Grant (1995: 149), indeed considers Antillean the source of Haitian, but designates Louisiana Creole, Guyanais, and Mauritian independent developments.

However, this metric is not as conclusive as FPC scholars appear to assume. The data lend themselves equally well to a reconstruction under which a parent French pidgin was unstable with respect to determiner fossilizations. Of course, the determiners are completely fossilized in the modern creoles, with lexical meanings long stabilized. However, this would not have been the situation at the pidgin stage. Variation is rife in pidgins, partly conditioned by a continuum of competences in the lexifier.

SPF, spoken at a trade post like St. Louis, would have been a pidgin used by people living mostly in their native tongue, not a full language. Meanwhile, French was readily available to Africans. In this context, the determination system would quite plausibly have been variable. Thus at St. Louis, the distinction in Mauritian between *diri* "rice" (<*du riz*) and *lari* "street" (<*la rue*) would not have been established yet. Some speakers would have had enough command of French to process the determiners at least approximately; some would have varied freely between partitives and definites with little sense of their distinction; some would have fallen in between these two poles. Such a scenario is based not on mere speculation, but upon well-documented variability in other pidgins like Hiri Motu and Pidgin Fijian. Only creoles misnamed "pidgins" (cf. Section 6.4.8), like Cameroonian "Pidgin" English and Tok Pisin "Pidgin" English, obscure this fundamental aspect of pidgin varieties.

This variability would have been transported to various colonies. In each, as the pidgin developed into a Medium for Interethnic Communication and native languages receded, the fossilizations would have stabilized. Certainly chance would dictate that the choices would differ from colony to colony. However, the variation in fossilizations is not counterevidence that there was a parent pidgin.

This is because it is an unremarkable process in language change for variability in an area of grammar to be resolved differently among descendant grammars. In Old English, pluralization varied according to noun class: *stanas* "stones," *word* "words," *guman* "men," *fēt* "feet." The paradigm became unstable, and by Shakespeare's time, the *-s* and *-n* plural varied freely in many dialects (*shoes* vs. *shoen*). While *-s* won out in the standard, *-n* persisted in other regions (such as Winchester, the English capital before London). Would anyone, from a collection of such homely facts, conclude that the two English dialects share no common parent and must have arisen independently?

Yet creolists often appear to work under an assumption that the tenets of language change are somehow only loosely applicable to creoles. Specifically, much genesis work proceeds according to the "obliteration" scenario, under which creoles taken from one colony to a new one were usually "repidginized" by large influxes of learners. As I noted in Sections 3.4. and 3.5., however, this hypothesis, though intuitively plausible, does not survive close examination.

It is useful to see that there are data from creoles themselves showing that instability in a coherent, transmissible pidgin is unremarkable. In Melanesian Pidgin English, the use of adjectival marker *-fela*, predicate marker *i*, and subject referencing "resumptive" pronouns were highly variable. Each of its modern descendants, Tok Pisin, Bislama, Solomon Islands Pijin, and Torres Strait Broken, have stabilized these features differently. No one, however, would suggest that these differences meant that all four had arisen separately.

Thus there is no reason to assume that the different choices among FPCs in fossilizing determiners are evidence of separate geneses. This by no means invalidates the studies in question. To be sure, the fossilizations are useful in demonstrating particularly direct relationships, such as between Mauritian and Seselwa or between the various Antillean dialects. Furthermore, Baker has usefully traced the particularly rampant fossilizations in Mauritian to the influence of Bantu noun class markers. To claim, however, that the difference between Haitian *pye* and Mauritian *lipye* for *foot* means that the two languages have no genetic relationship is equivalent to claiming the same thing based on *shoes* and *shoen*.

5.5.2 TENSE-MOOD-ASPECT MARKERS

FPC specialists may also point out that all FPCs do not match up in their TMA grids as precisely as Haitian and Mauritian. We have already seen that some of the Caribbean FPCs have *ka* as progressive marker and *ke* as irrealis. This is attributable to Portuguese pidgin influence (Section 5.2.1), and does not suggest that the FPCs with these markers were separate creations. There are other divergences which are not attributable to language contact, however. For instance, Louisiana Creole has not *pu* alone but *gẽ pu* (*gẽ* "to have") as a marker of futurity and obligation (Neumann 1983: 227–8), and appears to lack *fek*.

However, none of this is counterevidence to a common parent. In a group of genetically related creoles, what we would *not* expect is for them all to have identical TMA grids. This is because, as noted in Section 3.5.3., in identifying genetic relationship we do not seek to demonstrate that languages are identical, because then they would not be different languages. What we would seek would be a degree of overlap between their TMA grids impossible to attribute to chance. This is what we see. The sheer choice of *était* as a past marker in all of them is alone a powerful indication of common origin. Particularly striking, moreover, is that *any* two of the FPCs happen to have preserved all of the exact same markers, despite being separate languages with separate histories. This is conclusive evidence of a common origin.

Therefore, I have not intended to idealize the evidence in highlighting the particularly close likeness between Haitian and Mauritian. I claim not that the FPCs all make the exact same etymological choices for their TMA grid—they do not—but that the overlap among the choices is too great to attribute to chance, especially when two happen to pattern *exactly* the same—even when spoken on opposite sides of the world!

The divergences in the FPC TMA grids are due simply to divergences over time. Some of this divergence would have been due simply to chance loss: Louisiana Creole may have lost *fek* just as English happened to lose its past-tense modal *durst*. Other divergences are due to differing resolutions of an earlier variation. For example, Martiniquais has *ni pou* (*ni* "to have") as well as just *pou* (Neumann 1983: 227); Louisiana simply generalized the verbal expression at the expense of *pu* alone. Similarly, Italian has both a periphrastic past (*ho comprato* "I bought" or "I have bought") and an inflectional one (*comprai* "I bought"), while spoken French has eliminated the inflectional in favor of the periphrastic (*j'ai acheté* "I bought").

5.5.3 "APPROXIMATIONS OF APPROXIMATIONS"

Among French and some French Canadian creolists, creole genesis work is dominated by the "approximation" model espoused by Chaudenson (1979, 1992), now adopted by Mufwene (1992, 1996) for the AECs. The Afro-genetic approach to the FPCs, however, puts the essence of this model into question.

Chaudenson's hypothesis, in a nutshell, is that the initial stuff of creole genesis was a koine of regional dialects of a lexifier. Early slaves, on small farms, developed a second-language, but by no means pidginized, approximation of this koine. For later slaves, imported in such large number that they had more contact with the approximation than with the lexifier natively spoken, the approximation was the model. They developed an approximation of this which, autonomized and transmitted as a norm, was a creole. This model proposes no "break" in the transmission of the lexifier, and attributes most aspects of the creole to regional dialects of the lexifier, many now extinct. Mufwene is particularly explicit that the process is little more than one of gradual transformation of a language via language contact, and considers the very term *creole* vacuous as a linguistic concept (1994b: 71).

The "approximation" model, however, is ultimately based on sociohistorical extrapolations first and linguistic data second. Problems become apparent when we attempt to actually apply a wide cross-section of creole data to the framework. This section is a summary of ideas I have discussed in more detail in McWhorter (1998a).

5.5.3.1 "LE CRÉOLE, C'EST DU FRANÇAIS, COUDON!" (WITTMAN AND FOURNIER 1983)

The foundation of the superstratist argument is that in essence, creoles are merely continuations of regional lexifier dialects. Adherents of this framework believe that the only thing making plantation creoles look "exotic" is creolists' lack of familiarity with such dialects. The tone of the paper title above—translating roughly as "It's *French*, for goodness' sake!"—reflects the tone of much of this work.

The insight is valuable in itself, checking the excesses of both universalist and substratist arguments. Indeed, one is struck by how "creole" regional English dialects like that of Cornwall once looked (Hancock 1994). However, the claim that plantation creoles are essentially just "English" or "*du français*" must ultimately be judged a distortion of the facts.

French superstratist arguments are typically made on the basis of brief sentences. It is relatively easy to argue that FPCs are "*du français*" via selected citations such as *Bouki ap pale* "Bouki is speaking" (<*Bouki est après parler*). However, this imposes a rather artificial perspective on living languages which, in actual use, are extremely difficult to conceive of as mere varieties of their lexifiers.

Chaudenson (1992: 60, 167) has accused Anglophone creolists of being underqualified to address FPC issues because of insufficient familiarity with French. Lest I be accused of same, I will demonstrate my point with a creole based upon a language in which I have a fair competence, English. Here is a simple piece of Sranan (Adamson and Smith 1995: 231).

(23) Te   den   yonkuman fu wrokope yere na tori dis,
    when the-PL young-man for workplace hear the story this

    dan den e   lafu. Dati na   wan bigiman srefisrefi.
    then they PROG laugh that COP a   big-man self-self

Basedi   srefi ben   e   lafu tu   nanga ala den   tifi
Master Eddy self   ANT PROG laugh also with   all the-PL tooth

di   blaka fu soso tabaka. Noo a ben de   na   en yuru.
REL black for only tobacco now it ANT PROG LOC his hour

Whenever the boys at work heard this, they would burst out in laughter "That's one hell of a guy." Even Master Eddy would laugh too, baring all of his teeth which were black from pure tobacco. Now it was his turn.

Clearly there are features here derivable from regional English dialects, such as *den* from *them* as plural marker. Clearly there are features predictable as "approximations" of English, such as the elimination of plural inflection, the prevalence of CVCV structure, the overgeneralized plural *tifi* from *teeth*. One could easily make an "approximationist" case for Sranan via isolated sentences like *Den go waka* "they will walk," pointing to dialectal sentences such as African-American Vernacular English *dem's de ones* and *He gon walk*.

However, other features are utterly foreign to even the most hardscrabble dialect of English, and unelicitable from even the most disadvantaged learner of English. The postposition of *dis* (<*this*) is a West African inheritance (Bruyn 1995b: 111–24). Copula *na* is derived from *that*, not any form of *to be*, and one would look in vain for any English dialect with such a usage. The use of *self* (*srefi*) as an emphatic marker is extended in Suriname creoles far beyond anything conceivable in English of any kind (Rountree and Glock 1977: 133–4): never in the history of the English language, in any glen, cabin, or thicket has the sentence "That's a bigman self-self!!" ever been uttered (much less "That, that one bigman self-self!!"). Nor has any self-respecting Englishman ever stopped a card game dead informing a friend "It's your hour."

This only scratches the surface. Note the multifunctionality of the item *hebi:*

(24) a. *A saka hebi.* "The sack is heavy."

    b. *Na wan hebi saka.* "It's a heavy sack."

    c. *Apresina e-hebi i.* "Oranges are weighing you down."

    d. *Pur a hebi dis a m tapu.* "Pull this weight off of me."

    (Voorhoeve 1964: 241)

Surely no English speaker has ever used *heavy* in this many functions. In any case, isolating instances of multifunctionality in this regional English dialect or that would miss the point: no English dialect has ever had the *degree* of lexical multifunctionality that Sranan has.

The English contribution to Sranan is obvious. However, how plausible is it, in view of the above data, that Sranan as a living system is an "approximation," or even "an approximation of an approximation," of English? Sranan is many wonderful things, but when we let the language speak for itself, it could not be clearer that this language is in no sense of the word "English."

One could make similar cases for any number of plantation creoles. In the only approximationist engagement with Sranan, Mufwene (1996: 98–9) attributes the distance of Sranan from English to the fact that English was withdrawn from Suriname so early. However, the fact remains that however early the English departed, during their sixteen years of occupation Suriname was a quintessential *société d'habitation*. Both Chaudenson and Mufwene otherwise strongly associate *sociétés d'habitation* with second-language varieties and *not* creoles. It is unclear why Mufwene stipulates that sixteen years was not long enough for a second-language variety to emerge.

Besides, other data show that even when speakers of the lexifier occupied a colony for much longer, and furthermore under *société d'habitation* conditions, a creole could emerge and stabilize which was as vastly removed from its lexifier as Sranan. São Tomense Creole Portuguese emerged amidst Portuguese-African intermarriages in the late 1400s, and survived despite over a century of such intimate black-white contact—the Portuguese did not depart until 1586 (Ferraz 1979: 17). The approximationist model would predict that this intimate contact between whites and blacks would have created a second-language Portuguese. However, São Tomense is every bit as divergent from Portuguese as Sranan is from English. Approximationists would find it very difficult to make a case for this creole as "Portuguese" in any but the most forced sense.

Thus the distance of Sranan from English cannot be ascribed to the early departure of the English, because similar results have occurred where speakers of the lexifier remained for over a century. Sranan shows that plantation conditions indeed create contact languages much too far removed from their lexifiers to be considered mere dialects or koines thereof.

5.5.3.2 NO SUCH THING AS A CREOLE?

Another plank of the approximationist model is that there is no substantial difference between creole genesis and the heavy language contact that produced languages like Yiddish and Romanian. Mufwene takes this idea as far as to claim that the term *creole* is vacuous (1991b: 74), plantation creoles being no different qualitatively than other languages having undergone heavy use as second languages and contact with typologically disparate languages. This claim is related to the increasingly common one that *creole* is a sociohistorical term but not a linguistic one (Mufwene 1989; Chaudenson 1992: 135; Corne 1995a: 121; Jennings 1995b: 63).

Like the argument that plantation creoles are simply versions of their lexifiers, this claim simply is not true. All future claims that plantation creoles are simply the result of ordinary language contact, and that therefore *creole* is not a linguistic concept, might also identify a language in the world with the following characteristics which was *not* created a few centuries ago quickly by learners adapting a dominant language as a lingua franca:

(1)   Little or no inflectional morphology

(2)   No, or only marginally, lexically or syntactically constrastive use of tone

(3)   Derivational markers whose combinations with roots are always compositional.

Indeed, Tok Pisin has its adjectival marker -*pela*, etc., but no creole has more than one or two inflectional markers. Saramaccan has a few tonally contrasted lexical pairs, but these are mere epiphenomena of its adaptation of European stress as tone; for example, *bigí* from *begin*, *bígi* from *big*. Similarly, the distinction between *á* "negative marker" and *a* "he, she, it" is a recent innovation (McWhorter 1996a). Pidgin/creoles with richer uses of lexically or syntactically contrastive tone are almost always ones in which all of the source languages were tonal and closely related, such as Sango and Kituba, and even here, tone is relatively marginal. Papiamentu makes richer use of tone than almost any creole, because of an unusually close reproduction of Spanish stress patterns as tonal, due to unusually close contact with Spanish over time. The derivational marker trait distinguishes creoles from the few regular languages with no inflection or tone in Southeast Asia or Polynesia, where derivational morphology has developed into highly idiosyncratically lexicalized items. For example, in Khmer the causative marker is *pro-*. Sometimes its use is transparent; often, however, not: *kan* "to hold" but *prokan* "to discriminate" (Ehrman

1972: 60). On the other hand, derivational morphology in creoles is semantically transparent: Tok Pisin nominalizes *isi* "slow" with nominalizer *-pasin; isipasin* means "slowness" (Mühlhäusler 1985b: 625), not "applause" or "silverware."

Differences in the degree and duration of source language contact and in degree of typological divergence between source languages prevent all creoles from conforming precisely to these three traits. However, there are no languages which do conform to these traits, or even come close, that were not recently created by a community quickly adapting a dominant non-native language as a lingua franca. There quite simply are no regular languages which combine the three traits above. Any language which has existed for millennia has either developed inflection via concatenation of earlier syntactic constructions, developed tone via a wide range of processes, or both; meanwhile derivational items have had the time to semantically evolve far beyond their original meanings. As young languages, pidgins and creoles have not yet experienced change of this depth.

Crucially, however, this kind of language arises only under work and trade conditions involving constrained interethnic communication. Languages like this do not arise elsewhere: Romanian, Yiddish, and Singapore English are both products of heavy language contact and second-language acquisition, but none combine the three above traits.

Thus attributing creoles simply to language contact, as Mufwene does in particular (1996: 107), "undergenerates" the data. Plantation creoles combine three traits which are otherwise found only in pidgins. Pidgins clearly develop via a "break" in transmission, in that a lexifier is only partially acquired. Since plantation creoles and pidgins share this core of three features found together in no regular language, this suggests that plantation creoles, too, arose via a break in transmission. I prefer to suppose that creoles emerge *as* pidgins; others may work under different frameworks. The crucial point, however, is that a break in transmission occurred.

Some might argue that "creoles" like Lingala and Kituba make extensive use of inflection and tone. I have argued elsewhere (McWhorter 1997b) that the treatment of these highly elaborated languages as pidgins or creoles renders these terms rather empty, since reduction and reinterpretation of a lexifier is diagnostic of pidgins and creoles. These languages are conventionalized second-language varieties, best termed either *koines* or *semipidgins.*

Thus the point stands: plantation creoles differ crucially from regular languages which have experienced heavy contact. Mauritian cannot be analyzed as having simply "evolved" from French as Yiddish did from German. (Space does not permit a full exposition of this issue; see McWhorter 1998b.)

5.5.3.3 APPROXIMATION VERSUS PIDGINIZATION

A defense strategy here might be to claim that even if plantation creoles do form a natural class, languages of this sort could come at the end of a series of "approximations of approximations" just as easily as from a break in transmission. However, the "approximation" model is in fact unable to plausibly generate a creole. Chaudenson's demonstrations (1992: 156–67) of how "approximation" would produce a creole are based on highly selective fragments of evidence. How the model would generate the whole of a plantation creole system is elusive.

This becomes clear when we scrupulously apply Chaudenson's model to more than isolated sentences. Chaudenson claims that the absence of inflection in creoles is traceable to regional dialects in which inflectional paradigms were much more eroded than in European standards (1992: 158–62). The point that vernacular French dialects have often reduced the number of inflections in the present tense *-er* verb paradigm, for example, to a single one is well-taken (see Table 5.3).

However, Chaudenson evades a vital point, visible in the table: FPCs did not generalize the third-person singular, but the infinitive (Haitian *pale* [pale]). Therefore, the question is in what region of France people were using only the infinitive. The only hope here would be to claim that it was the second-person plural ending, also [e], that was generalized. However, Chaudenson gives only examples of some vernacular overgeneralizations of the *first*-person plural inflection, but not second-person plural (158–9). (Indeed, the second-person plural ending is generalized only very occasionally in FPCs, such as the common *vle* [<*voulez*] "to want," or Mauritian *bate* [<*battez*] "to beat").

Elsewhere, Chaudenson convincingly compares a verbal behavior in Réunionnais to Missouri French (1992: 159). However, Réunionnais is widely agreed to be a semicreole, and the construction Chaudenson treats is absent in Mauritian. Again, Chaudenson evades identifying a regional French source for the true creole, Mauritian.

Finally, not only is there no regional source for this overgeneralization of the infinitive, but regional dialects do not seem to even offer a source for its gradual overgeneralization via "approximation." Indeed, what they of-

Table 5.3. Comparison of *-er* verb present tense paradigms

English	Standard French	Canadian French	Haitian
I talk	*je parle*	*je parle* [parl]	*m pale*
you talk	*tu parles*	*tu parles* [parl]	*ou pale*
he talks	*il parle*	*il parle* [parl]	*li pale*
we talk	*nous parlons*	*on parle* [parl]	*nu pale*
you (pl.) talk	*vous parlez*	*vous parlez* [parle]	*nu pale*
they talk	*ils parlent*	*ils parlent* [parl]	*zot pale*

fer is a source for overgeneralization of the third-person singular—but this is exactly what the FPCS did *not* do.

Another example is the postposed third-person pronoun as plural marker in FPCs. It is unrecorded, to my knowledge, that an expression such as *chat-eux* cat-them "cats" was ever current in any regional French dialect. Thus Chaudenson (1992: 174) attempts to derive this from a rather nimble rebracketing of an erstwhile resumptive pronoun:

(30) [tous zapotes la]   yo   dire
     all   priest   DET they say
     Topic   Subj Pred

     [tous zapotes la   yo] dire
     all   priest   DET PL   say
     Subj   Pred

     All the priests say . . .

Chaudenson bolsters the plausibility of a given "approximation" by linking it to common diachronic changes (159–60). In this light, we must note that Example (30) is a highly unlikely change, raising more questions than it answers. What exactly would motivate the reinterpretation of a resumptive pronoun in a VP as a plural marker in a preceding NP? Changes of this sort result from the resolution of an ambiguity. In a language where the third-person *singular* pronoun was also used resumptively, as it has been and is in Mauritian Creole, there would have been nothing ambiguous about the similar use of the *plural* pronoun *yo*. Thus what motivated speakers to rebracket it? Chaudenson would be hard-pressed to find any examples of this happening cross-linguistically, a crucial component of a diachronic argument of this kind.

These problems sit unresolved. In the meantime, however, if we simply treat Mauritian as an erstwhile pidgin, we can readily explain the things the "approximation" model cannot. For example, while "approximation" cannot explain the recruitment of infinitives in FPCs, it is unproblematic that pidginization would lead to this situation, be this via overgeneralization and/or Foreigner Talk. Note, for example, that an unequivocally pidginized French, Tây Bôi, overgeneralizes the infinitive, not the third-person singular (*Toi napas savoir monsieur aller où?* "You don't know where the man went?" [Schuchardt 1888, cited in Holm 1989: 360]).

Zero copula is similarly unproblematic. We can be sure that no French speakers of any region were omitting the copula, saying *Je ø pêcheur,* or *Moi ø pêcheur.* Thus why do FPC speakers? On the other hand, zero copula is diagnostic of pidginization (Ferguson 1971, Ferguson and Debose 1977, Foley 1988: 165). Finally, while Chaudenson's account of the *yo* pluralizer fails, such wholesale reinterpretations of lexifier material are typical of pidgins (Chinese Pidgin English used *piece* as a noun classifier; Tok Pisin uses *fellow* as an adjectival marker; etc.).

Thus there is a mass of data which Chaudenson can neither trace to regional French dialects, nor plausibly present as the end product of a series of "approximations." Even if Chaudenson could somehow squeeze these things into his model, it would obviously be a very tight squeeze, in which case he would ensnare himself in one of his own nets. Chaudenson (1992: 44) makes an elegant argument that a viable theory must have "necessity" as well as coherence, meaning that there should be obvious grounds for preferring the hypothesis over others, his negative example being the old monogenesis hypothesis.

However, the "necessity" of Chaudenson's model is now elusive. Plantation creoles are not merely extensions of regional dialects of a lexifier (Section 5.5.2.1). Plantation creoles are not merely the result of heavy language contact (Section 5.5.2.2). Plantation creoles are not generable via a series of second-language "approximations" of a lexifier (this section). Thus there is no "necessity" to choose Chaudenson's model, while treating plantation creoles as erstwhile pidgins covers all of the data in one sure stroke.

5.5.3.4 RÉUNIONNAIS AND MAURITIAN

Thus at this point, the only thing that could save this model is a concrete demonstration of its operation. Chaudenson considers that demonstration to be a proposed relationship between Réunionnais and Mauritian.

There are two perspectives on the relationship between Réunionnais, a semicreole, and Mauritian, a typical plantation creole. Baker and Corne (1982) argue that Réunionnais never diverged sharply from French because of a long *société d'habitation* period during which slaves and whites lived in relative parity, while Mauritian is the product of a break in the transmission of French, because there was no such phase on Mauritius, large numbers of slaves having been imported shortly after settlement.

Chaudenson (1979, 1992), on the other hand, supposes that originally Réunionnais was a typical basilectal creole like Mauritian and—significantly—that this basilect developed via the unbroken series of "approximations" as per his genesis model. He considers this basilectal stage to now be preserved only in Mauritius, to which it was presumably brought by settlers from Réunion. This scenario is vital to the "gradual transformation" model of FPC genesis, because it casts Réunionnais as the preserved intermediate stage between French and what is now Mauritian. Presumably, if the alleged Réunionnais basilect had survived, we would see evidence of the entire progression on one island.

However, all evidence conspires against Chaudenson's interpretation. An outside observer of the ongoing debate between Chaudenson and Baker over this issue is forced to judge Baker the victor. For one thing, Baker and Corne (1982: 242) would seem to have conclusively demonstrated that what few settlers from Réunion came to Mauritius were hopelessly unlikely to serve as language models for Africans or Malagasies, having been a small band of hunters of runaway slaves. With the supposed link between Mauritian and Réunionnais broken, Réunionnais cannot be treated as the "lost" intermediate stage between French and Mauritian.

Meanwhile, Chaudenson's linguistic demonstration that Réunionnais once had a basilectal variety is easily dismissed. The first question that arises is why, in a context Chaudenson has so assiduously documented as a long-term *société d'habitation*, would a true creole emerge in the first place? Leaving aside that question, we first note Baker's (1987: 74) point that Chaudenson bases his claim mostly upon a single early text which was penned by non-native speakers of Réunionnais. It is unsurprising that *second-language* Réunionnais might appear somewhat more inflectionally reduced, and thus more like Mauritian, than the actual language.

Most important, however, Chaudenson seriously distorts the data upon which his claim is based. He demonstrates his point not with the texts in question, but with a list of eighteen features which early Réunionnais texts share with Mauritian (Chaudenson 1981a: 28–9). The problem with this list, however, is that only one of the features could be considered an idiosyncratic correspondence with Mauritian; all of the rest are mere garden-variety simplifications typical of language reduction of all kinds. The one remotely idiosyncratic feature early Réunionnais shares with Mauritian is the negator *napa*, and this one feature *all by itself* is hardly a sufficient case for genetic relationship. Moreover, Chaudenson inflates its significance by counting it as three features, each representing its use in a different construction. More properly it should be counted simply once, as a general negator, in which case his list has fifteen, not eighteen, features.

More to the point, Chaudenson's argument is based on brief citations rather than living language. It is one thing to isolate basilectal "features" from early Réunionnais texts, but ultimately, Chaudenson's claim can stand only if he can present an early Réunionnais text which, quite simply, looks like Mauritian. When we actually examine the texts in question, however, what we see is Réunionnais. Here is a representative selection from 1828 (Chaudenson 1981b: 10):

(26) Moi dir' à vous, mont' pas trop haut,

prends gard à caus' soleil li çaud;

si vous y fait comme vout' manière

vous là gagner mauvais affaire.

I tell you, don't go up too high,

Watch out because the sun is hot;

If you go about it in your typical way,

you're going to get in trouble.

This text is so far from a Mauritian-like basilect that word-for-word glossing is unnecessary for those familiar with French. To pick basilectal "tokens" from here and there vastly misrepresents this text.

In contrast, here is a sample text of Mauritian from just the previous year, 1827 (Chaudenson 1981b: 100):

(27) Acoute zaut' mo parlé. Enne zour ça nous té   la   sasse cerf
     listen you I speak one day that we PAST DET hunt deer

     Grand-Rivière.
     Grand-Rivière

     L'her solé lévé, mo pour allé prend mon poste   au pavé;
     when sun rise I   FUT go   take my position at road

> Listen, you all, I'm talking. One day we were hunting deer at Grand-
> Rivière. When the sun came up, I was off to take my position at the
> road.

Despite obvious transcription problems, the basic cast of Mauritian Creole is here, including the grammaticalized past marker, the conventionaliza-tion of *pu* (<*pour*) as a preverbal particle, and the grammaticalized use of *l'heure* for *when*. Thus Chaudenson's claim that Réunionnais preserves the "gradual transformation" which ultimately led to Mauritian is not only sociohistorically implausible, but is based upon a misrepresentation of a distinctly nonbasilectal text.

In sum, then, plantation creoles are not varieties of their lexifiers; plan-tation creoles do constitute, with pidgins, a distinct typological class, which mere "language contact" and "transformation" do not produce; the "ap-proximation" process cannot generate actual creole grammar; Réunionnais is not a preserved intermediate stage in Chaudenson's hypothesized "ap-proximation" scenario. We are left with no motivation for preserving this genesis model.

5.5.4 SUMMARY

My hypothesis is that FPC originated as a Senegalese Pidgin French used among free and enslaved Africans, possibly on Île Bocos starting in the late 1630s, perhaps at St. Louis after 1659. In the period between 1640 and 1670, a seed population of these Africans was transported to Martinique, where their speech became a model for the small slave population, which passed this pidgin on to the burgeoning numbers of new slaves. Before this, slave speech in the two previous French Caribbean settlements, St. Kitts and Tortuga, had been L2 approximations of French.

In order to have had influence, the seed population would have to have arrived before the massive influx of sale slaves after the sugar boom in the mid-1670s. For the pidgin to have formed only at St. Louis itself after 1659 would leave a rather small, but hardly implausible, window for appreciable conventionalization. This suggests that the pidgin may have begun form-ing at the earlier Bocos settlement; however, the surviving documentation of this early phase is silent on linguistic issues.

Expanding into FPC, this new language was transported to all of the other French Caribbean colonies via slaves brought to the initial settlement of each one, and perhaps later. While surely somewhat *bouleversée* at each transplantation because of second-language acquisition and language con-tacts, the essential structure of the language remained intact everywhere.

Sociohistorical documentation, at best, *allows* that this diffusion could have taken place—but it is the linguistic evidence which makes a positive case for it.

Meanwhile, in 1729 or the early 1730s, a development of this same pidgin was transported from Senegal to Mauritius by Africans brought to assist in establishing the colony, where it became Mauritian Creole. The development of Réunionnais was largely separate; by the time Africans were sent to Réunion, the colony was long established (with Malagasy slaves). Although there was a small current of slaves transported not from Réunion to Mauritius but in the other direction (Chris Corne, p.c.), there was neither reason to send castle slaves nor any way that the speech patterns of any sent could have had influence.

5.6 THE PORTUGUESE CREOLES

The Portuguese creoles provide no support for the limited access conception for reasons much simpler than among the English- or French-based. Namely, no Portuguese creole has developed amidst the conditions of sharp demographic disproportion thought crucial to the emergence of creoles of other lexical bases.

It is uncontroversial that a Portuguese pidgin formed at the site of what is now Guinea-Bissau for use between Portuguese settlers and Africans, and that this was the precursor of the creole spoken there today. It is unclear at this point whether this creole was the precursor to Cape Verdean Portuguese creole spoken nearby westward. However, the creoles are so similar today that one must have been precursor to the other, and in this light the Euro-African *grumete* assistants on the West African coast would seem to have been particularly likely creators (Kihm 1994: 4). I have argued that English Euro-African creoles were not the creators of AEC because it is documented that they were almost never transported to the New World, and they appear to have had no significant role in plantation slave societies there. However, there is no reason to suppose that Portuguese *grumetes* were not transported to nearby Cape Verde to serve in functions similar to the ones they fulfilled on the mainland, especially since such a migration would be much less disruptive than an irreversible one across the Atlantic Ocean. In any case, even if Cape Verdean by chance developed independently, plantation agriculture was always marginal on these islands, and mainly served merely to provision passing Portuguese ships. Thus massive African workforces cannot have been the source of the pidginization, rendering Cape Verdean inapplicable to the limited access conception.

Meanwhile, all of the other Portuguese creoles were the product of marriages between Portuguese men and local women. São Tomense emerged in this way before plantation agriculture was established (Ferraz 1979: 15–6; McWhorter 1998b) and seeded its sister creoles in the Gulf of Guinea. The Asian Portuguese creoles were not born amidst plantation conditions at all, with the centrality of the marriages in the birth of the creoles thus even clearer.

5.7 THE DUTCH QUESTION

Assessment of the limited access model is not technically complete until we have addressed the fourth and last group of New World plantation creoles, the Dutch ones. However, accidents of history make it difficult to draw any conclusions from them.

Brazil was the prime effort on behalf of the Dutch to establish large-scale plantation agriculture in the New World, and after they lost their foothold there in 1654, they concentrated their colonization efforts on Asia. In the New World, they became central as slave suppliers via Curaçao and St. Eustatius, but dealt only rather marginally in the establishment of plantation colonies, contenting themselves with Suriname (exchanged with the English in 1667 for what became New York) and Guyana (effectively run by the English by the late 1700s, officially in 1814).

For this reason, there have been only three Dutch-based plantation creoles. Berbice Creole Dutch has so heavy and deep-rooted a contribution from a single West African language, Eastern Ijo, that it in fact belongs more properly not to the creole, but the intertwined language class (e.g., Anglo-romani, Michif), having emerged under sociohistorical conditions crucially distinct from those which generate pidgins and creoles (Smith, Robertson, and Williamson 1987; McWhorter 1997b). This leaves just Negerhollands and Skepi Dutch. This already small basis of comparison is further restricted by the fact that both are now extinct, and Skepi was only sketchily documented before its death.

However, thus far the Dutch creoles offer no evidence in direct support of the limited access model, and a number of things have suggested that Dutch creoles did not arise as a response to limited access to Dutch. First, Sabino (1990: 28–30) hypothesizes that Negerhollands had emerged by the late seventeenth century, at which point St. Thomas had yet to develop beyond the *société d'habitation* stage. This is even more significant if Hesseling (1905) was right in placing its birth as early as the 1670s.

Secondly, under the limited access conception we would expect Negerhollands and Skepi Dutch to differ significantly. On the contrary, Robertson (1983: 14) likens their similarity to that between the French-based creoles of the Caribbean and those of the Indian Ocean, noting that "Skepi Dutch shows such remarkable similarity to Negerhollands that whatever origin is assigned to the one may be assigned to the other" (16). While Robertson does not illustrate this, we glean idiosyncratic shared traits by comparing available materials. For example, the two creoles shared an equative copula *da* derived from the same demonstrative out of many possible (Robertson 1989: 11; Stolz 1986: 153–4).

The assessment of the plausibility of a West African Dutch pidgin source has been hindered by certain misconceptions. For example, some have supposed that the Dutch merely used Portuguese and English pidgin in West Africa (e.g., Tonkin 1971: 142). However, while the Dutch clearly used these other pidgins on various occasions, they conducted business in reduced Dutch as well. In Jones (1985: 34) we find a reduced Dutch spoken by an African king's interpreter in 1682: *König Piter mie segge, ick juw segge, König Piter segge mi, segge König Piter, Dassie hebbe, mi segge, kike Dassie* ("King Peter has told me to say to you that he would like to see your present for him"). Nor was this an isolated instance: around 1680, Barbot observed Africans using Dutch in a "broken" fashion (Goodman 1985a: 67–106). These citations do not prove in themselves that Dutch castle slaves spoke a Dutch pidgin. However, since the Dutch did not withhold their language even when interacting with Africans on a passing basis, it is likely that they would have addressed their castle slaves in Dutch.

Van Rossem (forthcoming) has brought to attention a document describing a judicial session at the Elmina castle on the Gold Coast, in which Africans speak to the Dutch through an interpreter. Van Rossem interprets this as counterevidence to Afrogenesis for the Dutch creoles. However, these are Africans from the surrounding town, not castle slaves, and thus we would not expect them to speak a Dutch pidgin.

Further research on language use at Dutch West African trade castles, and possibly on Dutch population movements within the Caribbean, may shed more light on the origin of the Dutch creoles, although one senses that much is simply lost to history. However, to reiterate, there is no evidence ruling out a West African-born Dutch parent pidgin.

5.8 CONCLUSION

Through the past four chapters, I have demonstrated that the central assumption in creole genesis studies—that plantation creoles developed in response to sharp demographic disproportion—is not supported by the evidence. Creoles failed to appear despite massive demographic disproportion between blacks and whites in South America and Mexico, even when the disproportion set in quickly. AECs and FPCs are too much alike to have possibly arisen independently, eliminating the possibility of limited access creating any of them but the first ones. Meanwhile, in both cases, the first creoles were already spoken by the 1660s, when the Caribbean was devoted to small farms worked by Africans and white indentured servants together. On such farms, access to the target would have been rich, and thus the limited access model founders yet again.

The limited access model was an eminently logical response by early creolists to the presence of creoles in so many former plantation colonies. However, we must ask whether the evidence available to us today supports this anymore. The Chocó, Maroon Spirit Language dating Sranan to the 1660s, the 1671 Martiniquais document, and mountains of other evidence presented in the previous chapters strongly suggest not.

Judging from developments in the field as I write, a common response to some of these facts will be to suppose that AECs and FPCs could indeed have arisen on small farms, amidst intimate black-white interactions. In my view, the emergence of creoles on these farms strains sociolinguistic plausibility, but it would be almost impossible to argue this in a truly conclusive fashion.

However, the issue is broader than this, and the emergence of creoles on these farms would leave an uncomfortable number of large questions open. For one, again, why did no creoles emerge on either farms or plantations or in mines in the Chocó, Ecuador, Venezuela, Peru, or Mexico? Moreover, there is the linguistic evidence specifically suggesting that AECs and FPCs were born outside of the Caribbean. What about the mysterious Kwa transfer bias in AECs? What about the bizarre similarities between Haitian and Mauritian, united only by Senegalese trade settlements?

As noted in the introduction, however, my goal in this book is not simply criticism. The inadequacy of the limited access hypothesis and the evidence for Afrogenesis together point the way to a revision of how plantation creole genesis is conceived and classified. I present this revision in the next chapter.

6 Synthesis

6.1 GEOCENTRISM AND CREOLE STUDIES

In the fifteenth century, the consensus among the educated was that the
earth was the center of the universe. This scheme "described the heavens
precisely as they looked and fitted the observations and calculations made
with the naked eye. The scheme's simplicity, symmetry, and common sense
made it seem to confirm to countless axioms of philosophy, theology, and
religion." However,

> The system did not explain the irregularities observed in the motions
> of the planets. But the layman hardly noticed these irregularities, and
> anyway they seemed adequately described by the supposed movement
> of each planet within its own special ethereal sphere. Astronomers were
> adept at explaining away what seemed only minor problems by a variety
> of complicated epicycles, deferents, equants, and eccentrics, which gave
> them a heavy vested interest in the whole scheme. The more copious
> this peripheral literature became, the more difficult it became to retreat
> to fundamentals. If the central scheme was not correct, surely so many
> learned men would not have bothered to offer their many subtle correc-
> tions. (Boorstin 1983: 295–6)

One can draw a parallel between this situation and the one in creole studies today. The limited access model indeed fits the observations of the naked
eye, in deriving creoles from plantation conditions because they were spoken on plantations. There is also a pleasing "simplicity, symmetry, and common sense" to the idea. Furthermore, its influence is supported in part because of its compatibility with reigning "theologies." For universalists, the
"dilution" aspect of the plantation model potentially generates Universal
Grammar. For many Caribbeanists, the emergence of creoles as the result

of the removal of the white target helps to depict creoles as vehicles of cultural retention.

Unfortunately, however, the parallels continue into the second part of the preceding quotation. Just as Ptolemaic astronomy failed to explain exceptions, the limited access model cannot account for Spanish America, Suriname, the 1671 Martinique text, and dozens of other issues. Just as Ptolemaics supposed that each planet moved within its own "special ethereal sphere," a growing trend in creolist thought suggests that each context be treated individually, with a wariness of overarching models.

When the problems I have outlined are addressed, it is too often via "epicycles, deferents, equants, and eccentrics." In our case, this amounts to responses such as attributing SSG to "diffusion" without specifying the mechanism, maintaining the "obliteration" scenario (Section 3.4) no matter how alike two creoles may be, and advice to leave the most recalcitrant data "on the back burner."

The last thing I want to imply is that my ideas about creole genesis are of anything even approaching the urgency and learnedness of the work of Copernicus. I cite him for the sole reason of how uniquely instructive pre-Copernican astronomy was in showing how utterly plausible an analysis can appear even when ultimately founded upon premises later profoundly revised.

I began this book with a declaration that creole studies is on the brink of a mistake. I hope to have made my grounds for this assertion clear in the previous four chapters. With all of their divergences, all creole genesis models at this writing are founded upon a central conviction that plantation creoles were created by slaves barred from full acquisition of a language by sharp disproportions of black to white. Whether this be cast as "dilution" (Bickerton), exposure to "approximations" rather than the language itself (Chaudenson, Mufwene), relexification because of distance from the target (Alleyne, Lefebvre), or the "creative" forging of a new language in the absence of regular contact with the lexifier itself (Baker), the common core is constant—plantation creoles are linked to demographic disproportion. This conviction is so deeply ingrained that it is no longer even conceived as a hypothesis. In other words, creole studies has found a paradigm.

As intuitively sensible as that paradigm appears, however, a great deal of evidence makes it extremely difficult to support. In fact, the data in the past four chapters lead me to believe that *too* much evidence speaks against the limited access conception for it to be maintained. I would like to propose a revision of creole genesis theory which will surmount the problems I have noted.

6.2 THE AFROGENESIS HYPOTHESIS:
FUNDAMENTAL OUTLINE

Of all the anomalies we have seen, the most pressing is the scarcity of Spanish-based creoles. We have rejected the traditional explanations for this in Chapter 2: *bozal* Spanish was not a creole; the reconstruction of a once widespread Spanish creole now mysteriously extinct is implausible; the *société d'habitation* explanation accounts for only a few colonies; Iberians were not kinder, gentler slavemasters. Yet, the consistency with which creoles failed to appear under the Spanish indicates that the explanation for this anomaly lies in something unique to Spanish colonization.

One such factor that set Spain apart from England, France, Portugal, and Holland in the era of the slave trade was that Spain did not have West African trade settlements. With the Treaty of Tordesillas having allotted most of the New World to Spain but reserved the West African coast for the Portuguese, the Spanish generally obtained their slaves via contract (the famous *asiento*) from various powers over the centuries—first the Portuguese, then the Dutch, and later the English.

The only presence the Spanish established on the West African coast during the foundation of New World plantation colonies was in the Canary Islands, which were granted to them as an exception to the Tordesillas arrangement. The Spanish developed sugar plantations there which thrived during the first half of the 1500s. The plantations were staffed with Berber and black African labor, and indeed a small number of Canary Islands slaves were sent across the Atlantic (Thomas 1997: 121). However, this was to the Caribbean Islands, not the mainland (ibid.). Therefore, even if we cannot treat the absence of seasoned slaves from the West African coast as a crucial difference between the Spanish Caribbean *islands* and the English or French colonies, this difference remains valid for the *mainland* colonies. Furthermore, while as we have seen, the foundation of a new colony with slaves from an older one was standard practice under the English and French, this is undocumented under the Spanish. Therefore, while Mexico, Peru, and Venezuela were indeed being established in the 1500s at the same time as the islands, there is no evidence that Mexico was established with slaves from, for example, Cuba, or Peru with slaves from the Dominican Republic. Therefore, there was no pathway via which Canary slaves could have served as models in mainland colonies.

Connected with the Canaries was a small fort on the mainland coast opposite, in present-day Mauritania at Cape Juby, where the Spanish were permitted to catch slaves (Thomas 1997: 332–3). This, however, was not a permanently occupied castle and trading station, but a base from which the Spanish conducted occasional raids. Thus there was no crew of Africans employed there on a long-term basis who could have developed a Spanish pidgin, and the fort was overrun by local Berbers in the 1520s.

Of what relation could this be to the scarcity of Spanish-based creoles? Note that we are now presented with two sets of facts:

(1)   There are plantation creoles which emerged via encounters with English, French, Dutch, and Portuguese, but none with Spanish.

(2)   There were English, French, Dutch, and Portuguese trade settlements in West Africa, but none Spanish.

Could there be any causal relationship between these sets of facts? Taken simply thus, possibly not. However, we have justification for indeed drawing a causal relationship here, because of the evidence that West African trade settlements were the birthplace of pidgins which were later disseminated to plantation colonies.

Specifically, these facts lead to a crucial question. The Caribbean and Indian Ocean plantation creoles can be argued to have been disseminated from West African trade settlements. Meanwhile, creoles are strangely absent in *just the areas colonized by the one power that had no such trade settlements, and thus no West African pidgin.* Does not the evidence suggest that West African trade settlements were *pivotal* to the pidginization of English, French, Portuguese, and Dutch, and that plantation conditions themselves were only *incidental* to the appearance of plantation creoles?

If it were any power other than Spain who lacked West African trade settlements, then such a claim would lack motivation. For example, if France had lacked such settlements, but Haitian and other FPCs still existed, then there would be no reason to question the plantation-based models. However, since the power lacking trade settlements was Spain—just the nation which governed the regions where creoles consistently failed to emerge— we are obliged to consider that the trade settlements played a central, rather than marginal, role in plantation creole genesis. More specifically, we are brought to the following hypothesis.

The pidginization which created the plantation creoles did not occur on the plantations themselves. The pidginization took place in a very different social context: interaction between Europeans and Africans working in West

African trade settlements. In these settlements, Africans needed the lexifier only as a secondary linguistic medium, for utilitarian communication with Europeans. Thus pidginization was sparked simply by limited necessity for communication. These African workers had no reason to seek the lexifier as a primary mode of communication, and thus this type of pidginization cannot be seen as an attempt to develop a new primary language frustrated by inadequate input. Moreover, since the African workers were adults, young children had nothing to do with creating the pidgins in question.

The presence of creole languages in former European colonies is the result of these pidgins having been imported, with seed populations of castle slaves, to early Caribbean colonies, where they took their place as vernaculars expressive of black identity and expanded into creoles. The creoles were distributed to subsequently settled colonies via intercolonial traffic.

The full varieties of Spanish spoken by descendants of Africans in the Caribbean and Latin America are precious evidence that plantation conditions were not the impediment to language transmission which current theory stipulates. Spanish possessions were the only ones whose reigning power had no trade settlements in which a pidgin would have developed, and thus they were the only colonies where early slaves would not have brought in a preexistent pidgin to become a creole. The importation of these pidgins into early English, French, and Dutch colonies ultimately created the synchronic illusion that plantations themselves barred the slaves from richer acquisition, an illusion betrayed by the Spanish colonies.

6.3 THE AFROGENESIS HYPOTHESIS: ELABORATION

Under the Afrogenesis Hypothesis, various aspects of creole theory would be revised, as discussed in the following sections.

6.3.1 CHANNELS OF TRANSMISSION ON THE PLANTATION

The most fundamental aspect of the Afrogenesis Hypothesis (henceforth AH) is that it entails that large plantations did not significantly impede the transmission of a European language, especially to future black generations. The Chocó, the Chota Valley, Mexico, Venezuela, and Peru all strongly suggest that the conception of plantations as language filters be abandoned. The evidence that AECs and FPCs were not even created on plantations further supports this.

This becomes easier when we realize that the plantation-as-filter idea is based simply on the deduction that plantation creoles emerged on plantations. No one analyzing plantations before the advent of creole studies ever surmised that their structure would have hindered the transmission of a language to slaves. In fact, when examined through the lens of modern sociolinguistic theory, plantation structure reveals nothing which would prevent any slave from acquiring a viable second-language variety of a European language.

The traditional schematic conception of social structure on large colonial plantations depicted hundreds of Africans attempting acquisition of a European language via occasional interactions with white supervisors. However, it is now acknowledged that plantation personnel were organized in a pyramidal hierarchy, with house slaves, black overseers, and black artisans occupying levels between the whites and the field slaves (e.g., Lalla and D'Costa 1990: 85). In such a context, transmission of a lexifier to slaves is much more easily conceivable than under the older plantation model. Yet instead, creolists have adjusted the limited access conception to this new picture, supposing that the superstrate was diluted by degrees as it was passed from one social stratum down to the other, such that the input reaching field slaves would constitute the seeds of a pidgin.

In its compartmentalization of the black community on such plantations, the "trickle-down" model neglects basic sociolinguistic theory. Shared ethnicity, and the shared condition of slavery, surely delineated plantation blacks as a speech community within the plantation, which would have constituted a prototypical network of strong ties (as described by Milroy 1980). Blacks with richer access to the local standard were a part of this network, and thus input from the standard was readily available to other members of the black community. One channel of such transmission would have been interactions with black overseers, particularly likely to have served as linguistic intermediaries between the whites who trusted them and the blacks with whom they identified (recall the black *capitanejos* in the Chocó).

Surely, second-language acquisition, and the reinforcement of vernacular norms, transformed superstrate input on various levels—only a few Africans would have obtained near-native command. However, the assumption that a field slave could have achieved only pidgin-level command of a European lexifier is refuted by the Spanish colonies. The Spanish that even isolated black Hispanophones speak today shows that slaves, especially children, had free access to a lexifier in plantation settings. Settings like the Chocó prove that plantation settings did not strip a lexifier of its inflections and transmogrify it with typologically divergent West African structures rendering it incomprehensible to whites. What the evidence suggests is that adult slaves were capable of obtaining a viable second-language register of the lexifier: the synchronic evidence is all over South America and Mexico; the diachronic evidence is the *bozal* Spanish data from Cuba.

Many creolists may find it difficult to accept that a field slave could acquire an L2 version of a lexifier rather than a pidginized version of it. Again, however, the Spanish situations force us to accept this idea: black Chocoanos do not speak a creole Spanish and never have, and the existence of the exact same situation in several other Spanish colonies makes it clear that this is not a fluke. The imposing nature of massive importation figures for a given colony as a whole must not obscure the fact that the existence of a given slave took place within the contained context of a single plantation, a rich network of daily contacts, where all members were acquainted.

It must be clear that the AH stipulates that the lexifier was available to all slaves not only during early *société d'habitation* phases but even later, during the plantation stage. Again, this claim is based not on mere speculation, but upon demonstration—in the Chocó, the Chota Valley, Mexico, Venezuela, and Peru.

While adults' acquisition capacities and motivations surely varied, plantation-born children were even better situated to acquire the local standard than their parents. White and black children were often reared together on plantations (Patterson 1967: 154; Munford 1991: 597). In Martinique, for example, Du Tertre (1667: 510) observed that plantation slave children spoke French because of this practice.

The plantation-as-filter concept was an intelligent response to the database upon which creole studies was founded in the late 1960s: roughly that treated in Hall (1966). However, it was based neither upon observation (which would have been, and remains, impossible) nor upon sociolinguistic analysis (which is now possible), but upon an induction from the fact that creoles are spoken in former plantation colonies. The new data I have presented suggests that we revise this concept in favor of one which, while speculative in its own right, can account for both the old and the new data. There is a principled explanation for why creoles are so commonly encountered in plantation colonies, which will be outlined in Section 6.3.3. However, the explanation is not that plantations generated the creoles: the data do not allow this.

Turning the issue on its head, if blacks in *all* former plantation colonies spoke local standards as they do in former Spanish colonies, would the transmission of European languages to plantation slaves strike creolists as particularly perplexing?

6.3.2 THE ROLE OF DIGLOSSIA

The AH entails that during the *société d'habitation* phases in creolophone territories, slaves had a diglossic competence between an L2 variety of the lexifier and an imported pidgin. This contrasts with the general assumption that at this stage, slaves would have spoken only L2 varieties of the lexifier. This is intended as a constructive response to the finding that Sranan, Martiniquais, Louisiana French Creole, and Palenquero were both already spoken in *sociétés d'habitation*. Indeed, Sranan and Martiniquais appear to have already stabilized distinctly non-European norms by the 1660s, and thus would have been of little use in communication with bondservants. Yet since these same Africans were working cheek-by-jowl with these bondservants, they had ample opportunity to acquire the lexifier beyond the pidgin stage.

Combined with the other evidence suggesting that AEC and FPC were born in West Africa, a plausible reconstruction is that early slaves had already developed or learned the pidgins in West Africa, and had passed them on in the new world. Acquisition of the local standard would meanwhile have been necessary for communication with whites. The intimate conditions within which blacks and whites lived in *sociétés d'habitation* would have made acquisition of the lexifier even more compelling. Obviously, however, we cannot stipulate that upon exposure to the local standard, these slaves shed the pidgin and became monodialectal in the local standard. This would leave unexplained why the creoles exist.

We thus assume that founding slaves who spoke a pidgin (i.e., non-Spanish slaves), rather than treating the West African pidgin as a mere step on the path to the local standard, would retain it as a vernacular register, encoding in-group identity. This would have been a typical demonstration of the hardiness of vernaculars, as discussed in Section 2.4.2.

When colonies passed from the *société d'habitation* phase to the plantation phase, the creole would have gradually prevailed over the local standard in the slave speech community. The Spanish colonies show that even at this point, it is mistaken to assume that the lexifier was "unavailable" to these slaves because of demographic disproportion. More plausibly, the prevalence of creole competence was due to the creole becoming established as the linguistic expression of black identity, as blacks came to interact more exclusively with one another than with whites.

Thus the question, Why would slaves have maintained a creole if the lexifier was available to them? mistakenly presupposes that the lexifier was a necessary and desired target among all plantation slaves. Language choice is inextricably connected to identity. As such, in a community where a lexifier and a creole coexisted, the lexifier was a target strictly to the extent that a slave interacted with and/or identified with whites. Clearly, identity with whites was minimal among miserable field slaves working with each other from sunrise to sunset with no prospects for advancement of any kind.

A contemporary analogue is African-American Vernacular English. Many young, inner-city blacks speak mainstream standard English only as a subsidiary, out-group variety. Yet we would think rather naive the sociologist who found this odd in view of the rich standard input such blacks get from the media. Cultural factors align the identity of such young black people with the African-American community and the dialect which expresses it. Fluent competence in standard English comes from identity with the mainstream white community, such that middle-class African-Americans *are* comfortable in standard English. The availability of a target must not be confused with its desirability, especially when we are concerned with diglossic contexts. Rickford (1986a) offers a useful discussion of this point.

However, the recruitment of a West African-born pidgin as a vehicle of black identity occurred only where a pidgin had been imported in the first place. Early Spanish slaves in the Chocó, the Chota Valley, Mexico, Venezuela, and Peru imported no such pidgin. Meanwhile, plantations themselves did not pidginize input to slaves. Thus on Spanish plantations, there were not two targets—the local standard and the creole—but just one, the local standard. Therefore, Spanish slaves simply acquired a second-language Spanish, and passed this on to subsequent generations. There was no "pidgin" pole to express black identity through, and thus no movement among slaves towards such a pole as the black community grew and coalesced. The transmission of the standard, especially to children, was relatively nondisruptive, despite massive disproportion of black to white. This is not a mere speculation, but concretely demonstrated—by the Spanish spoken today by blacks in the Spanish colonies in question.

Thus black linguistic competence in Spanish colonies (other than Cartagena and Curaçao) encompassed a narrower band of variation than the diglossic one of slaves in the early English and French Caribbean. Black identity was thus expressed via a vernacular dialect of the local Spanish, with "blackness" encoded via slight phonological variations and above all, African lexical borrowings. The result was the local standard-like competence of even geographically isolated Hispanophone blacks today.

Since Portuguese creoles emerged in so many Portuguese colonies, it is easy to fall under the misimpression that the absence of a creole in Brazil is a massive contradiction to the AH. After all, it was formerly a plantation colony relying on vast numbers of Africans working large sugar plantations, and today many descendants of these blacks live in depressed conditions rather removed from contact with whites (Holm 1987). Various arguments that a creole once existed in Brazil but has since decreolized are tantalizing, but in my view it would be extremely unlikely that such a creole would disappear entirely in as large a country as Brazil, where so many dark-skinned people live in conditions ideal for preserving vernacular dialects.

In fact, however, Brazil is nothing less than further evidence in support of the AH. Recall that my argument is as follows

(1) Where creoles are spoken in former plantation colonies, they trace back to West African trade settlement pidgins.

(2) If no West African trade settlement pidgin was brought into a colony at the outset, then slaves simply learned the dominant language.

Clearly, in Brazil the slaves simply acquired Portuguese rather than developing a creole version of it; the Helvecian variety documented by Alan Baxter (De Mello, Baxter, Holm, and Megenney 1998), despite its interesting reductions and levelings, remains in essence a dialect of Portuguese, at best lightly "semicreolized," as he describes it. We have seen that slaves on large plantations could acquire the superstrate, since slaves in Spanish colonies were at this very time doing just that. What this appears to suggest, then, is that there was no founding contingent of trade settlement slaves speaking Portuguese pidgin brought to Brazil.

At this point it must be clear that the AH by no means stipulates that any power other than Spain brought such pidgin-speaking contingents to every single one of their new colonies. The evidence strongly suggests that this was the case for most of the English and French colonies. However, we have seen that there is no motivation to stipulate that the French brought castle slaves to Réunion, for example. The absence of a creole in Brazil can be read as evidence that Brazil is another case where there was no such shipment.

It may also be that a pidgin was indeed transported, but that the unusually long-term and widespread retention of African languages by slaves in Brazil made the pidgin unnecessary as a vehicle of black identity, as Holm (1987: 414–5) notes in a related point. Portuguese would have been needed solely for communication with whites, thus leading to acquisition and use of the local standard, not a pidgin.

The most important thing about Brazil under the AH, however, is that slaves acquired a relatively full variety of Portuguese despite massive disproportion of black to white. The question Brazil leaves is whether a castle slave contingent was brought to the colony at the outset, and if so, why they had no decisive linguistic influence. This, however, leaves intact my assertions that plantations were not language filters, and that when creoles emerged in plantation colonies they were imports rather than local creations.

6.3.3 THE ROLE OF DEMOGRAPHICS

The AH entails that the plantation creoles were born as utilitarian work pidgins in West African trade settlements. In these contexts, the cause of the pidginization was not input deprivation, but simply a low degree of motivation to acquire the lexifier, similar to the birth of Chinese Pidgin English or Tok Pisin.

Not only were the plantation creoles not generated by demographic disproportion, but we have also seen that demographic disproportion has not pidginized lexifiers in any plantation context: slaves under the Spanish simply learned Spanish. The irrelevance of demographic disproportion to creole genesis is even clearer when we recall that AEC and FPC were spoken in the Caribbean long before demographic disproportion set in. It is difficult to see how these facts could be reconciled with any conception of demographic disproportion as the engine of the pidginization which created the plantation creoles. Yet the fact remains that plantation creoles are most robust where demographic disproportion was high.

The explanation for this is that high disproportion of black to white *preserved* creoles, even though it had not *created* them. Thus demographics were indeed vital in a creole's life-cycle. However, their role was not to *generate* pidginization: if it were, Chocoanos would speak a creole. On the contrary, demographic disproportion has often *nurtured* a pidgin which was brought into a territory from elsewhere, by allowing for the development of a distinct black identity which naturally preserved the communication vehicle expressing that identity.

Note, then, that it is nothing less than predictable that creoles would establish themselves most typically in contexts of sharp demographic disproportion. However, the subsequent conclusion that the demographics *created*, rather than merely *preserved*, these languages is by no means the only one available, and contexts like the Chocó show its error. Again, in the Spanish contexts, even amidst great demographic disproportion, creoles did not emerge.

As an imported pidgin was more likely to survive to the extent that blacks outnumbered whites, an imported pidgin was less likely to survive to the extent that demographic parity obtained. Therefore, in contexts which never made the transition from the *société d'habitation* phase to the plantation stage, the black speech community was neither as large nor as discrete as it was on larger plantations. Interracial interactions would have been higher and richer, and the result would have been that pidgin competence would have eroded over time. This would have determined the fate of, for example, the Bajan creole spoken by many early slaves brought to South Carolina. In the Sea Islands, the development of large plantations and all-black work forces preserved the creole, which became Gullah. Elsewhere, where plantations were smaller and interracial interactions richer, the creole itself was not preserved, instead serving as one element in the mix which created African-American Vernacular English.

In other contexts, while plantation conditions first nurtured the creole, subsequent developments eroded it. For example, conclusive evidence shows that a typical mesolectal AEC was widely spoken in Barbados when it was a slave society (Rickford 1992; Rickford and Handler 1994). Yet today, this is largely confined to rural elderly people. The marginalization of Bajan is clearly due to the notoriously metropolitanized sociological terrain of that island, where black-white interaction has long been high, and blacks customarily identify strongly (if not completely) with English mores and speech styles.

Conversely, in a society like Haiti, where French speakers were ousted early in the colony's history, conditions have been perfect for the preservation of a basilectal creole. A related, but different, situation exists in Suriname, where Sranan has survived because the superstrate language is one it was not based on, Dutch. This discourages the dilution of Sranan, despite the highly bicultural orientation of urban Surinamese today. Given that Dutch nevertheless exerts a powerful lexical, and sometimes even structural, influence on Sranan (Healy 1993), we can surmise that if English were spoken in Suriname, Sranan would have developed into a "mesolectal" register closer to English, while its offshoot Ndjuka, spoken by maroon groups in the bush, would preserve the original language.

The crucial insight here is the following. Seeing on one hand lightly restructured varieties like African-American Vernacular English (AAVE) on small farms, and on the other hand true creoles like Mauritian on plantations, creolists have concluded that a lexifier was more deeply restructured according to how vastly blacks outnumbered whites. This is a thoroughly sensible interpretation of the data. However, it is not the only one, and runs into severe problems in the early Caribbean and in Spanish America. Under the AH, the same data are interpreted as evidence that an imported pidgin was nurtured by demographic disproportion, but was brought closer to the lexifier on smaller farms where interracial interaction was richer. This interpretation can account not only for dichotomies like AAVE and Mauritian, but also for dichotomies in the early Caribbean and Spanish America. This gives the AH more explanatory power than the limited access conception.

6.3.4 MOTIVATION IN PLACE OF DEMOGRAPHICS

The AH rejects any conception of a creole "beginning to appear" as slaves began to outnumber whites. In Suriname and Martinique, when slave numbers began to rise, a creole language had already existed for years. The emerging disparity in demographics did not create these languages.

What determined whether a lexifier was pidginized was degree of motivation to acquire the lexifier. In interethnic contexts where learner motivation is high, the result is, while usually not full transmission of the lexifier, a second-language register with viable inflectional morphology and relatively little L1 transfer. Taken alone, colonies like Suriname and Martinique might suggest that low ratios of learners to speakers would act as a brake on this. However, Spanish contexts like the Chocó, the Chota Valley, Mexico, Venezuela, and Peru suggest otherwise. Some might prefer to suppose the limited access model was somehow blocked in Spanish colonies but is still valid for the others. However, this must be seen in light of the other evidence, which has long suggested that the AECs and FPCs were not born in plantation colonies at all.

In a plantation context, for better or for worse, the language of universal communication and influence was the local standard. This led all slaves to a fundamental orientation towards acquiring competence in this language. To be sure, plantation slaves retained a degree of positive black identity. The retention of native languages for ritual purposes in many former colonies is a striking demonstration. However, black identity also shared space with a value placed upon the European, with African identity perceived as primitive (a typical example of the effects of what Bourdieu 1982 designates "symbolic domination"). The fierce retention of African identity by exceptionally resistant groups, such as maroons and rebels, were extremes. They were situated within a context where resigned acceptance of oppressive conditions was sadly, but understandably, prevalent.

Thus while hardly denying the pervasive African influences upon New World black identity, the fact remains that the subordinated psychology includes a tendency to internalize the values of the oppressor. We see this, for example, in the pejorative view within which recently arrived ("salt water") Africans were held by local-born blacks (e.g., Patterson 1967: 146). This bicultural orientation would have conditioned an investment in acquiring the local standard. A trenchant illustration of the effects of colonialism upon sociolinguistic orientation is offered by a Sango-speaking Central African, who wanted to learn French because "when you don't know the French language, you aren't a human being" (Samarin 1986).

Plantation-born blacks, in particular, had even less African social orientation than their parents. We note the watchcry among Barbadian slaves "Me Bajan!" (Pinckard 1806: 133), displaying a primary identification not with Africa but with the bicultural context within which they were born. Similar is the dismissive attitude of a former American slave describing his grandmother's African competence: "My granny could never speak good like I can . . . I can't talk no African" (Wood 1974: 168). Thus plantation children had a natural integrative, rather than segregative, orientation towards the local standard (in the terms of Meisel 1983).

On the other hand, in interethnic contexts where motivation to acquire the lexifier was low, the result was a pidginized variety. Again, this was the case whatever the demographic ratios. This is shown in hundreds of contexts giving rise to pidgins around the world. As we have seen, the AECs and the FPCs seem to have originally emerged under just such conditions, in West African trade settlements. Only the transportation of these pidgins to the New World leads to the illusion that plantation conditions created them.

In the New World, these pidgins became the main target of most plantation slaves, with the lexifier itself receding in importance. As noted, on Spanish plantations where there was no such pidgin; slaves were oriented instead towards acquiring Spanish itself. Slaves elsewhere can be assumed to have had a similar orientation towards the lexifier—but to have expressed it differently, because the lexifier was represented by a wider band of variation than on Spanish plantations; thus, *their acquisition of the creole was a form of acquiring the lexifier.* As is well known, the distinction between lexifier and creole is often fluid in the minds of creolophone speakers, such that the creole is seen as a form of the lexifier, not a second language. One need note, for example, only that Jamaicans are often insulted to be told that their patois is something other than "English."

Sociohistorical evidence (Lalla and D'Costa 1990: 79–92) also suggests that creolophone slaves controlled a range of registers, of which the basilectal creole was merely the pole furthest from English. Contemporary observers would naturally be most inclined to remark upon the creole end of this competence, even after having conversed with the same slaves in something closer to English. Slaves described as speaking "creole" are likely to have had wider competences, just as most creolophone Caribbeans do today. Even the 1671 Martinique document, comprising samples of the speech of three slaves, supports this: one speaker uses a clear FPC variety, but the other two speak something closer to French.

The speakers of Palenquero, of the maroon community El Palenque in Colombia, neatly demonstrate how slaves could identify with the lexifier via using a pidgin or creole based on it. As we saw in Section 2.3.2, the ancestors of the Palenques brought a Portuguese pidgin from Africa. They are documented as speaking Spanish by the 1700s when they were already maroons (Bickerton and Escalante 1970: 255), and since they could not have acquired Spanish in isolation, they must have learned it in contact with Spaniards. Theoretically, since they could have used Spanish with outsiders, they could have retained Portuguese pidgin as an in-group language. Instead, however, they retained the pidgin but only after relexifying it with Spanish. Thus they maintained a vehicle of black identity, but only within a fundamental allegiance to "Spanish."

The crucial insight, though, is that plantation conditions themselves would not have created Jamaican patois or Haitian Creole. Once established on the plantations, the West African pidgin varieties took their place within a sociolinguistic spectrum perceived as a range of varieties of the lexifier. However, the Spanish American evidence suggests that if such pidgins had not been imported with the founding slaves, new slaves would simply have learned the local standard itself. This would explain why blacks in the Chocó, the Chota Valley, Mexico, Venezuela, and Peru speak Spanish, not creoles.

Table 6.1. Motivation versus demographic disproportion

	Demographic Parity	Moderate Disparity	High Disparity
Low Motivation led to Pidgins and Creoles *regardless of ratios*	TÂY BÔI PIDGIN FRENCH: spoken by Vietnamese servants to French employers	SRANAN CREOLE ENGLISH: formed within roughly 1:2 ratios at Cormantin	NUBI CREOLE ARABIC: formed by 90% non-Arabic-speaking Sudanese army (Owens 1985)
High Motivation led to Second Language Registers *regardless of ratios*	BAJAN ENGLISH: developed in a colony where whites and blacks existed in relatively equal numbers	RÉUNIONNAIS FRENCH (1700s acrolect): semicreole born on small *sociétés d'habitation*	CHOCÓ SPANISH: developed among African mine gangs of as much as 500

The flaw in treating demographic disproportion as pivotal to plantation creole genesis is illustrated by Table 6.1, where we see that whether demographic disproportion is low, medium, or high, either a pidgin/creole or a full L2 can develop, with motivation the decisive factor.

6.4 THE AFROGENESIS HYPOTHESIS: PROBLEMS BECOME PREDICTIONS

I have observed that the limited access conception, though logical, is but a guess. I must emphasize that the AH is a guess as well. The fragmentary nature of the sociohistorical evidence could never, by itself, confirm any account of how plantation creoles of the New World and the Indian Ocean emerged. However, the AH is a better guess than the limited access hypothesis because, and only because, the AH accounts for the composition and distribution of the plantation creoles more thoroughly. Under the AH, myriad questions which the limited access model is incapable of answering become simple predictions.

6.4.1 THE KWA TRANSFER BIAS IN AECs

As was noted in Section 4.7.1, while slaves were brought to English colonies speaking an array of West African languages, the AECs have a clear stamp from one small group, the Kwa languages, and *no* discernible structural influence from *any* of the others. As we have seen, the data do not support Mufwene's proposal (1991a) that Kwa features were favored because of being maximally unmarked within the given mixture of languages.

Furthermore, the argument that Kwa languages, even if not a majority, were at least "consistently" present (LePage and DeCamp 1960: 75; Mufwene 1992) is circular, because other language groups were also represented consistently and often in larger numbers.

Limited access models show no signs of solving this puzzle. In locating the emergence of a creole among the sale slaves on the plantations themselves, all such models will run up eternally against this problem. Under the AH, the Kwa bias in AEC is merely predicted. LGPE can be assumed to have been, effectively, an Akan Pidgin English, whose Akan stamp was transported to the New World and retained in all AEC varieties.

6.4.2 THE ABSENCE OF SPANISH CREOLES

Under the limited access model, the absence of Spanish-based creoles is so peculiar that even undergraduates in pidgins and creoles classes often remark upon it before it has been pointed out. As we have seen, none of the attempts to answer this question effectively account for this massive anomaly.

Under the AH, the scarcity of Spanish-based creoles is another prediction. The scarcity of Spanish creoles is due to the Spanish having established no West African trade settlements from which a castle slave pidgin Spanish could have been exported. The powers under which plantation creoles *did* develop all had such settlements; the power under which plantation creoles did *not* develop had no such settlements. The connection between these two points would leap out at any layman presented with them. This is bolstered further by the fact that a coastal African Portuguese pidgin is documented to have played a significant role in the genesis context of *both* of the Spanish-based New World creoles: Guene in the case of Papiamentu, Cartagena slaves' comments about "the language of São Tomé" in the case of Palenquero.

6.4.3 CREOLES WHERE THEY SHOULDN'T BE

The existence of Sranan on small farms in Suriname by the 1660s, and the text which shows that Martiniquais existed on small farms at the same time, are severely damaging to limited access models.

Sranan and Martiniquais are by no means the only creoles which can be shown to have existed long before the limited access model would predict them. Klingler (1992: 56–7) and Speedy (1995: 102) are confronted with the appearance of Louisiana Creole in texts in the mid-1700s, when even the few large farms in existence had only twenty slaves, most slaveholders having only one or two: in other words, a classic *société d'habitation*. Klingler (1992: 56–7) proposes that a creole would have formed even among only twenty slaves. But how plausible is this if none formed among gangs of five hundred slaves in the Chocó, or three hundred in the Chota Valley? In any case, to accept this entails rejecting Chaudenson's (1979, 1992) and Baker and Corne's (1982) derivation of Réunionnais from small farm demographics, as well as Mufwene's (1992: 161) attribution of the absence of Gullah in most of the Deep South to the same cause. Thus to accept Klingler's account begs the Spanish question; to accept the traditional account begs the Suriname/Martinique question; to accept both of these accounts is to abandon theory.

Speedy (1995: 102) attributes the creole to the early termination of slave importation in Louisiana, in 1731. She proposes that at this point slaves would have not yet have developed an interethnic communication medium, and that this forced the first generation of slave children to build one anew. However, is this argument intended as an alternative to the general assumption that slaves would have acquired L2 registers on small farms? In depicting children as cobbling together a language from fragmentary input, this argument recalls Bickerton's earlier formulations of the Language Bioprogram Hypothesis, but even he has since conceded that creoles would not have formed on *sociétés d'habitation* (1983: 9). Again, why would slaves have been incapable of acquiring L2 French on small Louisiana farms when slaves acquired Spanish in gargantuan mining gangs? Here as well, then, to accept Speedy's account begs the Spanish question, to accept the traditional one begs the Suriname/Martinique question, and to accept both is not constructive. Clearly, the limited access model has forced these two scholars into an uncomfortable corner.

Under the AH, the existence of Sranan in the 1660s is simply predictable—indeed, the discovery of a Sranan document from even 1652 would be predictable, because Sranan is assumed to have been imported at the establishment of the colony. The existence of Martiniquais in 1671 and Louisiana Creole in the 1740s are similarly unproblematic. If just one creole appeared earlier in the record than we assumed, we might be able to reject it as a fluke. When we have several such cases, however, it behooves us to revise our theory.

6.4.4 THE ABSENCE OF KWA TRANSFER IN CARIBBEAN FPCs

It has been generally assumed in creole studies that Kwa languages were as important in the Haitian Creole substrate as in that of AEC (Baudet 1981), with Lefebvre (e.g., 1993) even famously arguing that Haitian is an out-right relexification of Fongbe specifically. However, Muysken (1994) points out that compared to Saramaccan, Haitian is significantly less reflective of Kwa patterns than might be expected. He notes the absence in Haitian of Kwa features such as reduplication to form participles and adjectives, post-posed nominals to encode spatial relations, or ideophones, all present in Saramaccan and other Suriname creoles.

Muysken presents this anomaly as an open question. The AH answers it: Haitian and the other FPCs were created by Wolof speakers in Senegal, not Kwa speakers on the Lower Guinea coast. Kwa influence on Haitian would have come during the "second pass" of substrate transfer, via the many Fongbe and Ewe-speaking sale slaves brought there. However, we would not expect Haitian or any FPC to have as extensive an impact from Kwa as the AECs do, since only the AECs retain the heritage of their origin in a Kwa-speaking region.

6.4.5 CORRESPONDENCES WITHIN AEC AND WITHIN FPC

As we have seen, the limited access model would lead us to expect that the AECs would be much less similar than they are. This would be partly due to differences in source language mixture. Equally important would be the crucial contribution of chance in creole genesis (an extremely important point; the reader is asked to review Sections 3.3.8 and 5.2.6 if recollection of the argument has faded). The same assessment applies to the FPCs.

In other words, the tenets of historical linguistics clearly classify the AECs as sisters, and the FPCs as sisters. Yet because of the limited access hypothesis, this basic fact must be soft-pedaled or outright denied, in favor of compensatory appeals to concepts like diffusion, which do not survive scrutiny.

The AH unravels this knot. The AECs are so much alike because they are descended from a single ancestor, Lower Guinea Coast Pidgin English. The FPCs are so similar because they, too, are descended from a single ancestor, Senegalese Pidgin French.

6.4.6 THE UNIFORMITY OF CREOLES

One question which creolists have rarely addressed is how, if a plantation creole really developed from interactions on single plantations, any creole is the single, coherent language that it is today. According to the plantation-based genesis scenario, we would expect *a different creole to have emerged on each plantation*. This should be especially clear given the role of chance in creole genesis, as discussed in Sections 3.3.8 and 5.2.6. Yet while creoles clearly have dialects (Haitian's North, Central, and Southern; Saramaccan's Upper River and Lower River; etc.), these dialects are certainly no more divergent than dialects of regular languages, if not usually much less.

Creolists have acknowledged this issue only in passing. Speedy (1995: 103) supposes that during slavery, interactions between slaves from different plantations would have leveled out the differences between each plantation's creole. However, it is unclear why such interactions would alter a slave's speech beyond the level of lexical items. A lifetime's interaction with speakers of other dialects, even warm intimates, can have no discernible effect upon the structure of one's language. According to Speedy's hypothesis, interactions between speakers of Scandinavian varieties or Czech and Slovak should long ago have reduced the dialects to a single variety.

Bickerton (1986: 232, 1988b: 303–4), on the other hand, speculates that the dialect leveling would have occurred after emancipation, when more permanent population mixtures could have led to such leveling. However, historical records refute the hypothesis that creoles differed considerably from plantation to plantation at all, thereby also rendering Speedy's hypothesis further unlikely. Records of creoles like Sranan and Negerhollands before emancipation reveal a single creole spoken across a colony, and furthermore, it is always clearly the creole spoken today.

As we have seen in Sections 3.3.8 and 5.2.6, for the limited access hypothesis to be correct, we would expect starkly different creoles to have emerged on each plantation, and for such differences to be regularly evident in historical citations. Under the AH, the uniformity of each creole is due to one system having been imported into the colony and transmitted.

6.4.7 THE RELEXIFICATION QUESTION

Lefebvre (e.g., 1986, 1993) argues that Haitian Creole was born via the relexification, morpheme by morpheme, of Fongbe, rather than developing from an erstwhile pidgin of any kind. Bickerton (1988c, 1990) has criticized this hypothesis on the basis that Fongbe speakers were by no means the only ones present in Haiti, and by his calculations were in fact a distinct minority. Later archival work has shown that Fongbe speakers were indeed a significant presence in early Haiti (Singler 1993), but the fact remains that speakers of Mande languages were viably represented as well. Lefebvre and Lumsden (1994) have recently addressed this via a slight revision, claiming that speakers relexified whichever West African language they spoke, and that subsequent dialect leveling created Haitian Creole.

One suspects that the debate over the Relexification Hypothesis will simply stagnate at this point. Lefebvre has indeed identified a number of correspondences between Haitian and Fongbe in her work. Nevertheless, there are many prominent, transferable Fongbe features absent in Haitian, and unlike classic cases of relexification like Media Lengua (Muysken 1981), Haitian does not retain morphological markers from Fongbe. The dialect leveling explanation technically can be used to account for both of these problems, but it also leaves the Relexification Hypothesis unfalsifiable. While, strictly speaking, it *could* be valid, as constructed, there is no way to test for this. It can be neither proven nor disproven.

The AH allows us to decide on this issue. Contrary to Lefebvre's hypothesis that Haitian had no pidgin stage, the AH entails that a French-based pidgin was brought to the Caribbean and became a target for slaves. In this situation, there was no need for slaves to simply relexify their native languages. The advantage of the AH is that the data allow no other explanation than this pidgin, because the FPCs reveal a common ancestor. On the other hand, the Relexification Hypothesis depends simply on the correspondences between Haitian and Fongbe, for which relexification is only one of many explanations. Substrate languages have had the same influence as Fongbe on Haitian in a great many pidgins and creoles where we are quite sure that pidginization, and not relexification, occurred (Tok Pisin, Chinese Pidgin Russian, etc.).

Besides, as we have seen, Haitian Creole, with no Fongbe morphological markers and missing many central Fongbe features, would actually be a rather unusual case of relexification compared to others. The AH explains why Haitian is unlike the definite cases of relexification: it was not created via relexification.

6.4.8 EXPANDED PIDGIN VERSUS CREOLE

In the early days, as in the work of Hall (1966), a creole was seen simply as an expansion of a pidgin: some pidgins stayed pidgins forever, like Chinese Pidgin English, while in other situations, such as plantations, a pidgin became a primary community language and thus expanded into a creole. Later developments in creole studies have taken us further from this basic formulation each year. Bickerton (1981, 1984a) sharply defines plantation creoles as the results of an eldritch circumstance in which children were exposed to nothing but a halting interlanguage spoken by their parents. This sets plantation creoles distinctly apart from the conditions producing pidgins, such as trade between English and Chinese adults at Canton. Thomason and Kaufman (1988) enshrine this classification: "pidgins" are treated in one chapter, but plantation creoles are treated in another as a distinct phenomenon called "abrupt creolization," entailing child acquisition amidst unusually limited input.

Meanwhile, Chaudenson (1979, 1992) treats plantation creoles as mere gradual evolutions from their lexifiers, mediated by some "approximation"; pidgins are considered a separate phenomenon. Mufwene, following Chaudenson, considers plantation creoles such unremarkable instances of language contact that he suggests eliminating the term *creole* completely (1994b: 71).

Alleyne (1980b: 2–3) remarked that there is no empirical evidence that plantation creoles developed from pidgins, and proposed a genesis account suggesting that creoles were, broadly speaking, relexifications of West African languages. Lefebvre's (e.g., 1993) model proposes relexification more specifically, and explicitly rules out that Haitian Creole was preceded by a pidgin (1993: 256).

An unfortunate result of these developments is a terminological problem. The term "creole" has for most creolists become a shorthand for "plantation creole," and thus most contact languages not born on plantations are simply called "pidgins." This distinction has lost any linguistic foundation, such that even natively spoken contact languages with all of the resources of a full language, like the West African "Pidgin" Englishes and the Melanesian ones, are referred to as "pidgins" even by trained creolists. The only concession made to the richness of these languages is the term "expanded pidgin." A question rarely asked, however, is what distinguishes an expanded pidgin from a creole.

From the terms themselves, one would expect that Tok Pisin, an "expanded pidgin," and Ndjuka, a "creole," would exhibit some qualitative difference in degree of structural expansion. However, they do not: anyone comparing comprehensive grammars of these two languages (Verhaar 1995; Huttar and Huttar 1995) would be hard pressed to see why they are categorized as two different classes of language. This is even clearer when comparing one of the New World AECs with one of the English-based "pidgins" of West Africa, in which case this terminological distinction has been imposed upon daughters of the same parent language. Comparing Huttar and Huttar's Ndjuka grammar with Faraclas's (1996) grammar of Nigerian "Pidgin" English, both published by the same house and organized according to the same outline, it becomes obvious that the term "expanded pidgin" is linguistically meaningless. Pointedly, it has been a Pacific creole scholar, separated from the plantation creole/limited access tradition, who has suggested that Melanesian Pidgin English be called Bislamic Creole (Goulden 1990).

This issue has implications far beyond creole studies. Beginning my first teaching job, I read a paper a graduate student had written before my arrival comparing phonology in pidgins versus creoles. Without a creolist to guide her, she had treated languages like Cameroonian "Pidgin" English in the same class with Chinook Jargon, grappling with the curious lack of qualitative difference between the "pidgin" phonology of Cameroonian and the "creole" phonology of Jamaican Creole. Todd (1984), a uniquely accessible work, presents Tok Pisin and Cameroonian to the public as "pidgins" despite the structural richness apparent on every page. Furthermore, referring to languages like Nigerian "Pidgin" English as "pidgins" helps maintain their perception as inferior by both speakers and observers; the term "creole" has a more legitimate connotation.

Creolists presumably suppose that the absence of any qualitative difference between "expanded pidgins" and creoles is simply a matter of different paths to the same mountaintop. However, the absence of qualitative difference also suggests that there may have been only one path to the mountaintop.

The AH presents a way of constructively addressing this. The sectioning off of the plantation creoles into their own category results from frameworks treating plantations as uniquely disruptive to language acquisition. We have seen that this conception is extremely problematic. On the other hand, under the AH, plantation creoles *are* descended from pidgins, born in West Africa. Thus, the lack of any qualitative distinction between "expanded pidgin" and creole is neatly explained, or, more properly, needs no explanation: there is no difference between them. Creoles *are* expanded pidgins. Expanded pidgins *are* creoles. Ndjuka and Nigerian Pidgin English are products of the same process: the pidginization of English followed by its reconstitution as a creole. There is no more justification for calling Tok Pisin an "expanded pidgin" than there would be for calling Lassie a "matured puppy."

6.5 THE AFROGENESIS HYPOTHESIS: CHANGING THE LENS

The AH transforms eight significant problems in creole studies into predictions. No variation on the limited access model can address even a single one of these issues. More to the point, the limited access model makes precisely the wrong predictions for creole data. Under the limited access conception, the following would hold:

(1) There would exist AECs with identifiable structural transfer from West Atlantic, Mande, and Bantu languages as well as Kwa.

(2) There would be Spanish creoles in the Chocó, Ecuador, Mexico, Venezuela, and Peru.

(3) Neither Maroon Spirit Language nor Saramaccan would specifically resemble Sranan, and no document in FPC would exist until past 1700.

(4) Some FPCs, especially Haitian, would have postposed nominals as adpositions, heavy serialization, and other Kwa features.

(5) The AECs would constitute a smorgasbord of distinct creoles, differing as widely as Sranan and Tok Pisin, some even relexifications of Twi or Kikongo; the FPCs would pattern similarly.

(6) There would be evidence in historical records of a different creole spoken on each plantation, and mutually unintelligible dialects persisting in some places, such as Haiti.

(7) French Guyanais, with its heavy Gbe substrate, would be a Gbe relexification, and Negerhollands an Akan relexification.

(8) Plantation creoles would constitute a perceptibly different language class than pidgins like Tok Pisin and Fanakalo.

Clearly, however, none of these eight things are true, but the limited access conception predicts them. Furthermore, there are *no questions which limited access models can answer that the AH cannot.* Since a hypothesis is evaluated according to its explanatory power, the AH is clearly preferable.

This is not true if the AH is founded upon invalid conclusions. However, I have hoped to show that many of the most plausible objections to Afrogenetic creole genesis theories are not as grave as often thought. The basic idea of a West African pidgin crossing the Atlantic and taking hold among slaves is problematic for many—but the Palenquero and Papiamentu cases empirically demonstrate that this happened (Section 4.10.3). Many are troubled by the idea of a small number of linguistic models having widespread effect—but the births of Bislamic Creole and Hiri Motu show how powerful a few models can be (Section 4.10.3). Others point to the lack of citations of LGPE or SPF. Yet while citations may be unearthed someday, the nature of the sociohistorical record is such that in this case, negative evidence is not counterevidence—unless Louis Leakey's life work has been worthless (Section 4.10.4).

The AH requires viewing the creole data through a new lens, through which eternal puzzles under the limited access model become mere predictions. Again, the AH cannot hold a candle to the significance of the Copernican revolution. However, the analogy is apt: Copernicus's heliocentric model required an analogous adjustment in perspective.

Certainly, the limited access model "looks" correct, just as geocentrism "described the heavens precisely as they looked and fitted the observations and calculations made with the naked eye," just as the earth looks flat, just as frog legs taste like chicken. To anyone standing in a field, geocentrism *still* "looks" correct. However, just as geocentrism proved incorrect when applied to a wide range of data, only supportable via "epicycles, deferents, equants, and eccentrics," limited access is incorrect, making all of the wrong predictions and only supportable via *ad hoc* adjustments.

Along the same lines, to be sure, the AH depends upon West African trade pidgins whose existence can be only deduced. Similarly, Kepler's and Galileo's expansions upon heliocentrism depended upon a postulation of "magnetic forces" in the heavens which at the time could be only deduced; only later did Newton and Einstein illuminate this as gravity. Continental drift must be deduced. The missing link must be deduced. And via the following points, the pivotal role of West African trade pidgins can be deduced:

(1) The earliest AECs (including the deepest, Sranan) appeared long before blacks outnumbered whites on English Caribbean plantations; meanwhile, a pidgin would easily have formed at the Cormantin trade settlement, which also regularly exported castle slaves to new colonies.

(2) The AECs all share a Kwa transfer bias which does not match substrate compositions in the colonies. At the Cormantin trade settlement, castle slaves would have spoken a Kwa language.

(3) Haitian and Mauritian French creole are too alike not to have a common ancestor, and their only sociohistorical intersection could have been via slaves in Senegalese trade settlements.

(4) Curaçao folklore traces Papiamentu to "Guene," descended from a pidgin or pidgins which arose as West African trade settlement pidgins.

(5) Spanish was never transformed into a creole in the New World, and the Spanish were also the only power lacking West African trade settlements.

6.6 THE CASE-BY-CASE ARGUMENT

In Section 2.7, I noted a growing tendency in creole studies to emphasize local sociohistorical research over broader theoretical claims. An example of the line of thought in question is Corne (1995b: 26–7):

> No assumptions about the nature of a creole emerging from its forma-
> tive period are safe in the absence of detailed study of the settlement
> history. As new creations, creole languages are sensitive to a wide
> range of factors, and cannot be understood without reference to them.
> By definition, the creativist position sees each act of creole genesis,
> i.e., vernacularization, as a unique event, and attempts to account for
> the linguistic result in terms of the particular society's social history.

This is welcome in itself, and discourages a natural tendency to impulsively construct grand theories upon a mere few shreds of evidence, neglecting crucial details that suggest a different picture.

Ironically, however, this eminently wise approach can also sometimes hinder us from engagement with larger messages that creole data world-wide might be telling us. Although Corne in no way intended this, the above quotation could be wielded to imply that creole studies will be properly conducted via methodically collecting complete data sets on each pidgin and creole, and theorizing later ("facts first, theory second"). Presumably, however, all creolists know that science does not proceed with a full data set. After a certain amount of data has been collected, a theory is proposed which presumably will predict the behavior of uncollected data and obviate the need to examine the entire corpus thereof. Astrophysics, for example, has not reached its current point via examining the movements of every star in the heavens. Yet there is a current in creolist thought (of which, it should be said, the late Corne was not a part) which casts all attempts at unified theories as "overambitious" and "hasty."

Yet the scientific method shows us that a unified theory of plantation creole genesis is not inappropriate simply because it is proposed before we have comprehensive data on all, or even most, contact languages. On the contrary, we should not only expect, but *require,* that hypothesizing begin long before that point. A hypothesis need respond only to a patterning in the data which suggests one. The limited access conception was developed in response to just such a patterning: the presence of creoles in so many former plantation colonies. The AH has been developed in response to a larger-scale pattern which has become obvious over the past three decades of further data collection—among other things, the absence of Spanish creoles and the uncanny similarities between AECs or FPCs. These factors suggest that forces were at work beyond idiosyncratic, unconnected language encounters in each colony.

The case-by-case approach would be a valid counterargument against the AH only if we saw no such patterns. In other words, there would be, perhaps, a Spanish creole in the Chocó and the Chota Valley, but perhaps not in Venezuela or Mexico; perhaps some AECs would trace to a West African ancestor, but others would look like independent encounters with English, and so on. But instead, we see patterns of distribution and composition which suggest that the AH is correct.

Thus creole studies will certainly depend crucially upon good field work and diligent sociohistorical research. However, the conclusion that creole studies will depend *solely* upon this condemns the field to butterfly collecting. Again, the AH pales hopelessly before heliocentrism, but solely for the usefulness of the analogy, there were scientists who dismissed Copernicus by claiming that each star had its own story, dwelling "within its own special ethereal sphere." We do not read those scientists today, because the aesthetic appeal of the "special ethereal sphere" idea misled them into reading this as a verity rather than as one of many possible alternatives. They missed the central point that general patterns in planetary and stellar movements revealed a mechanism which could explain the movements of all celestial bodies.

6.7 THE REALITY OF THE PARADIGM

A final possible objection to the AH might be for a creolist to claim that they do not subscribe to any "limited access model." As noted in the introduction, I am not claiming that limited access is the total of any creole genesis model. The models display a dazzling array of differing approaches to creole genesis: Bickerton (1981), Chaudenson (1992), and Lefebvre (1993) might as well have been written in different universes. However, I most firmly assert that limited access is pivotal to all of them. Very few working creolists could claim to consider disproportion of black to white unimportant to the emergence of plantation creoles. Examples:

> In the plantation situation, the preparatory phase of sugar colonization gave way . . . to the exploitative phase . . . requiring a rapid increase in the numbers of unskilled manual laborers; dilution of the original model

must have resulted . . . In fact, what took place . . . was second-language learning with inadequate input. (Bickerton [1988a: 271–2])

The year 1720 is significant because it marks both the year in which South Carolina became a crown colony and the onset of change in the coexistence of races, bringing about institutionalized segregation, with the consequence of reducing access to the native variety of English for the Africans. This is especially true of the large plantations, where the African-to-European ratio was often way above the two-to-one ratio suggested by the total population figures. It is precisely on these large plantations that Gullah must have developed as a creole. The conditions for creolization were hardly met on the small farms . . . (Mufwene [1992: 161])

L'évolution démographique des sociétés créoles fait apparaître . . . une phase initiale . . . durant laquelle les blancs sont plus nombreux que les noirs . . . Cette situation est évidemment très différente de celle qui peut s'établir plus tard, dans la "phase de la société de plantation," où ce rapport peut être de 1 à 10 ou même davantage . . . la créolisation se définit de façon essentielle par la mutation socio-économique qui fait passer de la "phase 1" ("société d'habitation") à la "phase 2" (société de plantation). Chaudenson (1992: 131–2)

In the New World, on sugar plantations, production was organized on the basis of a kind of occupational stratification according to which field slaves were most numerous and were furthest removed from contact with Europeans. Social intercourse of the field slaves was almost exclusively confined within the group; and so, among them, linguistic forms showing a high degree of divergence . . . were able to crystallize and achieve the appearance of stability. (Alleyne [1971: 180])

The greater the proportion of people of color in a Caribbean colony during the period of genesis, the more "radical" the creole that emerged, with "radicalness" being measured as distance from the lexifier language . . . [this assumption], linking the proportion of people of color in the population to degree of radicalness, is apparently uncontroversial. (Singler [1995: 219–20])

If it is accepted that Mauritian Creole emerged and jelled in that formative period (roughly fifty years or three generations long) of the eighteenth century and in demographic conditions which by definition rendered access to French next to impossible for most people . . . (Corne [1995b: 12])

Statements such as the above meet with no controversy. On the contrary, they clearly demonstrate my initial claim that the limited access conception has become canon in the field of creole studies, lying at the foundation of all work by our leading thinkers.

The AH is a revision of this canon. All of the above statements stem from considerable reflection and scholarship. However, not one of them is founded upon any address of the failure of Spanish to be pidginized in Mexico and South America, the existence of AEC and FPC on *sociétés d'habitation* in the 1660s, or the correspondences among the AECs and among the FPCs.

Thus when reading things like "bioprogram," *français approximatif,* "feature selection," "local mixtures of input," "relexification," and "language of resistance," we must immediately think about black Chocoanos speaking Spanish; about a slave on a little farm in Suriname greeting a fellow slave in Sranan after having picked tobacco all day alongside a white bondservant; about a slave describing a mermaid in creole that same day on an equally small farm up in Martinique; about a Sea Islander and a Jamaican happily conversing in what they consider variants of the same language. All of these things are fatal to any plantation-centered, limited-access-based hypothesis of plantation creole origin, and the weight of these things is a serious problem in creole studies. Because it would predict all of these things, plus many others lingering as paradoxes under the limited access conception, I propose the Afrogenesis Hypothesis as a solution.

7 Conclusion

At this point, many readers might ask, "Can't creole genesis be due to a combination of things, with Afrogenesis being only one process acting in concert with the others proposed over the years?" The answer to that question depends on what is meant by "combination." If after reading the preceding six chapters, the reader has decided that the AH accounts for creole genesis better than the limited access model, then clearly my argument has come through. Yet, even if the reader decides to reject the AH in favor of the limited access model, if the reader has come to this conclusion after evaluating my reasoning and finding it flawed, then I have still succeeded in making my argument.

However, if after the preceding six chapters, the reader is inclined to preserve the limited access model while also allowing some "influence" from West African trade settlement pidgins, then I have failed to communicate. In other words, the AH is not logically compatible with statements such as Mufwene's assessment of Hancock (1992: 173):

> It is debatable whether the role of GCCE, which suggests some sort of monogenesis (to which I do not subscribe) was as significant as that of second-language varieties of the lexifier spoken by the African and creole populations in the New World before the emergence of the creole. Nonetheless, these comments are not intended to deny the contribution that GCCE, like several African languages, must have made to the development of Gullah as a creole.

While politely acknowledging Afrogenesis hypotheses, positions like this ultimately imply that creoles would have appeared on plantations whether an imported pidgin was present or not. On the other hand, the AH stipulates that imported pidgins from West African trade settlements were nothing less than pivotal to the establishment of creoles on Atlantic and Indian Ocean plantations. The hypothesis is that without the West African pidgins, there would be no creoles spoken in these countries. This is a conclusion based, initially, upon the situation in Chocó, Ecuador, Venezuela, Peru, and Mexico, and bolstered by the history and composition of the AECs and FPCs. We can decide that Afrogenesis is merely a "component" only if the evidence precisely indicates this. It is unclear that the evidence does so in our case.

An analogy: were dinosaurs warm-blooded like mammals? This has been vociferously argued by Robert Bakker (1992) and other paleobiologists since the 1960s, and has revolutionized our image of dinosaurs. Previously depicted as sluggish, stupid reptilian failures, they are now reconstructed as dynamic, intelligent creatures.

This accepted, the evidence suggests that dinosaur metabolism was more like that of reptiles than the "dinosaur revolution" has depicted (Lessem 1992). Bakker has pointed out that dinosaur bone-growth patterns resemble mammalian ones, but in fact some reptiles have the same patterns. It is also difficult to accept that many of the environments dinosaurs inhabited could have supported the massive amounts of vegetation it would have required to support warm-blooded animals as massive as many dinosaurs. These and other observations show that the truth about dinosaurs lies in the middle: dinosaur metabolism was more like that of mammals than than that of many reptiles, and dinosaurs were not phlegmatic flubs of nature; nor, however, were they simply hairless mammals. This is surely a comfort to the paleontologists trained before the 1960s mavericks, who have predictably been resistant to the paradigm change.

However, all issues do not resolve this way, for better or for worse. We do not imagine scientists supporting Ptolemaic astronomy while courteously "not denying" that Copernicus' ideas might have "some validity." The earth cannot "kind of" revolve around the sun—heliocentrism cannot be "considered as a possible aspect of" geocentrism. The evidence simply does not allow this.

Similarly, science has not decided that natural selection operates in tandem with Lamarck's theory of the inheritance of acquired characteristics. Gymnasts do not pass their well-developed leg muscles on to their children, period. Perhaps one can conceive of an alternate universe in which these two processes operated in tandem: the idea even has a certain charm. But the evidence here on earth simply does not allow this. One imagines Lamarckians claiming, as Darwin's theory triumphed, that there was "room" for both theories. But as we now know, there was no such room in this case, whatever the pacific appeal of acknowledging all ideas.

In the same way, then, under the AH, the absence of Spanish creoles could not logically be "somewhat" due to the absence of Spanish trade settlements. Given the consistency with which creoles were absent under the Spanish, it is difficult to see any specific indication that some other factor was operating in tandem with the simple absence of West African trade settlements. On the contrary, the fact that some creolists have been tracing the AECs and FPCs to West African trade settlements for decades only bolsters the likelihood that West African trade settlements were the pivotal factor in the absence of Spanish creoles. Searching for these "other" factors would be motivated not by the evidence itself, but by a natural desire to preserve the traditional limited access model. I have suggested that the evidence may be telling us that this is no longer wise.

More to the point, what would these "other factors" be? In Chapter 2, we eliminated all of the ones previously proposed. Thus an argument that the trade settlements were merely "one factor" would include propositions as to what the other factors might be *which would operate consistently across colony after colony*. What offers itself? After-work Spanish classes on the plantations? A hitherto unknown "buddy system" where local whites were brought to mines and plantations to act as surrogates to slaves on Sundays? Is Spanish perhaps the world's easiest language to learn? Was it something in Spanish cuisine? What?

In the same way, under the AH, the appearance of AECs and FPCs cannot be "partly" due to LGPE and SPF. To say that the parent pidgins were only "one factor" in the appearance of AEC and FPC entails, quite simply, that "other factors" were capable of producing a creole even without the importation of a pidgin. If this were true, would not we expect that these "other factors" would have produced a Spanish creole in at least two or three of the countries where in fact there are none? To treat LGPE and SPF as "factors" requires explaining why the same factors never took effect in the Chocó, the Chota Valley, Mexico, Venezuela, or Peru, all colonies under a *single* power, and one which happened to be the *only* power to lack West African trade settlements.

Thus as formulated, the AH cannot be logically incorporated into a limited-access-based model. It must be either rejected or accepted.

7.2 THE DOMAIN OF THE AH

That said, however, I do not consider the AH to explain anywhere near everything about creole genesis. For one thing, it addresses only the plantation creoles of the New World and the Indian Ocean. I am not claiming that Tayo Creole French, Naga Pidgin, or Fanakalo trace back to West African trade pidgins. Closer to home, however, it will be helpful to outline what I consider the implications of the AH to be for other creole genesis theories.

7.2.1 THE LANGUAGE BIOPROGRAM HYPOTHESIS

Bickerton (1981, 1984a) claims that plantation creoles emerged when slaves' children were forced to construct a language anew because their parents' command of the lexifier was a mere structureless jargon, varying wildly according to native language of the speaker. The evidence in this book forces us to conclude that whatever the validity of the concept of a bioprogram itself, creole genesis has never offered a context in which children would have needed to fall back upon it. For example, we have seen that in English Suriname of the 1660s, when children were a subsidiary presence in Suriname at best (Arends 1995), Sranan already existed in recognizable form (Section 4.2); the existence of Martiniquan French Creole by the same time (Section 5.3) similarly reveals it as an adult creation. Furthermore, we must recall that these two creoles were parents to creoles in most of the New World colonies subsequently settled by the respective European powers they developed under, where their descendants are too similar to them to have possibly been created anew by the adults, much less the children.

This is hardly to say that when children finally began acquiring these contact languages, they did not play a vital role in "gelling" them into natural languages, via conventionalizing variations and instigating morphophonological processes (cf. Sankoff and Laberge 1980; Samarin 1997). However, this was more a minor "cleaning up" operation than the "catastrophic" transformation surmised by Bickerton: by the time children began acquiring these languages, they would have been elaborated far beyond the halting interlanguage Bickerton depicts as the spark for the bioprogram. The discovery of Nicaraguan Sign Language, created by deaf children previously reliant only on individually created homesigns used with their parents, appears to demonstrate the bioprogram in action and even confirm some of Bickerton's predictions (Kegl, Senghas, and Coppola 1996; Kegl and

McWhorter 1996). However, under the AH, the analysis of plantation creoles as child creations would be impossible.

There is one context Bickerton refers to which has not been treated in this book: Hawaiian sugar plantations, which Bickerton considers the birthplace of Hawaiian Creole English. If English was indeed pidginized on these plantations and expanded by children, then it is counterevidence to my thesis. The evidence, however, suggests otherwise. I have outlined my position on Hawaii in detail in McWhorter (1997a) and will present only a basic summary of the most pertinent facts here.

Bickerton proposes that Hawaiian Creole English (henceforth HCE) was created by children of immigrants to Hawaii around the turn of the twentieth century, on the basis of fragmentary and chaotic input from an English jargon spoken by their parents. Many scholars (Goodman 1985b; Holm 1986; and even myself [McWhorter 1994] in earlier work) have proposed that HCE was actually created by adults long before the turn of the century. New evidence unearthed by Roberts (1996; 2000), however, conclusively shows that HCE was indeed stabilized by children.

However, the problem is that the evidence also shows that while the children were creating HCE, they were surrounded by a continuum of Englishes, many of the varieties quite full. This input to the children would hardly have necessitated resort to a bioprogram, and shows that the halting jargon of Bickerton's elderly informants was merely a transient interlanguage, not the source of the children's HCE.

A newspaper editorial of 1887 makes specific reference to a "pigeon" English spoken by children (Roberts 1995b), dating HCE to this decade at the latest. Crucially, the same editorial includes the following description of a fuller English spoken by adults (Reinecke, Tsuzaki, DeCamp, and Wood 1975: 595, 609, cited in Goodman 1985b: 111–2):

> The colloquial English of Hawaii *nei* is even now sufficiently *sui generis* to be noticeable to strangers. It is not a dialect, but a new language with English as its basic element, wrought upon by the subtle forces of other languages, not so much in the matter of a changed vocabulary as a changed diction.

Roberts (1995b) has convincingly argued that although this appears to describe a pidgin, the author was in fact referring to a full, indigenized Hawaiian English. However, the citation still shows that the first children speaking HCE were doing so amidst a full variety of English. With input of this richness, children would not have needed to create a language from the ground up.

Furthermore, Roberts (1996) has shown that even the pidginized English spoken by many adults in late nineteenth-century Hawaii, while not fully stabilized, was by no means as structureless as the data from Bickerton's elderly informants. Finally—a fact markedly de-emphasized in Bickerton's writings—the children who created HCE attended schools where they were taught in English. Alone, this fact eliminates any reason for supposing that their English input was limited to any jargon or pidgin.

All of this refutes Bickerton's claim that the creators of HCE had only the most rudimentary of English as input. He must be judged as having mischaracterized the halting, variable speech of his "pidgin" speakers as the general state of English in turn-of-the-century Hawaii. This was by no means the only English available to the children who created the creole, and may well have been quite marginal in its development. Several decades before 1900, pidgin English and varieties closer to English had been established in Hawaii via interethnic interactions between adults, just as pidgins and lectal continua develop around the world. Going to school in standard English and surrounded by a Hawaiian English indigenized along the lines of Indian or Australian English, these children created HCE not out of deprivation, but as a vehicle of identity.

Bickerton's responses to this have been oddly brief. One guesses that he considers these Englishes somehow irrelevant to the birth of HCE, perhaps considering these developments separate from what was occurring on the plantations. However, Roberts (1995a) shows that the main lingua franca on the Hawaiian plantations was a pidginized Hawaiian, not English. English came to be used on the plantations only after the turn of the century (43). What this suggests is that HCE evolved outside of the plantations, while pidgin Hawaiian was used on the plantations themselves. (Roberts [p.c.] concurs on this point.)

Thus while the absence of Spanish creoles, the existence of AEC and FPC on *sociétés d'habitation*, and the correspondences between AECs and between FPCs all eliminate the possibility that plantations pidginized lexifiers in the Caribbean, South America, or the Indian Ocean, the data above show that Hawaiian plantations did not pidginize English either. What room is there for the Language Bioprogram Hypothesis under the AH, then?

For one, while the AH refutes Bickerton's identification of children as the creators of creoles, it takes no issue with the assumption that creoles are closer to Universal Grammar than regular languages are. For example, typological and acquisitional studies of regular languages (Givón 1979, Cziko 1989) suggest that aspects of Bickerton's creole TMA prototype are indeed fundamental to language in general. Under the AH, it simply becomes clear that adults are capable of reverting to Universal Grammar to a greater extent than Bickerton allows.

Therefore, without accepting Bickerton's dismissal of substrate influence, we can retain the more promising universals even without attributing them to children. Contrary to Bickerton (1984b), adults are thoroughly capable of creating "optimal" languages reflecting innate linguistic fundamentals.

7.2.2 THE SUBSTRATE HYPOTHESIS

The AH does not stipulate that substrate influence on plantation creoles was exerted only by castle slaves in West Africa. It merely proposes that a preliminary imprint was made by substrate languages there, which then persisted on plantations even in the presence of slaves speaking different substrate languages. On plantations, creoles can be assumed to have undergone a "second pass" of substrate influence. However, this was relatively nondisruptive, and the basic outlines of the language survived.

An example of this is Saramaccan. Born as LGPE in Ghana, the "first pass" of substrate influence in Saramaccan would have been based on Akan when it was still LGPE, with some influence also from Igbo. However, Saramaccan fairly drips with very specific Gbe inheritances absent in any AEC outside Suriname (McWhorter 1996c). Since Gbe speakers would have constituted roughly half of the sale slaves brought to Suriname in the late seventeenth century (Postma 1990: 111), we can attribute this Gbe influence to a "second pass" of transfer in Suriname itself.

Gullah is an especially useful illustration of the persistence of castle slaves' substrate influence in creoles used and developed by slaves speaking other languages. Cassidy (1983) notes that the Kwa influence in Gullah is more fundamental than the primarily lexical influence from languages of other groups. Mufwene (1992) attempts to square this with a combination of the "approximation" model and slave shipments, but the data are resistant. At best, in early South Carolina slaves from the Kwa-speaking region were a "constant" presence (166), but never remotely a majority, and often as low as 17.2 percent of the total. Contrary to the Suriname data, where during a lengthy crucial period, Gbe speakers were half or more of the slave total, in South Carolina Kwa speakers were almost always outnumbered by speakers of Mande, Kru, and/or Bantu languages. Bantu speakers, for example, can also be considered to have been a "constant" presence, and yet there is no Bantu structural transfer in Gullah.

Mufwene strengthens the role of the Kwa speakers via his argument that Kwa structures were preferred because of being "unmarked" (1992:

167–8), but we have seen that this argument is not supported by the actual linguistic data (Section 4.7.1). A more economical solution is that the Kwa influence on Gullah is traceable to Akan speakers creating LGPE, one of whose descendants was Gullah. West Atlantic, Mande, Kru, and Bantu speakers did not create Gullah, nor did those Kwa speakers sold to South Carolina. Gullah was ultimately created by castle slaves in Ghana as LGPE, and simply acquired by sale slaves elsewhere. To be sure, such acquisition entailed second-language acquisition effects, including transfer. This, however, left the core structure of LGPE intact.

7.2.3 THE APPROXIMATION MODEL

The AH model concurs with the approximation model in stipulating that slaves would have been capable of acquiring L2 varieties of a lexifier on *sociétés d'habitation*. However, the AH stipulates that while slaves were acquiring L2 varieties, a pidgin had been imported into such settings and that this, not "approximation," was the source of the plantation creoles.

To make clear the preferability of the AH over the approximation scenario, we will test whether the "approximation" conception can answer the eight questions which the AH can, as we saw in Section 6.4.:

(1) *Why is there a Kwa transfer bias in the AECs?* Chaudenson and Mufwene are both highly skeptical of substrate influence in plantation creoles, emphasizing the role of superstrate sources (the "founders" in Mufwene's Founder Principle are primarily the whites). However, certain features are too blatantly transfers to be denied: there is no English dialect with the Sranan sentence type exemplified by *mi de na a tafra ondro* "I am under the table," while Kwa languages do have this construction. Mufwene, somewhat more open to substrate influence, attributes the Kwa bias to markedness factors. However, as we have seen in Section 4.7.1, the data do not support this.

Under the AH, the Kwa bias is due simply to AEC having emerged as LGPE, developed by Kwa speakers.

(2) *Why are there no Spanish creoles?* Chaudenson purports to address this, but restricts his discussion to the Caribbean islands, where long *société d'habitation* periods happen to provide an answer.

Under the AH, there are no Spanish creoles because there were no Spanish West African trade settlements where a parent pidgin could have formed.

(3) *Why were there creoles on* sociétés d'habitation? No "approximation" adherents have addressed Suriname nor the 1671 Martinique text.

Under the AH, Maroon Spirit Language and the 1671 Martinique text simply confirm what we would have expected; AEC and FPC were in place in the founding colonies alongside the developing L2 varieties of the lexifiers.

(4) *Why is there so little Kwa transfer in FPCs?* No adherents have discussed this issue, presumably because substrate influence is considered to be marginal.

Under the AH, the low Kwa transfer in FPCs is due to FPCs having begun as a Wolof-influenced pidgin French.

(5) *Why do AECs look so much alike? Why the FPCs?* Approximationists would attribute this to similar superstrates, but as we have seen, the chance factor would predict greater differences nevertheless. Why would French, regional or standard, lead slaves all over the world to develop a strictly sentence-final copula?

Under the AH, this is simply because the AECs all stemmed from one parent, as did the FPCs.

(6) *Why are creoles so uniform within themselves?* Among approximationists, only Mufwene has briefly touched upon this (1993b: 204, 1996: 102), relying on the post-emancipation contact argument refuted in Section 6.4.6.

Under the AH, this is because each creole stems from a single pidgin having been introduced into the colony.

(7) *Are plantation creoles relexifications of single West African languages?* As noted (Section 6.4.7), the relexificationists' appeal to dialect leveling to

explain discrepancies between Haitian and Fongbe leaves this model un-falsifiable. Only a concrete demonstration that another process was at work would be a constructive response. Chaudenson's claims for Mauritian as de-scended from Réunionnais do not stand, and this deprives the approxi-mation model of its single concrete demonstration. Approximationists can now point only to the correspondences between plantation creoles and re-gional lexifiers. However, as we have seen, approximationists have exag-gerated the likeness between creoles and their lexifiers, and contrary to the approximationist timetable, creoles already coexisted with L2 varieties in *sociétés d'habitation*. Approximationists and relexificationists can thus ar-gue only past one another at this point.

Under the AH, we can decide on this: there was no need for relexification on plantations because a pidgin was imported to serve as a target.

(8) *Why is there no qualitative difference between expanded pidgins and plantation creoles?* No approximationist argument addresses this question.

Under the AH, the reason for the lack of difference is that they are the same thing.

It would appear that the "approximation" process would, at best, yield a re-structured variety like Réunionnais or Afrikaans, not a pidgin or creole. Short of a specific response to all four arguments in Section 5.5.3 plus the above observations, it is difficult to see a motivation for preserving the ap-proximation model.

7.2.4 THE RELEXIFICATION HYPOTHESIS

As discussed in Section 6.4.7, the presence of imported pidgins on planta-tions would have obviated the need for slaves to directly relexify their na-tive languages. Thus the AH does not support the characterization of plan-tation creoles as the deliberate manifestations of African cultural retention inherent in, for example, Mervyn Alleyne's work. The life cycle of the plantation creole began as a pidgin in West African trade settlements. At this point, the pidgin could only tenuously be considered to express the castle slave's "identity," just as Melanesian Pidgin English was only mar-ginally reflective of the "identity" of the Australian Aboriginals and Melanesian whalers who created it. Such pidgins were simply expedient work/ trade facilitators, only obliquely connected to a "soul." Only when transplanted to the New World were these pidgins recruited as expressions of identity, but by this point it was being acquired, not created.

The point is not a hair-splitting one, because we must recall that where such pidgins were not imported, in Spanish colonies, the expression of a new bicultural identity was expressed merely via a vernacular form of the local standard. The evidence suggests that, for better or for worse, the heavy retention of West African structure visible in creoles was an accident of the life cycle of these languages, and not evidence of slaves having fiercely "retained" part of their heritage. Such structures were typical of a utilitarian work pidgin at a trade settlement, but were never retained in the New World unless such a pidgin were imported to serve as a model. Without such a pidgin, Africans were simply oriented towards acquiring the local standard: this is demonstrated by the Spanish colonies.

7.2.5 THE CREATIVITY HYPOTHESIS

Baker (1990, 1995b) depicts plantation creoles as dynamic responses to new interethnic identities, taking issue with the depiction in many genesis models of creoles as frustrated attempts at full acquisition. The AH, too, takes issue with this Sisyphean element in genesis models. Just as modern creoles and vernaculars are regarded with a covert prestige, slaves would have identified with creoles as expressions of black identity. Slaves' conception of "English" or "French" would have been much broader and more fluid than our own.

However, the AH departs from Baker's hypothesis where it is extended to suggest that "every creole is its own story," to borrow the etymologist's adage about words. Under the AH, every creole does have its own story— but only as a second chapter, its first chapter having unfolded as a pidgin arising at a West African trade settlement. If this were not true, we would not see the uncanny patterning under which no creoles emerged under just the power which had no such trade settlements. More to the point, AECs would not correspond so closely, and FPCs would not correspond so closely. How would slaves in separate places "create" such similar languages? The creolophone speakers certainly approached their language "creatively" on plantations. However, its original "creators" had developed it as a utilitarian work pidgin, not as a Medium for Interethnic Communication.

Another extension of the creativity hypothesis is Baker's observation that many features thought to date to the beginning of a creole's history actually occur only rather late in its documentation (1995b). Baker interprets these attestations to mean that the emergence of plantation creoles in their current form was very gradual. This interpretation challenges the AH, because some features in a given creole are documented so late that their appearance at that time would disqualify them from having been in a parent pidgin, seemingly supporting polygenesis.

While historical documentation is crucial to the study of creoles, however, the documents can be responsibly used only in full cognizance of three unfortunate facts about creoles and their documentation. First, most such documents were written by Europeans with non-native competence, if any, in the creole. Even when the Europeans' competence appears to have been "good," we must ask ourselves how confidently we would chart the history of English based solely on materials written by Chinese missionaries whose competence in English was "good." Second, creoles are denigrated oral vernaculars, usually spoken alongside prestigious, written lexifiers. The authors of the early documents, even native speakers, often shifted the creole towards the lexifier considerably, which betrays itself in suspiciously "written" constructions highly unlikely to have ever been current among black plantation workers. Finally, documentation generally begins so long after the creole emerged that there is a question as to whether the documentation captures creole "genesis" at all. For example, we have no remotely substantial document in Sranan until about 125 years after the colonization of Suriname.

Because of this, such documents can play only a supplementary role in a genesis argument. Tracing the development of a language in documents like these is analogous to tracing the artistic maturation of a film actress most of whose early films are lost or survive only in fragments, and in which she was hemmed into small parts that did not allow her to show her range.

A thought experiment will illustrate this. The reader is asked to imagine the following corpus: three letters written by planters in Virginia to the British government in 1690; a four-page agreement by a Hessian general to fight alongside the American colonists during the Revolutionary War; a diary written in 1810 by the Swedish-born wife of a Congressional representative; fifteen letters home written by African-born Civil War soldiers; a phrasebook for French travelers to the United States from 1882; and the transcript of a radio broadcast by an Austrian-born comedian in 1936.

Now, imagine that the year is 2250, and that a cadre of scholars count the occurrences of pronouns, articles, and copulas in these documents—few written by native speakers of English—and submit them to quantificational analysis. Finally, imagine the results presented as depicting the development of vernacular American English! It is in this light that we must see the "late attestation" of a feature in a creole. It is not that these documents can shed no light on such issues: however, they can do so only in tandem with other approaches.

Crucially, this will entail that at times these other approaches will reveal that the documentation gives a misleading impression. One suspects that the case of the progressive marker *ape* in early Mauritian documents is one such case. Baker observes that this marker is not attested until 1822 (Baker 1995b: 7–8). However, this is extremely odd when viewed in comparison with all of the other FPCs. Since (1) so many of them also chose *après* as a progressive marker, (2) even the few using *ka* today appear to have begun with *ape*, the exact same progressive marker, and (3) there are *so very many other idiosyncratic correspondences between the FPCs*, the more economical explanation is that the documents simply do not happen to have captured *ape* until 1822, but that the marker had existed and had been inherited as part of SPF.

Baker (1995b) argues against this on the grounds that before 1822, there is no overt progressive marker at all in the texts, even where *ape* would be obligatory today, suggesting that the very semantic concept itself had yet to emerge before the 1820s. However, there are only two such texts, both only "moderately long." How do we know that the occurrence of *ape* was not simply less obligatory in early Mauritian (and SPF) than it is now?

Another question that arises is whether Mauritian Creole speakers plausibly went without a progressive marker for almost a century: there exists no creole which has no overt progressive marker. This is another suggestion that *ape* was being used, but happened not to have been written, until 1822. In Section 5.5.2 I presented similar arguments regarding Baker's dating of Mauritian's sentence-final copula *ete* to the late 1800s (Baker and Syea 1991; Baker 1995b: 11). I hope not to appear *ad hoc* in framing the early Mauritian documents in this fashion; I myself have concluded (and before I had developed the AH) that early documents give a misleading picture of the development of predicate negation in Saramaccan (see, for example, McWhorter 1996a). Thus in sum, the AH retains the central insight of the Creativity Hypothesis, but questions some of the implications scholars have drawn from it.

7.3 STANDARDS OF EVALUATION

The AH is based upon a claim that the *co-occurrence* of the following three things signifies that plantation creoles are traceable to West Africa:

(1) No creoles emerged under the Spanish, who were the only power with no West African trade settlements.

(2) AECs correspond too closely not to trace back to a single ancestor; the FPCS are the same.

(3) The ancestral AEC and the ancestral FPC existed on *sociétés d'habitation* where creoles would not have formed, suggesting, in tandem with linguistic evidence, that they were imported from West African trade settlements.

The AH is explicitly *not* based upon a claim that any single one of these things makes a viable case for Afrogenesis. Most important, the AH is constructed as a way of deriving the most explanatory power from evidence which often lends itself to many interpretations. Therefore, in many cases, to evaluate the AH on the basis of only one of the observations at a time would not, properly speaking, be a constructive engagement.

For instance, a creolist might suggest an interpretation of the sparse records of seventeenth-century Ghana which would make the emergence of LGPE there unlikely. However, an interpretation which makes the emergence of LGPE likely is possible as well (Sections 4.6, 4.7). The main point, however, is that LGPE is only one plank of the AH argument. In rejecting Afrogenesis in favor of a plantation-based scenario, this creolist must be always aware that *no* creoles emerged under classic plantation conditions in a welter of colonies owned by the very power that lacked West African trade settlements. Technically, to refrain from addressing this is to address the AH in incomplete fashion.

In general, alternative explanations of isolated bits of the data supporting the AH are less interesting as criticism than engagements with the underpinnings of the hypothesis itself. Certainly, many of the problems I have noted are, taken individually, amenable to solutions other than this one. However, this is true of any theory, valid as well as invalid. What is important is whether after the inevitable nibbles of this sort, the hypothesis remains more powerful than the traditional one.

For example, even if *unu* could be traced to a hitherto unknown contingent of Igbos in early Suriname, so be it: *da* and the four other idiosyncratic

AEC commonalities would remain, and thus would the case for an AEC ancestor. Similarly, even a locally based explanation for the absence of a Spanish creole in, say, Venezuela, would leave a passel of other Spanish colonies unexplained. As discussed in Sections 2.7 and 6.6, the point is how vastly unlikely it would be that the absence of Spanish creoles *in general* is due to a variety of unconnected outcomes, different in each colony. Given the myriad directions sociohistory can take, why would independent rolls of the wheel of fate lead to the absence of a creole so consistently *only under the Spanish?*

As Bugliosi (1996: 215) notes, the evidence supporting a viable theory is analogous not to a chain, where removal of one link destroys the entire enterprise; a theory is analogous to a rope. Removal of two or three strands does not invalidate the usefulness of the rope. Thus, alternate possible explanations of, say, *unu* and Venezuela would not invalidate the AH. The issue is great quantities of evidence all pointing in one direction, suggesting a single process at work allowing a decision between the myriad explanations possible for any isolated piece of data.

Thus there are two truly constructive criticisms of the AH. One is to show how the limited access conception could account for all of the data I have called attention to. This would entail the following:

(1) A unified explanation of why creoles did not appear in Spanish colonies unless a Portuguese-based creole was imported previously.

(2) A sociologically grounded explanation of why creoles were spoken on *sociétés d'habitation* in the seventeenth century Caribbean.

(3) A model of language contact explaining how an array of grammatical items can be borrowed without a lexicon, without bilingualism, including an identification of what factor rendered this unexpected result so typical on plantations.

Alternatively, one could easily directly refute the AH, via any one of these four strategies:

(1) A unified explanation of why creoles did not appear in Spanish colonies unless a Portuguese-based creole was imported previously.

(2) Presentation of a natively spoken creole created by plantation conditions; specifically, a creole which emerged in a setting in which (a) social domination of lexifier speakers, in combination with a large number of substrate languages, conditioned the need for a lin-

gua franca based on that lexifier; (b) the resultant lingua franca was a pidgin/creole; and (c) children grew up in this setting and learned not the lexifier itself but only this pidgin/creole (the AH predicts that in such settings, adults learned an L2 variety of the lexifier, and children acquired an even fuller command, unless an imported pidgin became the target for the subordinated).

(3) An explanation for how all or most (not just one or two) of the AEC and/or FPC correspondences could plausibly be contributed to *several separate creoles* by the lexifier, the substrate, or universals.

(4) Concrete evidence that no pidginized varieties of European languages developed among castle slaves in West Africa in the seventeenth century (specifically, a description of a need for interpreters to speak to castle slaves in general, or a comment that they do not speak any form of the lexifier).

7.4 CURTAIN

The very nature of science dictates that we devote more attention to confirming a reigning theory than to formulating a new one (Kuhn 1970: 35–8). Ultimately, however, this can be classified as seeking truth only to the extent that the theory continues to provide elegant and complete explanations of the data which confront it. This book has been written in the belief that creole genesis theory no longer meets this standard. Creole studies is founding an ever-growing literature upon an artificially constrained data set, the result being the reconstruction of a scenario of language transmission which may never have occurred.

This book leads to the conclusion that there has arisen no situation in the world in which a large group of people seeking a lexifier as a Medium for Interethnic Communication so outnumbered lexifier speakers that they could glean only enough input to produce a pidgin or creole. Be this via "dilution," "approximation," "transformation," "relexification," or "creation," the scenario would appear to have simply never taken place. As heretical as this declaration may seem, this is what my reading of the data suggests. Properly, then, "plantation creole" ought to be conceived as a mere cultural and geographical designation, but not a distinct language contact phenomenon. Any impression otherwise is the result of a distributional *trompe-l'oeil* which obscures the actual origins of these creoles as trade settlement work pidgins on the West African coast. It follows from this that creoles were not created by children, were not merely "approximations" of their lexifiers, were not relexifications of West African languages, and were not deliberate creations of a new interethnic identity. The plantation creoles were simply transplanted work pidgins, plain and simple.

Some may charge that this statement takes us back to the conception of creoles as simply nativized pidgins. This is unabashedly true. However, it is less a charge than a compliment. An assessment of the explanatory power of modern creole genesis theory suggests that the classification of plantation creoles as a *sui generis* type of language transmission has been less an advance than a drift. This is because this evolution in thought has shunted creole studies into a paradigm incapable of explaining an uncomfortably large mass of data. Reflexively couched in a plantation-based genesis model, our theories founder upon the mainland Spanish colonies. Constrained by a localist, polygenetic orientation, we are unintentionally blinded to the sisterhood of the AECs and FPCs. Forced to trace substrate influence to local sale slaves whose origins do not match that influence well, our theory of transfer is permanently tentative. Taught to link the depth of a creole to sharpness of demographic disproportion, we are left to sweep the 1671 Martinique document and similar discoveries under the rug. I propose the AH as a way of escaping from these traps and moving ahead.

"Transplanted work pidgin" may seem to have a wan ring in comparison to "Universal Grammar *ab ovo*," "language of resistance," or "relexification." However, in fact, plantation creoles are as exciting in this new role as in the traditional ones.

Plantation creoles carry the heritage of a truly bracing life cycle. Created in West Africa by castle slaves, a hitherto shadowy presence in written history, work pidgins were transported across oceans where they took on new roles as lingua francas among the enslaved. After emancipation, these creoles have survived, blessing their speakers with fascinating languages more their own than any European one, serving as one pole in rich multilectal language competences.

Furthermore, in establishing that the AECs are sister creoles, and that the FPCs are as well, the AH presents plantation creoles as a fertile ground for the study of the many directions which a system can take as the result of change and contact. Distributed from colony to colony, one pidgin became a dazzling array of sister creoles, each molding the parent pidgin material in its own fashion. Lower Guinea Pidgin English, for example, in Suriname became a highly basilectal Gbe-influenced creole; in Jamaica a classic lectal continuum now disseminated throughout the world by reggae music; in South Carolina one of the sources of African-American Vernacular English; in Cameroon a lingua franca gravid with a French lexical con-

tribution. Framing the data in this fashion will be an excellent way for creole studies to incorporate itself further into mainstream linguistics.

Finally, in revealing plantation creoles to have emerged as pidgins just
like all other contact languages, the AH takes these languages out of the
rarefied limited access hothouse. In particular, it removes the recalcitrant
boundary between Atlantic and Pacific creole studies. The AH allows us to
conceive of all contact languages as a single data set, with endless comparative applications to one another.

This book has been written out of a simple desire to bring order to a body
of data. Despite its stance towards most of the hypotheses upon which creole studies has been built, the Afrogenesis Hypothesis is not simply a mere
hubristic stunt.

I stand in awe of the creolists before me who brought these fascinating
languages to world attention, who gathered the data which I can now simply
access at a library, and who formulated the initial hypotheses which stimu-
lated my own.

Out of this awe, however, I have hoped to steer creole studies out of the
holding pattern into which the limited access model has led it. Of course, I
hope to have convinced the reader that the Afrogenesis Hypothesis is a solution. However, if this book instead simply releases creole studies from
the clutches of an illusion, it has accomplished its ultimate goal.

References

Abraham, R. C. 1958. Dictionary of modern Yoruba. London: University of London Press.

Acosta Saignes, Miguel. 1967. Vida de los esclavos negros en Venezuela. Caracas: Hespérides.

Adamson, Lilian, and Norval Smith. 1995. Sranan. In Pidgins and creoles: An introduction, ed. Jacques Arends, Pieter Muysken, and Norval Smith, 219–32. Amsterdam: John Benjamins.

Aguirre Beltrán, Gonzalo. 1958. Cuijla: Esbozo etnográfico de un pueblo negro. México: Fondo de Cultura Económica.

Alleyne, Mervyn C. 1971. Acculturation and the cultural matrix of creolization. In Hymes 1971, 169–86.

———. 1980a. Comparative Afro-American. Ann Arbor, MI: Karoma.

———. 1980b. Introduction. In Valdman and Highfield, eds. 1980, 1–17.

———. 1987. Predicate structures in Saramaccan. In Studies in Saramaccan language structure, ed. M. Alleyne, 71–86. University of Amsterdam: Instituut voor Algemene Taalwetenschaft.

———. 1993. Continuity versus creativity in Afro-American language and culture. In Mufwene 1993, 167–181.

Allsopp, Richard, ed. 1996. Dictionary of Caribbean English usage. London: Oxford University Press.

Alvarez Nazario, Manuel. 1961. El elemento afronegroide en el Español de Puerto Rico. San Juan: Instituto de Cultura Puertoriqueña.

Arends, Jacques. 1989. Syntactic developments in Sranan. Ph.D. diss., University of Nijmegen.

———. 1995. Demographic factors in the formation of Sranan. In The early stages of creolization, ed. J. Arends, 233–85. Amsterdam: John Benjamins.

Bachiller y Morales, Antonio. 1883. Desfiguración a que está expuesto el idioma castellano al contacto y mexcla de razas. Revista de Cuba 14: 97–104.

Bailey, Beryl. 1966. Jamaican creole syntax. Cambridge: Cambridge University Press.

Baker, Philip. 1972. Kreol: A description of Mauritian Creole. London: C. Hurst.
———. 1984. Agglutinated nominals in Creole French: Their evolutionary significance. Te Reo 27: 89–129.
———. 1987. Combien y a-t-il eu de genèses créoles à base lexicale française? Études Créoles 10: 60–76.
———. 1990. Column: Off Target? Journal of Pidgin and Creole Languages 5: 107–19.
———. 1993. Australian influence on Melanesian Pidgin English. Te Reo 36: 3–67.
———. 1995a. Some developmental inferences from the historical studies of pidgins and creoles. In Arends, ed. 1995, 124.
———. 1995b. Motivation in creole genesis. In From contact to creole and beyond, ed. P. Baker, 3–15. London: University of Westminster Press.
———. 1996. Review article: Pidginization, creolization and *français approximatif*. Journal of Pidgin and Creole Languages 11: 95–120.
———. 1998. Investigating the origin and diffusion of shared features among the Atlantic English Creoles. In St. Kitts and the Atlantic creoles, ed. P. Baker and Adrienne Bruyn, 315–64. London: University of Westminster Press.
Baker, Philip, and Chris Corne. 1982. Isle de France creole: Affinities and origins. Ann Arbor, MI: Karoma.
———. 1986. Universals, substrata, and the Indian Ocean creoles. In Muysken and Smith 1986, 163–83.
Baker, Philip, and Anand Syea. 1991. On the copula in Mauritian Creole, past and present. In Byrne and Huebner 1991, 159–75.
Bakker, Robert T. 1992. The dinosaur heresies. New York: Zebra.
Balmer, W. T. , and F. C. F. Grant. 1929. A grammar of the Fante-Akan language. London: The Atlantis Press.
Barbot, John. 1732. A description of the coasts of North and South-Guinea . . . London: Churchill.
Baudet, Martha M. 1981. Identifying the African grammatical base of the Caribbean creoles: A typological approach. In Highfield and Valdman 1981, 104–18.
Baugh, John. 1979. Linguistic style-shifting in Black English. Ph.D. diss., University of Pennsylvania.
Bentley, Rev. W. Holman. 1887. Dictionary and grammar of the Kongo language. London: Baptist Missionary Society.
Berlin, Ira. 1996. From Creole to African: Atlantic Creoles and the origins of African-American society in mainland North America. The William and Mary Quarterly 53: 251–88.
Bernabé, Jean. 1987. Grammaire Créole. Paris: L'Harmattan.
Bickerton, Derek. 1981. Roots of language. Ann Arbor, MI: Karoma.
———. 1983. Notice of P. Baker and C. Corne, Isle de France Creole (Karoma, 1982). The Carrier Pidgin 11: 8–9.
———. 1984a. The Language Bioprogram Hypothesis. The Behavioral and Brain Sciences 7: 173–88.

————. 1984b. The Language Bioprogram Hypothesis and second language acquisition. In Universals of second language acquisition, ed. William Rutherford, 141–61. New York: Academic Press.

————. 1986. Column: Beyond *Roots:* The five-year test. Journal of Pidgin and Creole Languages 1: 225–32.

————. 1988a. Creole languages and the Bioprogram. In Linguistics: The Cambridge Survey, vol. 2, Linguistic theory: Extensions and implications, ed. Frederick J. Newmeyer, 268–82. Cambridge: Cambridge University Press.

————. 1988b. A dialog concerning the linguistic status of creole languages. In Linguistics: The Cambridge survey, vol. 2, Linguistic theory: Extensions and implications, ed. Frederick J. Newmeyer, 302–6. Cambridge: Cambridge University Press.

————. 1988c. Relexification. Journal of Pidgin and Creole Languages 3: 277–82.

————. 1989. Squawks and ruffled feathers. Carrier Pidgin 17: 2–3, 5–6.

————. 1990. Haitian demographics and creole genesis. Canadian Journal of Linguistics 35: 217–19.

————. 1991. The Lexical Learning Hypothesis and the pidgin-creole cycle. In Wheels within wheels, ed. Martin Pütz and Rene Dirven, 11–32. Frankfurt: Peter Lang.

————. 1994a. Reply to McWhorter. Journal of Pidgin and Creole Languages 9: 65–77.

————. 1994b. The origin of creoles in Surinam. Unpublished Ms.

————. 1995. A sociohistoric examination of Afrogenesis. Unpublished Ms.

————. 1998. A sociohistoric examination of Afrogenesis. Journal of Pidgin and Creole Languages 13: 63–92.

Bickerton, Derek, and Aquilas Escalante. 1970. Palenquero: A Spanish-based creole of northern Colombia. Lingua 24: 254–67.

Bilby, Kenneth. 1983. How the "older heads" talk: A Jamaican Maroon Spirit possession language and its relationship to the creoles of Suriname and Sierra Leone. Nieuwe West-Indische Gids 57: 37–88.

————. 1992. Further observations on the Jamaican Maroon Spirit Language. Paper presented at the 1992 Annual Meeting of the Society for Pidgin and Creole Linguistics, Philadelphia.

Birmingham, John C., Jr. 1976. Papiamentu's West African cousins. In 1975 Colloquium on Hispanic Linguistics, ed. Frances M. Aid, Melvyn C. Resnick, and Bohdan Saciuk, 19–25. Washington, DC: Georgetown University Press.

Blackburn, Robin. 1997. The making of new world slavery. London: Verso.

Bolingbroke, Henry. 1799–1806. *A voyage to Demerary.* London.

Boorstin, Daniel J. 1983. The discoverers. New York: Vintage.

Boretzky, Norbert. 1983. Kreolsprachen, Substrate und Sprachwandel. Wiesbaden: Harrassowitz.

Bourdieu, Pierre. 1982. Ce que parler veut dire. Paris: Fayard.

Bouton, J. 1640. Relation de l'établissement des François depuis l'an 1635 . . . en l'isle de la Martinique . . . Paris: Cramoisy.

Bowser, Frederick P. 1974. The African slave in colonial Peru, 1524–1650. Palo Alto: Stanford University Press.

Brauner, Siegmund 1974. Lehrbuch des Bambara. Leipzig: VEB Verlag Enzyklopädie.

Bruyn, Adrienne. 1995a. Relative clauses in early Sranan. In Arends, ed. 1995, 149–202.

———. 1995b. Grammaticalization in creoles: The development of determiners and relative clauses in Sranan. Amsterdam: IFOTT.

Bugliosi, Vincent. 1996. Outrage. New York: W. W. Norton.

Byrne, Francis. 1984. Instrumental in Saramaccan. York Papers in Linguistics 11: 39–50.

———. 1987. Grammatical relations in a radical creole. Amsterdam: John Benjamins.

———. 1990. Pre-clausal forces in Saramaccan. Linguistics 28: 661–88.

Byrne, Francis, and Alexander Caskey. 1993. Focus, emphasis, and pronominals in Saramaccan. In Focus and grammatical relations in creole languages, ed. Francis Byrne and Donald Winford, 213–29. Amsterdam: John Benjamins.

Byrne, Francis, and John Holm, eds. 1993. The Atlantic meets the Pacific: A global view of pidginization and creolization. Amsterdam: John Benjamins.

Byrne, Francis, and Thom Huebner, eds. 1991. Development and structures of creole languages: Essays in honor of Derek Bickerton. Amsterdam: John Benjamins.

Cabrera, Lydia. 1954. El monte. Paris: Gallimard.

Carden, Guy, Morris Goodman, Rebecca Posner, and William Stewart. 1990. A 1671 French Creole text from Martinique. Paper presented at the Society for Pidgin and Creole Linguistics meeting.

Carrington, Lawrence, D. R. Craig, and R. Todd Dandare, eds. 1983. Studies in Caribbean language. St. Augustine, Trinidad: Society for Caribbean Linguistics.

Carroll, Patrick J. 1991. Blacks in colonial Veracruz. Austin: University of Texas Press.

Carter, Hazel. 1987. Suprasegmentals in Guyanese: Some African comparisons. In Gilbert 1987, 213–63.

Cassidy, Frederic G. 1964. Toward the recovery of early English-African pidgin. In Symposium on multilingualism, (no ed.), 267–77. Louvain, Belgium: Ceuterick.

———. 1980. The place of Gullah. American Speech 55: 3–16.

———. 1983. Sources of the African Element in Gullah. In Carrington et al. 1983, 76–81.

———. 1986. Barbadian Creole: Possibility and probablility. American Speech 6: 195–205.

———. 1994. Gullah and the Caribbean connection. In Montgomery 1994, 16–22.

Cassidy, Frederic G., and Robert B. LePage. 1980. Dictionary of Jamaican English. Cambridge: Cambridge University Press.

Castellanos, Jorge, and Isabel Castellanos. 1992. Cultura Afrocubana. Vol. 3. Miami: Édiciones Universal.

de Castro, Padre Francisco Manuel. 1933. Apontamentos sobre a língua èmakua. Lourenço Marques: Imprensa Nacional.

Cauna, Jacques. 1987. Au temps des isles à sucre. Paris: Éditions Karthala et A. C. C. T.

Chatillon, M. 1984. L'évangélisation des esclaves au XVIIe siècle: Lettres du R. P. Mongin. (Extract from) Bulletin de la Société d'histoire de la Guadeloupe, 61 and 62.

Chaudenson, R. 1979. Les créoles français. Évreux: Nathan.

———. 1981a. Continuum intralinguistique et interlinguistique. Études Créoles 4: 19–46.

———. 1981b. Textes créoles anciens. Hamburg: Helmut Buske.

———. 1990. Recherche, formation et créolistique. Revue québécoise de linguistique théorique et appliqué 9: 287–303.

———. 1992. Des îles, des hommes, des langues. Paris: L'Harmattan.

Christaller, Rev. J. G. 1875. A grammar of the Asante and Fante languages called Tshi. Republished 1964 by Gregg Press, Ridgewood, NJ.

———. 1933. Dictionary of the Asante and Fante languages called Tshi. Basel: Basel Evangelical Missionary Society.

Corne, Chris. 1977. Seychelles Creole grammar. Tübingen: Narr.

———. 1984. On the transmission of substratal features in creolisation. Reply to Bickerton 1984. The Behavioral and Brain Sciences 7: 191–2.

———. 1995a. A contact-induced and vernacularized language: How Melanesian is Tayo? In Baker, ed. 1995b, 121–48.

———. 1995b. Métchif, Mauritian and more: The "Creolisation" of French. The 1995 Samuel Weiner lecture delivered before the University of Manitoba. Winnepeg: Voices of Rupert's Land.

Coronel Feijóo, Rosario. 1991. El valle sangriento: de los indígenas de la coca y el algodón a la hacienda cañera jesuita: 1580–1700. Quito: FLACSA/ABYA-YALA.

Creissels, Denis. 1983. Elements de grammaire de la langue Mandinka. Grenoble: Publications de l'Université des Langues et Lettres.

Crespo, Alberto. 1977. Esclavos negros en Bolivia. La Paz: Academia Nacional de Ciencias de Bolivia.

Crouse, N. N. 1940. French pioneers in the West Indies, 1625–1664. New York: Columbia University Press.

Crowley, Terry. 1989. Serial verbs and prepositions in Bislama. In Melanesian Pidgin and Tok Pisin, ed. John W. M. Verhaar, 57–89. Amsterdam: John Benjamins.

———. 1990. Beach-la-Mar to Bislama: The emergence of a national language in Vanuatu. Oxford: Clarendon Press.

Cultru, P. 1910. Histoire du Sénégal du XVe siècle à 1870. Paris: Émile Larose.

Curtin, Phillip D. 1969. The Atlantic slave trade: A census. Madison: University of Wisconsin Press.

Cziko, Gary. 1989. A review of state-process and punctual-nonpunctual distinctions in children's acquisition of verbs. First Language 9: 1–31.

Davies, K. G. 1957. The Royal African Company. London: Longmans.

Dayley, Jon P. 1979a. Belizean Creole: Grammar Handbook. Brattleboro, VT: The Experiment in International Living.

———. 1979b. Belizean Creole: Glossary. Brattleboro, VT: The Experiment in International Living.

Debien, Gabriel. 1974. Les esclaves aux Antilles Françaises: XVIIe–XVIIIe siècles. Basse-Terre: Société d'Histoire de la Guadeloupe.

De Chanvallon, Thibault. 1763. Voyage à la Martinique. Paris: Bauche.

Delafosse, Maurice. 1931. Afrique occidentale française. Histoire des colonies françaises et de l'expansion de la France dans le monde, Tome IV, ed. Gabriel Hanotaux and Alfred Martineau, 1–356. Paris: Société de l'Histoire / Librairie Plon.

Delcourt, André. 1952. La France et les établissements français au Sénégal entre 1713 et 1763. Mémoires de l'Institut français de l'Afrique Noire 17. Dakar: I. F. A. N.

De Mello, Heliana R., Alan N. Baxter, John Holm, and William Megenney. 1998. O português vernáculo do Brasil. In Perl and Schwegler 1998, 71–137.

Devitt, Dan. 1990. Beingness and nothingness: Zero allomorphy in copula constructions. SUNY Buffalo MS.

Doane, Nick, Joan Hall, and Dick Ringler, eds. 1992. Old English and new: Essays in language and linguistics in honor of Frederic G. Cassidy. New York: Garland.

DuCoeurjoly, S. J. 1802. Manuel des habitans de Saint-Domingue. Paris: LeNoir.

Dunn, Richard S. 1972. Sugar and slaves: The rise of the planter class in the English West Indies, 1624–1713. Chapel Hill: University of North Carolina Press.

Du Tertre, J-B. 1667. Histoire générale des Antilles habitées par les François, vols. 1–2. Paris: Thomas Jolly.

Dutton, Tom. 1985. Police Motu: Iena sivarai. Port Moresby: University of Papua New Guinea Press.

Edwards, Jay. 1974. African influence on the English of San Andres Island. In Pidgins and creoles: Current trends and prospects, ed. David DeCamp and Ian Hancock, 1–26. Washington, DC: Georgetown University Press.

Ehrhart, Sabine. 1993. Le créole français de St-Louis (le tayo) en Nouvelle-Calédonie. Hamburg: Helmut Buske.

Ehrman, Madeline. 1972. Contemporary Cambodian. Washington, DC: Foreign Service Institute.

Emenanjo, E. Nolue. 1978. Elements of modern Igbo grammar: A descriptive approach. Ibadan: Oxford University Press.

Escure, Genevieve. 1983. The Belizean copula: A case of semantactic shift. In Carrington et al. 1983, 190–202.

Fal, Arame, Rosine Santos, and Jean Léonce Doneux. 1990. Dictionnaire Wolof-Français. Paris: Éditions Karthala.

Faraclas, Nicholas. 1996. Nigerian Pidgin. London: Routledge.

Fauquenoy-St. Jacques, Marguerite. 1979. Le créole guyanais. Atlas des départements français d'outre-mer 4: La Guyane, ed. Guy Lasserre. Bordeaux and Talence: Centre des Études de Géographie Tropicale du Centre National de Recherche Scientifique.

Ferguson, Charles A. 1971. Absence of copula and the notion of simplicity. In Hymes 1971, 141–50.

Ferguson, Charles A., and Charles E. DeBose. 1977. Simplified registers, broken languages, and pidginization. In Pidgin and creole linguistics, ed. Albert Valdman, 99–125. Bloomington: Indiana University Press.

Ferraz, Luis Ivens. 1979. The creole of São Tomé. Johannesburg: Witwatersrand University Press.

———. 1984. Fanakalo: A pidgin caught in a crisis. York Papers in Linguistics 11, ed. Mark Sebba and Loreto Todd, 107–116. York: University of York.

Fiagã, Kwasi. 1976. Grammaire Eve. Lomé: Institut National de la Récherche Scientifique.

Fields, Linda. 1995. Early Bajan: Creole or non-creole? In Arends, ed. 1995.

Foley, William A. 1988. Language birth: The processes of pidginization and creolization. In Linguistics: The Cambridge survey, vol. 4, Language: The sociocultural context, ed. Frederick J. Newmeyer, 162–83. Cambridge: Cambridge University Press.

Fournier, Robert. 1987. Le bioprogramme et les français créoles: vérification d'une hypothèse. Ph.D. diss., Université du Québec à Montréal.

Fox, James A. 1974. Russenorsk: A study in language adaptivity. Master's thesis. University of Chicago.

Fyfe, Christopher. 1962. A history of Sierra Leone. London: Oxford University Press.

Fyle, Clifford N., and Eldred D. Jones. 1980. A Krio-English dictionary. Oxford: Oxford University Press.

Gal, Susan. 1978. Peasant men can't get wives: Language change and sex roles in a bilingual community. Language in Society 7: 1–16.

Gálvez Ronceros, Antonio. 1975. Monólogo desde las tinieblas. Lima: Inti-Sol Editores.

Gamble, David P. 1987. Elementary Mandinka. San Francisco: Gambian Studies, no. 20.

Garfield, Robert. 1992. A history of São Tomé island, 1470–1655: The key to Guinea. San Francisco: Mellen Research University Press.

Gérmain, Robert. 1976. Grammaire créole. Villejuif: Éditions du Levain.

Gildea, Spike. 1993. The development of tense markers from demonstrative pronouns in Panare (Cariban). Studies in Language 17: 53–74.

Gilbert, Glenn G., ed. 1987. Pidgin and creole languages. Honolulu: University of Hawaii Press.

Givón, Talmy. 1979. Tense-aspect-modality: The creole prototype and beyond. In Tense-aspect: Between semantics and pragmatics, ed. Paul J. Hopper, 115–63. Amsterdam: John Benjamins.

Glock, Naomi. 1986. The use of reported speech in Saramaccan discourse. In Pragmatics in non-Western prespective, ed. George Huttar and Kenneth

Gregerson, 35–61. Summer Insititute in Linguistics and University of Texas at Arlington.

Goodman, Morris. F. 1964. A comparative study of creole French dialects. The Hague: Mouton.

———. 1985a. The origin of Virgin Islands Creole Dutch. Amsterdam Creole Studies 8: 67–106.

———. 1985b. Review of Bickerton 1981. International Journal of American Linguistics 51: 109–37.

——— 1987. The Portuguese element in the American creoles. In Gilbert 1987, 361–405.

———. 1992. Review of Holm (1989). Journal of Pidgin and Creole Languages 7: 352–61.

Görlach, Manfred, and John Holm, eds. 1986. Focus on the Caribbean. Varieties of English around the world, vol. G8. Amsterdam: John Benjamins.

Goulden, Rick J. 1990. The Melanesian content in Tok Pisin. Canberra: The Australian National University.

Gragg, Larry. 1995. "To procure Negroes": The English slave trade to Barbados, 1627–60. Slavery and Abolition 16: 65–84.

Granda, German de. 1978. Estudios lingüisticos hispánicos, afrohispánicos, y criollos. Madrid: Editorial Gredos.

Grant, Anthony P. 1995. Article agglutination in Creole French: A wider perspective. In Baker, ed. 1995b, 149–76.

———. 1996. Zamboangueño, Papiamentu, and "Spanish-based Creoles." Unpublished ms. York University.

Guerra y Sánchez, Ramiro. 1964. Sugar and society in the Caribbean. New Haven: Yale University Press.

Günther, Wilfried. 1973. Das Portugiesische Kreolisch der Ilha do Príncipe. Marburg-an-der-Lahn: Marburger Studien zur Afrika- und Asienkunde.

Hagman, Roy S. 1977. Nama Hottentot grammar. Bloomington: Indiana University Publications.

Hall, Robert A. 1966. Pidgin and creole languages. Ithaca: Cornell University Press.

Ham, William. 1999. Tone sandhi in Saramaccan: A case of substrate transfer? Journal of Pidgin and Creole Languages 14: 45–91.

Hancock, I. 1969. A provisional comparison of the English-based Atlantic creoles. African Language Review 8: 7–72.

———. 1980. Gullah and Barbadian: Origins and relationships. American Speech 55: 17–35.

———, ed. 1985. Diversity and development in English-related creoles. Ann Arbor, MI: Karoma.

———. 1986. The domestic hypothesis, diffusion and componentiality: An account of Atlantic Anglophone creole origins. In Muysken and Smith 1986, 71–102. Amsterdam: John Benjamins.

———. 1987. A preliminary classification of the Anglophone Atlantic creoles with syntactic data from thirty-three representative dialects. In Gilbert 1987, 264–333.

———. 1992. Review of Holm 1989. Journal of Pidgin and Creole Languages 7: 352–61.

———. 1993. Creole language provenance and the African component. In Mufwene, ed. 1993, 182–191.

———. 1994. Componentiality and the creole matrix: The Southwest English contribution. In Montgomery 1994, 95–114.

Handler, Jerome S., and Frederick W. Lange. 1978. Plantation slavery in Barbados. Cambridge: Harvard University Press.

Hashimoto, Anne Yue. 1969. The verb "to be" in Modern Chinese. In The verb "be" and its synonyms: Philosophical and grammatical studies, ed. John W. M. Verhaar, 72–111. New York: Humanities Press.

Hazaël-Massieux, Guy. 1990. Le guyanais et les langues créoles atlantiques à base française. Études Créoles 13: 95–110.

Hawkins, Emily. 1982. A pedagogical grammar of Hawaiian: Recurrent problems. Honolulu: University Press of Hawaii.

Healy, Maureen. 1993. The parallel continuum model for Suriname: A preliminary study. In Byrne and Holm 1993, 279–89.

Herskovits, Melville, and F. S. Herskovits. 1936. Suriname folklore . . . Columbia University Contributions to Anthropology, 37. New York: Columbia University Press.

Hesseling, D. C. 1905. Het Negerhollands der Deense Antillen. Leiden: A. W. Sijthoff.

Highfield, Arnold, and Albert Valdman. 1981. Historicity and variation in creole studies. Ann Arbor, MI: Karoma.

Holm, John. 1978. The creole English of Nicaragua's Miskito Coast: Its sociolinguistic history and a comparative study of its lexicon and syntax. Ph.D. diss., University College, University of London.

———. 1980. The creole "copula" that highlighted the world. In Perspectives on American English, ed. J. L. Dillard, 367–75. The Hague: Mouton.

———. 1984. Variability of the copula in Black English and its creole kin. American Speech 59: 291–309.

———. 1986. Substrate diffusion. In Muysken and Smith 1986.

———. 1987. Creole influence on Popular Brazilian Portuguese. In Gilbert 1987, 406–29.

———. 1988. Pidgins and creoles. Vol. 1. Cambridge: Cambridge University Press.

———. 1989. Pidgins and creoles. Vol. 2. Cambridge: Cambridge University Press.

———. 1992. Atlantic input in Pacific pidgins and creoles. Paper presented at the Society for Pidgin and Creole Linguistics meeting, Philadelphia.

Hornby, Ove. 1980. Kolonerne i vestindien. Copenhagen: Politiken.

Huber, Magnus. 1999. Atlantic English creoles and the Lower Guinea coast: Afrogenesis reconsidered. In Huber and Parkvall 1999, 81–110.

Huber, Magnus, and Mikael Parkvall, eds. 1999. Spreading the word: The issue of diffusion among the Atlantic Creoles. London: University of Westminster Press.

Hull, Alexander. 1979. On the origin and chronology of the French-based creoles. In Readings in creole studies, ed. Ian F. Hancock, Edgar Polomé, Morris Goodman, and Bernd Heine, 201–16. Ghent: E. Story-Scientia.

Huttar, George, and Mary Huttar. 1992. Reduplication in Ndjuka: Phonology, syntax, and semantics. Paper presented at the Society for Pidgin and Creole Linguistics meeting, Philadelphia, January.

Huttar, Mary, and George Huttar. 1995. Ndjuka. Newbury, MA: Routledge.

Hymes, Dell, ed. 1971. Pidginization and creolization of languages. Cambridge: Cambridge University Press.

Isert, Paul Erdman. 1793. Voyages en Guiné et dans les Isles Caraïbes. Paris.

Janson, Tore. 1984. Articles and plural formation in creoles: Change and universals. Lingua 64: 291–323.

Jaramillo Perez, Cesar. 1962. Historia del Ecuador. Quito.

Jennings, William. 1995a. The first generations of a Creole society: Cayenne 1660–1700. In Baker, ed. 1995b, 21–40.

———. 1995b. Saint-Christophe: Site of the first French creole. In Baker, ed. 1995b, 63–80.

Jobson, Richard. 1626. The golden trade. London.

Jones, F. C. 1983. English-derived words in Sierra Leone Krio. Ph.D. diss., University of Leeds.

Jones, A. 1985. Brandenburg sources for West African history. Stuttgart: F. Steiner.

Jourdain, Élodie. 1956. Du français aux parlers créoles. Paris: Klincksieck

Joyce, P. W. 1910. English as we speak it in Ireland. London: Longmans.

Katupha, José Mateus Muária. 1983. A preliminary description of sentence structures in the e-Sáaka dialect of e-Mákhuwa. Ph.D. diss., University of London.

Keesing, R. (1988). Melanesian pidgin and the Oceanic substrate. Stanford: Stanford University Press.

Kegl, Judy, and John McWhorter. 1996. Perspectives on an emerging language: Creolization and critical periods. Proceedings of the 28th Annual Child Language Research Forum. Palo Alto: CSLI.

Kegl, Judy, Anne Senghas, and Marie Coppola. 1996. Creation through contact: Sign language emergence and sign language change in Nicaragua. In Comparative grammatical change: Language creation and language change, ed. Michel DeGraff, 179–237. Cambridge: MIT Press.

Kihm, Alain. 1980. Aspects d'une syntaxe historique: Études sur le créole portugais de Guiné-Bissau. Thèse de Doctorat de 3e Cycle, Université de Paris III, Sorbonne Nouvelle.

———. 1989. Lexical conflation as a basis for relexification. Canadian Journal of Linguistics 34: 351–76.

———. 1994. Kriyol syntax. Amsterdam: John Benjamins.

Klein, Herbert S. 1967. Slavery in the Americas. Chicago: University of Chicago Press.

Klingler, Thomas A. 1992. A descriptive study of the Creole speech of Pointe Coupée Parish, Louisiana with focus on the lexicon (Volumes 1 and 2). Ph.D. diss., Indiana University.

———. 1997. Louisiana Creole: The multiple geneses hypothesis reconsidered. Paper presented at the Society for Pidgin and Creole Linguistics meeting, London.

Knight, Frank. 1970. Slave society in Cuba during the nineteenth century. Madison: University of Wisconsin Press.

Kouwenberg, Silvia. 1987. Morphophonemic change in Saramaccan pronominal forms. In Alleyne, ed. 1987, 1–15.

Kozelka, Paul R. 1980. Ewe (for Togo)—grammar handbook. Brattleboro, VT: The Experiment in Modern Living.

Kuhn, Thomas S. 1970. The structure of scientific revolutions. Chicago: University of Chicago Press.

Labat, J. B. 1730. Voyages des marchais en Guiné, isles voisines, et à Cayenne faits en 1725, 1726, et 1727. Paris: Saugrain.

Ladhams, John. 1999. The Pernambuco connection? An examination of the nature and origin of the Portuguese elements in Surinam creoles. In Huber and Parkvall 1999, 209–40.

Lalla, Barbara, and Jean D'Costa. 1990. Language in exile: Three hundred years of Jamaican Creole. Tuscaloosa: University of Alabama Press.

Laurence, Kemlin M. 1974. Is Caribbean Spanish a case of decreolization? Orbis 23: 484–99.

Lawrence, A. W. 1969. Fortified trade-posts: The English in West Africa, 1645–1822. London: Jonathan Cape.

Lefebvre, Claire. 1986. Relexification in creole genesis revisited: The case of Haitian Creole. In Muysken and Smith 1986, 279–300.

———. 1992. Travaux de recherche sur le créole ha{id}tien, no. 8. The clausal determiners of Haitian and Fon. Montréal: Université du Québec à Montréal.

———. 1993. The role of relexification and syntactic reanalysis in Haitian Creole: Methodological aspects of a research program. In Mufwene, ed. 1993, 254–79.

Lefebvre, Claire, and John Lumsden. 1994. Relexification in creole genesis. Paper presented at the MIT Symposium on the Role of Relexification in Creole Genesis: The Case of Haitian Creole. Research Report edited by Claire Lefebvre and John Lumsden, Université du Québec à Montréal.

Lefebvre, Claire, and Diane Massam. 1988. Haitian Creole syntax: A case for DET as head. Journal of Pidgin and Creole Languages 3: 213–43.

LePage, Robert, and Andre Tabouret-Keller. 1985. Acts of identity. Cambridge: Cambridge University Press.

LePage, Robert, and David DeCamp. 1960. Jamaican Creole. London: Macmillan.

Lessem, Don. 1992. Kings of creation. New York: Simon and Schuster.

Li, Charles N., and Sandra A. Thompson. 1977. A mechanism for the development of copula morphemes. In Mechanisms of syntactic change, ed. Charles N. Li, 419–44. Austin: University of Texas Press.

Ligon, Richard. 1657. A true and exact history of the island of Barbados. London: Humphrey Moseley.

Lipski, John. 1986a. Sobre lingüística afroecuatoriana: el valle del Chota. Anuario de Lingüística Hispanica (Valladolid) 2: 153–76.

———. 1986b. The Portuguese element in Philippine Creole Spanish: A critical reassessment. Philippine Journal of Linguistics 17: 1–17.

———. 1994. Latin American Spanish. London: Longmans.

Louden, Mark L. 1993. The evolution of prepositional complementizers: Parallels between English-based creoles and Germanic. Paper presented at the Society for Pidgin and Creole Linguistics Conference at the annual meeting of the Linguistics Society of America, Los Angeles, 1993.

Luo, Cheng. 1991. Cross-categorial formal identity: A functional account. Unpublished ms. University of Manitoba.

Ly, Abdoulaye. 1955. L'évolution du commerce français d'Afrique noire dans le dernier quart du XVIIe siècle: la compagnie du Sénégal, 1673 à 1696. Thèse pour le Doctorat ès Lettres, Université de Bordeaux.

Makepeace, Margaret. 1989. English traders on the Guinea Coast, 1657–1668: An analysis of the East India Company archive. History in Africa 16: 237–84.

Marchese, Lynell. 1986. Tense/aspect and the development of auxiliaries in Kru languages. Dallas: Summer Institute of Linguistics and the University of Texas at Arlington.

Martinus, Frank. 1989. West African connection: The influence of the Afro-Portuguese on the Papiamentu of Curaçao. In Estudios sobre español de América y lingüística afroamericana (no ed.). Bogotá: Publicaciones del Instituto Caro y Cuervo.

McWhorter, John H. 1992a. Substratal influences on Saramaccan serial verb constructions. Journal of Pidgin and Creole Languages 7: 1–53.

———. 1992b. Ni and the copula scenario in Swahili: A diachronic approach. Diachronica 9. 15–46.

———. 1994. Rejoinder to Derek Bickerton's Reply to McWhorter 1992 "Substratal Influence in Saramaccan Serial Verb Constructions." Journal of Pidgin and Creole Languages 9: 79–93.

———. 1995. The scarcity of Spanish-based creoles explained. Language in Society 24: 213–44.

———. 1996a. The diachrony of predicate negation in Saramaccan Creole. Studies in Language 20: 285–311.

———. 1996b. A deep breath and a second wind: Reassessing the substrate hypothesis. Anthropological Linguistics 38: 461–94.

———. 1996c. It happened at Cormantin: Tracing the birthplace of the Atlantic English-based creoles. Journal of Pidgin and Creole Languages 10: 289–333.

———. 1996d. Looking into the void: Zero copula in the creole mesolect. American Speech 70: 339–60.

———. 1997a. Towards a new model of creole genesis. New York: Peter Lang.

———. 1997b. A creole by any other name: Streamlining the terminology in creole studies. In Huber and Parkvall 1999, 5–28.

———. 1998a. The word on the street: Fact and fable about American English. New York: Plenum.

———. 1998b. Identifying the creole prototype: Vindicating creoles as a typological class. Language 74: 788–818.

Megenney, William W. 1984. Traces of Portuguese in three Caribbean creoles: Evidence in support of the monogenetic theory. Hispanic Linguistics 1: 177–89.

———. 1985. Africa en Venezuela: su herencia lingüística y cultura literaria. Montalbán 15. 3–56.

———. 1988. Black rural speech in Venezuela. Neophilologus 73: 52–61.

Meintel, Deirdre. 1984. Race, culture, and Portuguese colonization in Cabo Verde. Syracuse: Maxwell School of Citizenship and Public Affairs.

Meisel, Jürgen M. 1983. Strategies of second language acquisition: More than one kind of simplification. In Pidginization and creolization as language acquisition, ed. Roger W. Andersen, 120–57. Rowley, MA: Newbury House.

Migge, Bettina. 1995. The emergence of creole copulas: Evidence from Belize Creole. In Studies in synchronic and diachronic variation (Ohio State University Working Papers in Linguistics, no. 46), ed. Elizabeth Hume, Robert Levine, and Halyna Sydorenko, 63–85. Columbus: The Ohio State University Department of Linguistics.

Milroy, Lesley. 1980. Language and social networks. Oxford: Basil Blackwell.

Mintz, Sidney W. 1971. The socio-historical background to pidginization and creolization. In Hymes 1971, 481–98.

Mittelsdorf, Sibylle. 1978. African retentions in Jamaican Creole: A reassessment. Ph.D. diss., Northwestern University.

Montgomery, Michael, ed. 1994. The crucible of Carolina: Essays in the development of Gullah language and culture. Athens, GA: University of Georgia Press.

Mufwene, Salikoko S. 1986a. Notes on continuous constructions in Jamaican and Guyanese creoles. In Görlach and Holm 1986, 167–82.

———. 1986b. Les langues créoles peuvent-elles être définies sans allusion à leur histoire? Études Créoles 9: 135–50.

———. 1990. Transfer and the substrate hypothesis in creolistics. Studies in Second Language Acquisition 12: 1–23.

———. 1991a. Pidgins, creoles, typology, and markedness. In Byrne and Huebner 1991, 123–43.

———. 1991b. Is Gullah decreolizing? A comparison of a speech sample of the 1930s with a speech sample of the 1980s. In The emergence of Black English, ed. Guy Bailey, Natalie Maynor, and Patricia Cukor-Avila, 213–30. Amsterdam: John Benjamins.

————. 1992. Africanisms in Gullah: A re-examination of the issues. In Old English and New: Studies in language and linguistics in honor of Frederic G. Cassidy, ed. Joan Hall, Nick Doane, and Dick Ringler, 156–82. New York: Garland.

————, ed. 1993a. Africanisms in Afro-American language varieties. Athens: University of Georgia Press.

————. 1993b. African substratum: Possibility and evidence. In Mufwene 1993a, 192–208.

————. 1994a. Creole genesis: A population genetics perspective. In Caribbean language: Issues old and new, ed. Pauline Christie. Mona, Jamaica: University of the West Indies Press.

————. 1994b. On decreolization: The case of Gullah. In Language and the social construction of identity in creole situations, ed. Marcyliena Morgan, 63–99. Los Angeles: Center for Afro-American Studies, UCLA.

————. 1996. The Founder Principle in creole genesis. Diachronica 13: 83–134.

————. 1997. Jargons, pidgins, creoles, and koines: What are they? In Spears and Winford 1997, 35–70.

Mühlhäusler, Peter. 1976. Samoan Plantation Pidgin English and the origin of New Guinea: An introduction. Journal of Pacific History, 122–5.

————. 1985a. Syntax of Tok Pisin. In Wurm and Mühlhäusler 1985, 341–421.

————. 1985b. The scientific study of Tok Pisin: Language planning and the Tok Pisin lexicon. In Wurm and Mühlhäusler 1985, 595–664.

Munford, Clarence J. 1991. The Black ordeal of slavery and slave trading in the French West Indies, 1625–1715. Vol. 2. Lewiston, NY: Edwin Mellen.

Munteanu, Dan. 1991. El papiamento: Origen, evolución y estructura. Bochum-Essener: Beitrage zur Sprachwandelforschung XV. Bochum: Brockmeyer.

Muysken, Pieter. 1981. Halfway between Quechua and Spanish: The case for relexification. In Highfield and Valdman 1981, 52–78.

————. 1994. Column: Saramaccan and Haitian: A comparison. Journal of Pidgin and Creole Languages 9: 305–14.

Muysken, Pieter, and Norval V. Smith, eds. 1986. Substrata versus universals in creole genesis. Amsterdam: John Benjamins.

Neumann, Ingrid. 1983. Le créole de Breaux Bridge, Louisiane. Hamburg: Helmut Buske.

Niedzielski, Henry. 1989. A French-based pidgin in Burundi. In Wheels within wheels, ed. Martin Pütz and René Dirven, 81–107. Frankfurt: Peter Lang.

Niles, Norma A. 1980. Provincial English dialects and Barbadian English. Ph.D. diss., University of Michigan.

Njie, Codu Mbassy. 1982. Description syntaxique du Wolof de Gambie. Dakar: Les Nouvelles Éditions Africaines.

Northern Rhodesia and Nyasaland Joint Publications Bureau. 1954. The White Fathers' Bemba-English dictionary. London: Longmans, Green and Co.

Nylander, Dudley K. 1983. Étude déscriptive du Krio (langue créole de la

Sierra-Léone): phonologie et syntaxe. Ph.D. diss., Université des Langues et Lettres de Grenoble.

Ogunbowale, P. O. 1970. The essentials of the Yoruba language. London: University of London Press.

Otheguy, Ricardo. 1973. The Spanish Caribbean: A creole perspective. In New ways of analyzing variation in English, ed. C-J. Bailey and Roger Shuy, 323–39. Washington, DC: Georgetown University Press.

Owens, Jonathan. 1985. The origin of East African Nubi. Anthropological Linguistics 27. 229–71.

———. 1990. East African Nubi: Bioprogram vs. inheritance. Diachronica 7: 217–50.

Paquette, Robert L. 1988. Sugar is made with blood. Middletown, CT: Wesleyan University Press.

Parkvall, Michael. 1995a. A dual approach to creole genesis. Unpublished ms. University of Stockholm.

———. 1995b. The role of St. Kitts in a new scenario of French Creole genesis. In Baker, ed. 1995b, 41–62.

———. 1999. Feature selection and genetic relationships among Atlantic creoles. In Huber and Parkvall, eds. 1999, 29–66.

Patterson, Orlando. 1967. The sociology of slavery. London: McGibbon and Key.

Patterson, W. 1880. A glossary of words in use in the counties of Antrim and Down. London: Trübner.

Pelleprat, P. 1655. Relation des missions des pères de la Compagnie de Jésus . . . Paris: Cramoisy.

Perl, Matthias, and Armin Schwegler, eds. 1998. América negra: panorámica actual de los estudios lingüísticos sobre variedades hispanas, portuguesas y criollas. Frankfurt: Vervuert.

Petit Jean Roget, J. 1980. La société d'habitation de la Martinique: un demi-siècle de formation, 1635–1685. Paris and Lille: Librairie Honoré Champion and Atelier Reproduction des Thèses de l'Université de Lille.

Phillips, John Seward. 1975. Vietnamese contact French: Acquisitional variation in a language contact situation. Ph.D. diss., Indiana University.

Phillips, Judith Wingerd. 1982. A partial grammar of the Haitian Creole verb system. Ph.D. diss., SUNY Buffalo.

Pichardo, E. 1862. Diccionario provincial casi razonado de voces cubanas. Havana: Imprenta la Antilla.

Pinckard, George. 1806. Notes on the West Indies. London: Longman, Hurst, Rees, and Orme.

Plag, Ingo. 1993. Sentential complementation in Sranan. Tübingen: Max Niemeyer.

Porter, Robert. 1989. European activity on the Gold Coast, 1620–1667. Ph.D. diss., University of South Africa.

Postma, Johannes. 1990. The Dutch in the Atlantic slave trade. Cambridge: Cambridge University Press.

Price, Richard. 1976. The Guiana maroons: A historical and bibliographical introduction. Baltimore: Johns Hopkins University Press.

———. 1983. First Time: The historical vision of an Afro-American people. Baltimore: Johns Hopkins University Press.

Rajemisa-Raolison, Régis. 1969. Grammaire malgache. Tananarive: Fianarantsua.

Reinecke, J. E., S. M. Tsuzaki, D. DeCamp, I. F. Hancock, and R. E. Wood, eds. 1975. A bibliography of pidgin and creole languages. Honolulu: University Press of Hawaii.

Rens, L. L. E. 1953. The history and social background of Surinam's Negro English. Amsterdam: North Holland.

Restrepo, Vicente. 1886. A study of the gold and silver mines of Colombia. Trans. C. W. Fisher. New York: Colombian Consulate.

Rickford, John R. 1980. How does DOZ disappear? In Issues in English creoles, ed. Richard R. Day, 77–96. Heidelberg: Julius Groos Verlag.

———. 1986a. The need for new approaches to social class analysis in sociolinguistics. Language and Communication 6: 215–21.

———. 1986b. Social contact and linguistic diffusion: Hiberno-English and New World Black English. Language 62: 245–90.

———. 1987. Dimensions of a creole continuum. Stanford: Stanford University Press.

———. 1988. Connections between sociolinguistics and pidgin-creole studies. International Journal of the Sociology of Language 71: 51–7.

———. 1992. The creole residue in Barbados. In Old English and new: Essays in language and linguistics in honor of Frederic G. Cassidy, ed. Nick Doane, Joan Hall, and Dick Ringler, 183–201. New York: Garland Publishing.

Rickford, John R., and Jerome S. Handler. 1994. Textual evidence on the nature of early Barbadian speech, 1676–1835. Journal of Pidgin and Creole Languages 9: 221–55.

Roberts, Julianne. 1995a. Pidgin Hawaiian: A sociohistorical study. Journal of Pidgin and Creole Languages 10: 1–56.

———. 1995b. Letter to the Editor. Journal of Pidgin and Creole Languages 10: 221–3.

———. 1996. Formation of Hawaii pidgin English and diffusion. Paper presented at the meeting of the Society for Pidgin and Creole Linguistics, San Diego, January 1996.

———. 2000. Nativization and the genesis of Hawaiian Creole. In Language change and language contact in pidgins and creoles, ed. John McWhorter, 257–300. Amsterdam: John Benjamins.

Robertson, Ian E. 1983. The Dutch linguistic legacy in Guyana: Berbice and Skepi Dutch. Carib 3: 11–23.

———. 1989. Berbice and Skepi Dutch: A lexical comparison. Tijdschrift voor Nederlandische Taal- en Letterkunde 105. 3–21.

Rodney, Walter. 1970. A history of the Upper Guinea coast, 1545 to 1800. Oxford: The Clarendon Press.

Romaine, Suzanne. 1992. Language, education, and development: Urban and rural Tok Pisin. Oxford: Clarendon Press.

Rongier, Jacques. 1988. Apprenons L'Ewe. Paris: Éditions l'Harmattan.

Rountree, S. Catherine. 1972. Saramaccan tone in relation to intonation and grammar. Lingua 29: 308–25.

Rountree, S. Catherine, and Naomi Glock. 1977. Saramaccan for beginners. Paramaribo: Summer Institute of Linguistics.

Rout, Leslie B. 1976. The African experience in Spanish America: 1502 to the present day. Cambridge: Cambridge University Press.

Rowlands, E. C. 1969. Teach yourself Yoruba. London: University of London Press.

Roy, John D. 1986. The structure of tense and aspect in Barbadian English Creole. In Görlach and Holm 1986, 141–56.

Ryder, A. F. C. 1965. Dutch trade on the Nigerian coast during the seventeenth century. Journal of the Historical Society of Nigeria 3: 195–210.

Sabino, Robin. 1990. Towards a phonology of Negerhollands: An analysis of phonological variation. Ph.D. diss., University of Pennsylvania.

Sadler, Wesley. 1964. Untangled CiBemba. Kitwe, N. Rhodesia: The United Church of Central Africa in Rhodesia.

Samarin, William J. 1986. French and Sango in the Central African Republic. Anthropological Linguistics 28: 379–87.

———. 1989. The colonial heritage of the Central African Republic: A linguistic perspective. The International Journal of African Historical Studies 22: 697–711.

———. 1997. The creolization of pidgin morphophonology. In Spears and Winford 1997, 175–216.

Sanderson, G. Meredith. 1954. A dictionary of the Yao language. Zomba, Nyasaland: The Government Printer.

Sandoval, A. de. 1987 (1627). De instauranda aethiopum salute. Introduction and transcription by Enriqueta Vila Vilar. Madrid: Alianza Editorial.

Sankoff, Gillian, and Suzanne Laberge. 1980. On the acquisition of native speakers by a language. In The social life of language, ed. Gillian Sankoff, 195–209. Philadelphia: University of Pennsylvania Press.

Schuchardt, Hugo. 1888. Kreolische Studien. VIII. über das Annamito-französische. Sitzungsberichte der kaiserlichen Akademie der Wissenschaften zu Wien 116: 227–34.

———. 1980. Notes on the English of American Indians: Cheyenne, Kiowa, Pawnee, Pueblo, Sioux, and Wyandot. In Pidgin and creole languages: Selected essays, ed. and trans. Glenn G. Gilbert, 30–37. Cambridge: Cambridge University Press.

Schwegler, Armin. 1991a. El habla cotidiana del Chocó (Colombia). América Negra 2: 85–119.

———. 1991b. Negation in Palenquero: Synchrony. Journal of Pidgin and Creole Languages 6: 165–214.

———. 1993a. Rasgos (afro-) portugueses en el criollo del Palenque de San

Basilio (Colombia). In Homenaje a José Perez Vidal, ed. Carmen Díaz D. Alayón, 667–96. La Laguna, Tenerife: Litografía A. Romero S. A.

———. 1993b. Subject pronouns and person/number in Palenquero. In Byrne and Holm 1993, 145–61.

———. 1996a. La doble negación dominicana y la génesis del español caribeño. Hispanic Linguistics 8: 246–315.

———. 1996b. Chi ma nkongo, chi ma ri Luango: lengua y rito ancestrales en El Palenque de San Basilio (Colombia). 2 vols. Frankfurt/Madrid: Vervuert Verlag.

———. 1996c. Palenquero pronouns—person/number markers. Paper presented at the University of California, Berkeley.

———. 1998. El palenquero. In Perl and Schwegler 1998, 219–291.

———. (forthcoming) El vocabulario africano de Palenque (Colombia). Segunda parte: compendio de palabras (con etimologías).

Seidel, A., and I. Struyf. 1910. La langue congolaise. Paris: Jules Groos.

Sharp, William Frederick. 1976. Slavery on the Spanish frontier. Norman, OK: University of Oklahoma Press.

Shnukal, Anna. 1988. Broken: An introduction to the creole language of Torres Strait. Canberra: Australian National University.

Siegel, Jeff. 1987. Language contact in a plantation environment. Cambridge: Cambridge University Press.

Singler, John V. 1981. An introduction to Liberian English. East Lansing: Michigan State University, African Studies Center/Peace Corps.

———. 1986. Short note. Journal of Pidgin and Creole Languages 1: 141–5.

———. 1988. The homogeneity of the substrate as a factor in pidgin/creole genesis. Language 64: 27–51.

———. 1993. African influence upon Afro-American language varieties: A consideration of sociohistorical factors. In Mufwene, ed. 1993a, 235–53.

———. 1995. The demographics of creole genesis in the Caribbean: A comparison of Martinique and Haiti. In Arends, ed. 1995, 203–32.

Smith, Norval. J. 1987. The genesis of the creole languages of Surinam. Ph.D. diss., University of Amsterdam.

———. 1997a. Ingredient X: The common core of African words in the Atlantic creoles. Paper presented to the Society for Pidgin and Creole Linguistics, London.

———. 1997b. Pernambuco to Surinam 1654–1655? The Jewish slave controversy. In Huber and Parkvall 1999, 251–98.

Smith, Norval J., Ian E. Robertson, and Kay Williamson. 1987. The Ijo element in Berbice Dutch. Language in Society 16: 49–90.

Sordam, Max, and Hein Eersel. 1985. Sranantongo/Surinaamse Taal. Baarn, the Netherlands: Bosch and Keuning.

Spears, Arthur K., and Donald Winford, eds. 1997. The structure and status of pidgins and creoles. Amsterdam: John Benjamins.

Spears, Richard A. 1973. Elementary Maninka-kan. Unpublished ms. Northwestern University.

Speedy, Karin. 1994. Mississippi and Tèche Creole: A demographic and linguistic case for separate geneses in Louisiana. Master's thesis. University of Auckland.

———. 1995. Mississippi and Tèche Creole: Two separate starting points for Creole in Louisiana. In Baker, ed. 1995b, 97–114.

Spencer, John. 1971. West Africa and the English language. In The English language in West Africa, ed. John Spencer, 1–34. London: Longman.

Sreedhar, M. V. 1985. Standardized grammar of Naga Pidgin. Mysore: Central Institute of Indian Languages.

Stark, Elsie L. 1969. Malagasy without moans. Tananarive: Trano Printy Loterana.

Stenson, Nancy. 1981. Studies in Irish syntax. Tübingen: Günter Narr.

Stewart, W. A. 1971. Sociolinguistic factors in the history of American negro dialects. In Black-white speech relationships, ed. Walt Wolfram and N. Clarke, 74–89. Washington, DC: Center for Applied Linguistics.

Stoller, Paul. 1985. Toward a phenomenological perspective in pidgin and creole studies. In Hancock, ed. 1985, 1–12.

Stolz, Thomas. 1986. Gibt es das Kreolische Sprachwandelmodell? Vergleichende Grammatik des Negerholländischen. Frankfurt: Peter Lang.

Stolz, Thomas, and Pieter Stein. 1986. Social history and genesis of Negerhollands. Amsterdam Creole Studies 9: 103–122.

Swartenbroeckx, S. J. Pierre. 1973. Dictionnaire Kikongo et Kituba-Français. Banbundu, Zaire: Ceeba.

Sylvain, Suzanne C. 1936. Le créole Haïtien: Morphologie et syntaxe. Port-au-Prince: Imprimerie de Meester.

Taylor, Douglas. 1956. Language contacts in the West Indies. Word 13: 399–414.

———. 1977. Languages of the West Indies. Baltimore: Johns Hopkins University Press.

Thomas, Hugh. 1997. The slave trade. New York: Simon and Schuster.

Thomason, Sarah Grey, and Terence Kaufman. 1988. Language contact, creolization, and genetic linguistics. Berkeley: University of California Press.

Thompson, Laurence C. 1965. A Vietnamese grammar. Seattle: University of Washington Press.

Thompson, R. W. 1961. A note on some possible affinities between the creole dialects of the Old World and those of the New. In Creole Language Studies II: Proceedings of the conference on Creole Language Studies (University of the West Indies, Mona 1959), ed. Robert B. LePage, 107–13. London: Macmillan.

Todd, Loreto. 1973. "To be or not to be"—What would Hamlet have said in Cameroon Pidgin? An analysis of Cameroon Pidgin's "Be"-verb. Archivum Linguisticum 4: 1–15.

———. 1984. Modern Englishes: Pidgins and creoles. Oxford: Basil Blackwell.

Tonkin, Eizabeth. 1971. Some coastal pidgins of West Africa. In Social anthropology and language (Association of Social Anthropologists, Monograph 10), ed. E. Ardener, 129–55. London: Tavistock.

Turner, Lorenzo D. 1949. Africanisms in the Gullah dialect. Ann Arbor: University of Michigan Press.

Valdman, Albert. 1978. Le créole: structure, statut et origine. Paris: Klincksieck.

Valdman, Albert, and Arnold Highfield, eds. 1980. Theoretical orientations in creole studies. New York: Academic Press.

Van Rossem, Cefas. Forthcoming. Short Note: No Dutch-based pidgin in Elmina in 1760. Journal of Pidgin and Creole Languages.

Veenstra, Tonjes. 1994. The acquisition of functional categories: The creole way. In Creolization and language change, ed. Dany Adone and Ingo Plag, 99–115. Tübingen: Max Niemeyer.

Verhaar, John W.–M. 1995. Toward a reference grammar of Tok Pisin: An experiment in corpus linguistics. Honolulu: University of Hawaii Press.

Voorhoeve, Jan. 1964. Creole languages and communication. Symposium on Multilingualism (Commission de coopération technique en Afrique, publication 87). London.

———. 1973. Historical and linguistic evidence in favor of the relexification theory in the formation of creoles. Language in Society 2: 133–45.

———. 1985. A note on epenthetic transitive /m/ in Sranan Tongo. In Hancock, ed. 1985, 89–93.

Voorhoeve, Jan, and Ursy M. Lichtveld. 1975. Creole drum. New Haven: Yale University Press.

Wakeman, Canon C. W. 1979. A dictionary of the Yoruba language. Ibadan: University Press, Ltd.

Washabaugh, William. 1975. On the development of complementizers in creolization. Stanford University Working Papers on Language Universals 17: 109–40.

Watts, David. 1987. The West Indies: Patterns of development, culture, and environmental change since 1492. Cambridge: Cambridge University Press.

WEC International. 1992. Wolof learning manual. Banjul, Gambia: WEC International.

Welmers, Beatrice F., and William E. Welmers. 1968. Igbo: A learner's dictionary. Los Angeles: African Studies Center.

Welmers, William E. 1973. African language structures. Berkeley: University of California Press.

West, Robert C. 1957. The Pacific lowlands of Colombia. Baton Rouge: Louisiana State University Press.

Westermann, Diedrich. 1928. Ewe-English, English-Ewe dictionary. Berlin: Dietrich Riemer.

———. 1930. A study of the Ewe language. London: Oxford University Press.

Whinnom, Keith. 1965. Contacts de langues et emprunts lexicaux: The origins of the European-based creoles and pidgins. Orbis 14: 509–27.

———. 1971. Linguistic hybridization and the "special case" of pidgins and creoles. In Hymes 1971, 91–115.

Williams, Jeffrey P. 1988. Women and kinship in creole genesis. International Journal of the Sociology of Language 71: 81–9.

Winford, D. 1985. The syntax of *fi* complements in Caribbean English Creole. Language 61: 588–624.

———. 1993. Predication in Caribbean English creoles. Amsterdam: John Benjamins.

Wittman, H., and Robert Fournier. 1983. Le créole, c'est du français, coudon! Revue de l'association québécoise de linguistique 3: 187–202.

Wood, Peter. 1974. Black majority. New York: Knopf.

Wurm, S. A., and Peter Mühlhäusler, eds. 1985. Handbook of Tok Pisin (New Guinea Pidgin). Canberra: Australian National University.

Wylie, Jonathan. 1995. The origins of Lesser Antillean French Creole: Some literary and lexical evidence. Journal of Pidgin and Creole Languages 10: 77–126.

Index

Page references in italics indicate tables.

Text: 10/13 Aldus
Display: Aldus
Compositor: G&S Typesetters
Printer and Binder: Thomson-Shore, Inc.